200 YEARS

OF

AMERICAN

BUSINESS

200 YEARS OF AMERICAN BUSINESS

Thomas C. Cochran

A DELTA BOOK

A DELTA BOOK

Published by
Dell Publishing Co., Inc.
1 Dag Hammarskjold Plaza
New York, New York 10017

For information address: Basic Books, Inc., Publishers, New York, New York 10022.

Delta ® TM 755118 Dell Publishing Co., Inc.

Reprinted by arrangement with Basic Books, Inc., Publishers.

ISBN: 0-440-58779-4

Printed in the United States of America

First Delta printing—March 1978

VB

CONTENTS

IV

The Age of Demand, 1930-1976

ACKNOWLEDGMENTS

I am deeply indebted to the Eleutherian Mills-Hagley Foundation for an eighteen-month visit as Senior Resident Scholar, during which I found their library extremely convenient and helpful for this synthetic type of writing. I also wish to extend my gratitude to E. P. Douglass of the University of North Carolina and Reavis Cox of the University of Pennsylvania, who have read and criticized large portions of the manuscript.

INTRODUCTION

John Maynard Keynes said that "events start with the actions of businessmen."[1] Although much of his time was spent in the cloistered environment of England's Cambridge, this great theorist had a penetrating understanding of the real operations of life. Clearly he saw that unpredictable man may, by unusual actions, continually upset all theories. Granting this is true, as I think most business executives would agree, practical aids to decision making have to be derived from analyzing the actions of men in somewhat similar past situations.

But situations and their results are seldom simple. Aside from some flash of brilliant intuition, from which business decisions have often benefited, the more pedestrian business or scholarly approach must be to try to break down the baffling overall picture of reality into understandable parts. Application of this process in the ubiquitous world of business may start with an initial division of problems into those arising from managing the activities of buying, processing, and selling. But each of these in itself is an extensive and varied category, and each presents different challenges to the inquiring entrepreneur that differ in both type and complexity. The businessman has learned by the hard experience of many centuries that buying is a relatively understandable matter of judging quality, price, and probable supply. Processing, however, depends on the type of business. It may require the mastering of new scientific theory, better technology, or simply more diligent supervision of well-known routines; all three involve both knowledge and its application, but the variable elements can usually be understood. Selling or marketing, on the other hand, is a step into the truly unpredictable. Guides of many types, such as market research, may help, but the great unknowns of how to reach and influence customers can defeat the best laid plans. Taste may change, markets may suddenly become glutted, a sales campaign may not reach the right people, the selling staff may make the wrong appeal, or the physical process of marketing may prove inefficient—these are just a few of the common difficulties. Put another way, stages one and two in the business trilogy are largely governed by physical or institutional limitations, while stage three depends on all the vagaries of human psychology, personal relations, and often the unforeseen desires of people in ethnic, regional, or foreign cultures.

Fundamental problems of management are present in all stages of the classic triology. The generic or ideal administrative structure is that of the master craftsman who knows all that is commercially useful about his suppliers, his technology, and his prospective customers. Once he adds a worker he is depending for profit on a less highly motivated employee turning out enough in his part of the business to more than cover his wages. When the number of employees mounts and hired supervisors become necessary, the rates of productivity per worker begin to depend not only on technology and personal motivation but also on the efficient functioning of a human organization. Put very simply, no one but the proprietor is motivated by profit. Bureaucratization necessarily adds employees with less motivation. The problem is to administer diminished individual efficiency well enough so that the larger total production is still profitable.

Occasionally, to be sure, technology has made available new products so desirable that even poor managers could make a profit in an assured market. But this production-oriented stage has tended to pass away in all advanced nations, sometimes without the local businessmen even realizing it, leaving as its heritage "the production myth": what could be made economically could be sold. In recent times the concept that what could be most profitably sold could usually be produced is closer to the truth. Business history, therefore, is in part an account of diminishing emphasis on what economists would call the supply side of the market and an increasing preoccupation with how to create and sustain demand for particular goods or services.

In between the initial stage of supply and the final one of stimulating demand there has been a gradual change toward greater complexity. Here again, the early years of machine production involved alertness to new technology and improved methods of handling, but as time passed and the average business grew bigger, the efficient functioning of the intermediate levels of managerial organization became more important. While generally offering less complex problems than those of marketing, innovations in business structure assumed increasing importance.

Consequently, while economic history has elected to be primarily concerned with production and transportation—usually seeing trade only in measures of volume, and business firms as collections of units that automatically maximize profits—business history is chiefly concerned with how the policy decisions, the organizational structure of the enterprise, and the methods of selling have led to profits (maximum only by chance) or losses. As one approaches the present, the business emphasis is on the structure for making decisions, especially ones that affect marketing. Such advantages as American business may for a time have had over that of Europe are ascribed by foreign analysts to an earlier shift to market rather than production orientation.

So far nothing has been said of the environment in which the three stages of buying, processing, and selling take place, but it inevitably determines how each stage is carried on. Social customs, values, and types of government all directly affect the form of business organizations, the way they can operate, and most of all the demands of the market and what will stimulate them. The way businessmen perceive these external forces is, in turn, limited and conditioned by the fact that they also are members of the society in which their businesses function. For more than a century Frenchmen viewed market opportunities differently from Americans and, therefore, came to different conclusions. People often do not see indicators that they are not looking for, and hence seldom recognize signs of how future social change will affect their business.

A powerful factor shaping social change in the history of the United States has been a strong feeling of national economic and physical superiority. One of the initial sources of this belief was the fact that by 1840, America had an average standard of living far superior to that of continental European nations, and, within another generation, one superior to that of world leader, Great Britain. That this ethos of confidence had declined by the late twentieth century needs no emphasis, but it has left many heritages that still hinder a more humble and analytical approach to the complexity of business processes. One of the old simplistic myths was that of an oversimplified view of American economic growth. Since by 1890 the United States was bigger and produced more than any other Western nation, American management, business practices, and technology were assumed to have been superior, a belief applied to most facets of the national history. When American business corporations, because of the huge domestic market, became bigger than their European counterparts, it was assumed that they had grown large because of brilliant entrepreneurship and efficient operation; when migrants flowed westward, scholars saw the process as uniquely favorable to the economic welfare of the nation; and when, between the conflicting jurisdictions of state and nation, government remained for more than a century confused and weak, it was acclaimed for pursuing laissez-faire policies and avoiding bureaucracy.

The fact that much of this business, social, and economic belief has always been false is only beginning to penetrate academic and management circles in the 1970s. As late as 1972, an able writer on the history of American management could say: "In Europe, American managerial ability is so superior to that of indigenous talent that it poses a threat to the economic goals of many nations."[2] Yet as American income per capita sank below that of Sweden, Denmark, West Germany, and Switzerland, and its *rate* of growth in this universal measure declined close to the bottom of the scale of the leading industrial nations, the old simplistic self-assurance had to crumble. Discouraged in a time of rapid change by the mounting confusion of theories, practical men needed more than ever to turn to history to understand the meaning for them of what was actually happening.

In trying to provide some answers this book starts with the assumption that entrepreneurs control the use of economic factors in all stages of business, and that, therefore, either growth or decline is largely the long shadow of management. Against such an assumption traditional economics would urge the importance of capital, land, and resources operating through the market. Yet history shows that rapid economic advance has occurred without major initial dependence on any of this trio, as for example in Japan; and that, therefore, there must be social and business forces at work.

This line of reasoning has a host of corollaries. If economic growth lags at a later stage in development, for example, the governmental or business systems should be assumed, until proven otherwise, to be at fault. If, on the other hand, business in a nation is able to secure the help it desires from government, this political achievement may be far more important than deposits of iron ore. Similarly, the ability to interpret and utilize correctly the large masses of information that flow to management in the twentieth century may be more important than economies coming from size. One could go on at length with such a list, but the conclusion should now be clear: the pervasive values, interests, and attitudes of a society and the resulting business structure constitute causal forces that shape the nature of both executive action and the markets in which companies operate.

The proposition that social structure and cultural values underlie economic change has been widely accepted in principle by leading economists, but it has too frequently been regarded as a given from the standpoint of theory. Almost equally well-accepted is the hypothesis that technological change or invention accelerates in response to effective demand. What this book will try to illustrate by the American experience is that these factors are not only the given, or platform from which economic growth takes off, but that by shaping and reshaping business forms and relationships, they are continuously active forces in daily economic operations and in the longer run processes of growth. The relations between business forms and practices, in turn, and the market are reciprocal, or, put another way, beyond the necessities of subsistence the market results from a fostered demand for what business has to offer.

The remarkable advances in commercially useful technology over the last two centuries have obscured the fact that the general use of a new product or service comes about only through the business system. For example, in the first decade of the twentieth century the Germans and French knew rather more about automobile technology than did Americans, but the foreign business leaders did not try to create a demand for inexpensive automobiles or apply the commonly understood machine processes necessary to make them. One may point out that this was a rational response to a smaller and poorer domestic market with less demand for middle-distance private transportation, but these controlling variables arose from the political and social structure, not from automobile technology.

Going a step further, for administrators seeking returns that more than cover costs, fabricating is one of the expenses, but it has usually been directed by salaried specialists who were not commonly thought of by top executives as businessmen. Knowledge of possible improvements in such processes may influence or even revolutionize business practices, but the change comes because executives above the plant level foresee a new demand and seek to satisfy it by employing new means. Unfortunately the tangible and relatively simple fact of new types of fabrication has led historians to put the cart before the horse and become preoccupied with manufacturing, rather than with the forces and decisions that control it. In contrast, we need to view our economic progress as one dependent on evolving associations of people in business who may make good or poor use of organizational forms and technology.

Neither definitive nor detailed, this is a suggestive book. The international background is limited to the four largest nations that have historically rivaled the United States in business efficiency and economic growth—the nations from which America could, and still can, learn by making comparisons. Even in the cases of France, Germany, Great Britain, and Japan, the information here is only a sampling of that available in English.

Business is narrowly conceived as the entrepreneurial or managerial operation of organizations, and closely allied areas such as the efficiency of labor and its use are not explored. This is not because one type of management might not be superior to another in its labor relations, but because comparisons regarding the cost, productivity, attitudes, and organization of labor on an international level involve vast unstudied areas, mere entrance into which would double the length of this book and produce highly questionable conclusions.

In short, this is an outline for what may properly constitute the field of business as distinct from economic or labor history. The synthesis is concerned primarily with human relations and organizational innovation. Economic measurements, for example, are used chiefly as one but not the only test of performance. My hope is that younger scholars, questioning what has been said here, will soon supply better information for the international and comparative history of business.

I

The
Business
Revolution,
1776-1840

1

The Social Bases of Enterprise

BUSINESS PRACTICES, inevitably reflecting the forms of society and culture, have roots far back in the past with offshoots in unexpected directions. The rise in the early modern period of interest in exactness and quantification, for example, accompanied by a shift from religious sanctions toward recognition of utility as self-justifying, was part of the basis for a phenomenal rise of commercial enterprise. These new attitudes spread in the sixteenth century in Western Europe, in contrast to the prolonged hold of older religious and aristocratic values in the rest of the world. Italy pioneered in the use of arabic numerals and the keeping of orderly accounts, England in the new secular emphasis on utility.[1] By the time the American colonies were established, the so-called modern attitude toward the world was part of the English heritage that the settlers brought with them.

This interest in finding out how to perform the tasks of life in ways that saved time and energy was probably the basic factor in the advance of material civilization. Since almost every action in life can be performed in several ways, better understanding may vary from innovation in physical processes to a new scientific or philosophical grasp, and the possible combinations of the specific thoughts or actions that enter into any complicated process are almost infinite. The key question is what lines of thought and activity are perceived as possible by a group wanting to accomplish certain ends; the answer is a product of the group's common knowledge, social structure, accepted values, normal roles (behavior), and physical opportunities. These psychological and environmental factors shaped the new American business institutions during the half-century following the end of the war for independence—the period of the Business Revolution.

AMERICAN PERCEPTION

Since people usually see only what they are prepared to see, generally held knowledge and values are basic factors that largely control the perception of opportunities. This proposition is so self-evident and widely accepted by philosophers and social scientists that elaboration seems superfluous.[2] Granting a widely held store of appropriate knowledge, however, not everyone will perceive opportunities in the same way, since personal elements enter into perception and may cause either useful innovation or barriers to change. It was extremely important that people in America of the late eighteenth century had brought with them or inherited the general business and technological knowledge of England and northwestern Europe, the most advanced areas of the world. Since there was little technical or business literature available to practical men, direct experience and personal instruction had to be the means of dissemination, and both were available in the new United States. While the market for luxury goods was still dominated by imports, and would be for many decades, domestic artisans were capable of copying those items for which there was wide demand. Similarly, not all American merchants used double entry bookkeeping and profit and loss accounts, but as demand rose toward the end of the eighteenth century, they readily made use of these more exact methods.

The lack of ability to execute intended policy is one of the principle causes of entrepreneurial failure, but because of the need to be jacks-of-all trades in new areas, Americans were rather well possessed of the perception and know-how necessary to carry out their plans. Thomas Hamilton, an astute British observer, said at the end of the early period, "In that knowledge . . . which the individual acquires by himself by actual observation, which bears an immediate market value, and is directly available in the ordinary avocations of life, I do not imagine the Americans are excelled by any people in the world."[3] Hamilton's remarks emphasize that relatively good preparation for business and interest in technology were not the results of a high level of general education. Outside of New England the level of public education was low, and it may well have declined between 1775 and 1825.[4] Rather, knowledge was transmitted through apprenticeship, small part-time business schools, and a trend toward including business subjects in the curricula of private academies. Parents of all classes who wanted their children to acquire special skills would bind them out in apprenticeships of many types for from four to seven years. Included were the sons of owners of big southern plantations, who were often apprenticed to merchants. Young men in the bigger cities could take evening courses at business academies, later to be called colleges, where within a few months they could learn arithmetic, bookkeeping, commercial geography, or navigation. The inroads of business education in the previously theological and classical private academies is illustrated in 1796 by the remark of Reverend David Barnes of Darby Academy in Massachusetts that business arithmetic was the international common language.[5]

LACK OF SOCIAL BARRIERS

While the American fund of social knowledge useful for production and trade was probably somewhat inferior to that in England or limited areas of northwestern Europe, nowhere was the social structure so favorable to rewarding business activity. The lack of prestigious governmental, military, or religious orders is so well-known that it needs no elaboration, but it should also be remembered that in America even landowning was in part a business pursuit. With a very few exceptions, American farmers bought and sold properties on a purely profit-making basis, and even Southern planters moved frequently to take advantage of new opportunities.[6] In the East coast ports where the Business Revolution occurred, no landowners, as such, ranked higher than the well-established mercantile leaders.

The most obvious characteristics of American social structure were its truncated form, with no legally privileged elite and wide horizontal levels of near equality. It was still in the old language a "class society," but not an authoritarian or carefully graded hierarchical one. As in other primarily agrarian societies, three classes could readily be distinguished, but they rested on property rather than governmental, religious, or social sanctions. There were no poor samurai or indigent noblemen in the United States. Upper class status rested on wealth (with some regard to birth), but such wealth could be won or lost within a generation.

Similarly, at the other end of the scale, laborers in the North were not numerous and most, except for slaves, regarded their status as temporary. In the years after 1830, when the urban industrial structure became more widespread, native-born whites tended to rise to middle class status, while their former places were taken by newly arrived immigrants. Compared to the European nations with much higher population density, free, male, native labor continued to be relatively scarce.

In the middle class level of small businessmen, farmers, and professionals the horizontal character of the social structure was most apparent. Geographical or occupational movement went on continuously and no one had a fixed place in a hierarchical order. From the standpoint of growth or the improvement of processes this extreme, competitive horizontalism had its weakness. It was hard for the successful businessman to boss his neighbors in the office or shop to the degree necessary for a well-run firm. Loyalty based on looking up to a man as leader could not be relied on, as it could, for example, in Germany or Japan. Respect was situational and temporary rather than institutionalized and lasting. Frequent movement from place to place also tended to interfere with the highest development of skills.

In this loosely structured, mobile society government was as much a utility as an authority. Central government only gradually gained nationalistic support and perhaps, in this early period, achieved little beyond a vague feeling of loyalty toward the flag.[7] State and local governments were looked upon as agencies to protect and promote their own areas in the intercity and interstate race for development. The entire period from 1787 to 1837 was characterized in economic terms by extensive schemes for internal development by the states, greater in relation to the populations involved than any ever undertaken by foreign governments before 1917.[8]

Law also became a utility for the businessman. In the Colonial period the common law doctrines regarding real property had been reshaped in the interest of easy transfer of ownership. As the courts recovered from the disruption of the Revolution, with the accompanying distaste for English precedents, the law was shaped to favor the active developer rather than the rights of either society as a whole or absentee owners.[9] Justice was expeditious, locally oriented, and nonlearned—qualities that might be harmful in a stable well-coordinated nation but were probably stimulating to the competitive advance of the Eastern seaports.[10]

EDUCATION FOR SUCCESS IN BUSINESS

With what values would families in such a society try to indoctrinate children? According to foreign visitors the whole process of child socialization was less rigorous than in Europe. Such writers saw American parental relations to children as permissive. The father had less authority than abroad, and although the mother's influence was increasing, it was still relatively weak. Since the father administered the severe punishments, he also generated a resentment or combativeness in his sons that was not suppressed by internal values placed on authority, as such, and was later transferred to relations with other adult males.[11]

There is a large contemporary childrearing literature, mostly by clergymen, that probably reflects parental desires more than it does reality. The books and articles stress devotion to work, effective use of time, saving money, abhorrence of debt, and obedience. But it is impossible to tell whether these were the values actually inculcated in the child or whether such widespread invocations were inspired by an obvious lack of these values in the young.[12] Some present writers fail to find any unusual dedication to work among the offspring of the American family system.[13] Since young males tended to migrate to new areas in search of opportunity, except among the rich the extended or patriarchal family within a town or village existed only in the more backward parts of the nation.

Therefore, while competitiveness was, in part, a product of the horizontal social structure, it was also stimulated by both the permissive family and the effects of continual migration on the bonds of kinship. The effort by most men, made insecure by strange surroundings, to find some firm values for self-justification may well account for the strong religiosity of many educated Americans but it also stimulated a desire for money. Competitiveness, weak personal ties, and ready movement from place to place aided in adjusting men and their lives to the demands of the market and the rational needs of business. Perry Miller, one of the most important historians of American thought, found the business values dominant by 1815.[14]

VALUES AND SOCIAL ROLES

The conditioning force of both business and migration contributed to a number of widely held values that were more useful in the early stages of business development than in meeting the complex problems that came later. In new areas activity was highly valued, and perhaps habitual, on the part of the aspiring middle class, whereas reading and contemplation savored of femininity and indecision. Necessarily, experience rather than theoretical knowledge was the accepted guide for decisions.[15] Before science and bureaucracy entered much into business affairs these values, more pronounced in America than in England or the European Continent, may have been a stimulant to growth.

Values, particularly those internalized in childhood, are principal factors in shaping the social roles that constitute business behavior. And business behavior, in turn, controls the standard of living and rate of economic growth. Role analysis, therefore, is inseparable from understanding economic performance. Unfortunately, role terminology varies somewhat from one discipline to another, but essentially a social role indicates the way a man in a certain position is expected to behave in performing the functions that go with his status. In a traditional economy where social and technological processes have changed but slowly, expectations can be quite exact, or, where ceremony is involved, exacting. In an economy or society undergoing rapid change, expectations are much less certain. Since the new United States represented an extreme form of the latter case, one is not surprised to find roles loosely structured and expectations of behavior correspondingly indefinite. Continual migration of businessmen and others to new areas accentuated the uncertainty.

From the business standpoint, loosely defined roles offer more chance of innovation and require more thought about problems than would be required in a rigidly fixed society. On balance, the history of the period of the Business Revolution in America indicates a net positive value in what might be called open-ended roles. New forms were more readily tried, cooperation appears to have been relatively easy, and traditional resistances weak. But loose roles also had some disadvantages. Men were easily made overconfident by chance success when they really had only a poor comprehension of what they were doing. Americans probably took risks more readily than Europeans, but because of lack of proper understanding, the risks often turned out badly. The absence of traditional community sanctions on conduct and the ease of movement to new states to avoid obligations undoubtedly led to more dishonesty in American business transactions than in those of more stable societies. Yet, against this petty dishonesty or local corruption must be balanced the class privilege and influence of nations with feudal traditions. It was not regarded as corrupt for established business leaders, members of the aristocracy, and top administrative officials of post-Napoleonic France, for example, to limit corporate charters to applicants from their own ranks.[16]

Whether the Calvinistic emphasis on "calling" and salvation led to more ardor in business activities may be uncertain, but the local control of religion surely encouraged the use of the church as a type of business club, where members of the same denomination gathered together to promote their locality and their individual ventures.

American role playing since the Revolution, at least, has tended to be characterized by its friends as highly individualistic. In the United States and Western Europe, individualism meant relative individual freedom in the control of property, what has been called entrepreneurial freedom rather than the Latin or Eastern type of inward feeling of personal uniqueness.[17] Probably the real desire for individual, including family, control of operations was stronger in France and much of the rest of Europe than in America, where the need for cooperation in settling new areas was a strong force.[18] In fact, the tempering of personal and familial individualism by the need of the migrant to conform and cooperate may have been a modification particularly valuable for the advance of more highly-organized and widely-financed business.

Emphasis on equality of rights among the members of any group became another strong element in American individualism. While often these rights were connected with the ownership or use of property, under most circumstances each person tended to be assertive about his equality with all others.[19] Whether this horizontalism was strongly present in the Colonial period is doubtful. Equality as a value or a component of role playing was unquestionably strengthened by the Revolution, migration to the interior, and urbanization. These same forces also continued to lessen the already comparatively low value placed on ascribed status. Even the rapid growth of corporations controlled by directors elected by the stockholders, through emphasizing impersonality and equality of rights, may be seen, in part, as a manifestation of American horizontalism.

European travelers almost universally saw Americans exhibiting the traits we would today ascribe to an inferiority complex: a desire to be more than they were and a corresponding overassertiveness. Fanny Kemble wrote in her journal: "Such an unhappy sensitive community surely never existed in the world." The travelers saw Americans as inordinately somber, serious, and without real pleasure outside their business. Although such qualities are not necessarily admirable components of society as a whole, they are important for business success.

Perceived opportunity is, of course, basic to business decisions that produce change and growth. In a sparsely inhabited country with rich farming land, timber close to the water, a seacoast suited to trade, and a rapidly growing population, opportunities seemed to abound. Motivation for achievement must also be in part a function of perceived opportunities as well as internalized values. At all events, compared with the entrepreneurs of other nations Americans appear to have been overly optimistic, to have been too ready to assume risks, with the result that there were many starts and many failures.[20] Yet, at an early stage of business development this may constitute the most rapid road to progress.

Once such behavioral or culture patterns are well established they tend to outlast for long periods the operation of the factors that originally gave them birth. This hypothesis, with which few historians would quarrel, suggests the possibility of using behavioral characteristics for forecasting purposes. In later chapters the process will be illustrated from successive stages of the past, yet there is no reason why such "ordinal variables" (ranked in relation to estimated comparative strength) should not be projected into the future.

The American business society that had reached an initial level of maturity by 1840 was the product of all of these interacting social forces operating in an area of good, although not outstanding, economic opportunity. The fact that the United States achieved the most rapid economic advance in the world during this first half-century of its constitutional life was more the result of a combination of fortuitous external events, the absence of hampering traditions or customs, and the mutual stimulation of government and business than any unique geographical or technological circumstances.

2

Innovations in Structure
and Processes

SCHOLARS in history, economics, and technology have called a
series of physical and social changes in Western society between
1750 and 1850 the Industrial Revolution. In keeping with this language,
the focus of attention has been on the gradual growth of machinery
using nonmanual power. When such machines became economically
productive they were housed in factories that, in turn, drew workers
from other activities, produced new business forms for distribution,
created new opportunities for the use of capital, and greatly raised the
standard of living. Exemplifying this approach, David Landes writes:
"The heart of the Industrial Revolution was an interrelated succession
of technological changes. The material advance took place in three areas:
. . . substitution of mechanical devices for human skills; . . . inanimate
power—in particular steam—took the place of human and animal
strength; . . . a marked improvement in the getting and working of
raw materials . . . ."[1] Although not always so explicitly stated, this
general or classic approach assigns a primary and basic function to
technology.

Yet, most of the same writers would agree that certain social conditions were, and still are, essential to a rapid growth of production in

Parts of this chapter have appeared in the *American Historical Review* 79 (Dec.
1974) under the title "The Business Revolution," and are reprinted with permission.

factories using power machinery.[2] Even those who adhere closely to measurable economic factors admit that something has to accelerate growth in the existing or traditional economy. Greater understanding may come, therefore, from reversing the traditional approach of focusing on technology, while assuming the entrepreneurial decisions necessary for its economic use, and instead seeing the technological advances as following the demands of men motivated by new elements in the business-political-social system.

THE PATTERN OF CHANGE

A general model of the progress from relatively fixed or traditional patterns of economic life to those characterized by new adjustments promoting higher productivity runs as follows. Such social change requires as an initial condition the existence of an entrepreneurial group enjoying relative security and freedom of action, as well as access to requisite knowledge. Given this condition, an increase in the demand for goods so substantial as to exceed the capacity of the existing system of production and exchange will induce entrepreneurs to enlarge their scale of operations.[3] The process of enlargement, in turn, entails and indeed depends upon innovations in forms of organization—such as the specialization of a number of functions previously performed by one individual businessman. Specialization increases the efficiency of the system as a whole (much as the division of labor does in production) and stimulates a greater flow of information. For example, a better capital market and faster turnover increases the availability of this classic factor, while each specialized business unit enhances the operating efficiency of the labor and management factors. At this point the operation of the model has been described; yet an additional element, efficient relations between the specialized units, determines the over-all performance of the system; and among the institutions strongly affecting this efficiency are those of government.

The realism of this approach through social or business structure can be readily substantiated from the history of Great Britain or Holland, but the interrelationships are both more rapid and clearly defined in the United States.[4] Here changes that had been gradual in England, stretching over three-quarters of a century, occurred within a generation, with developments in business structure clearly preceding the use of new technology.[5]

In addition to dealing with a different nation and period, the business approach also places more emphasis on human planning and behavior than has been done by economic historians. To my knowledge, few scholars have stressed business organization rather than technology or capital as the leading sector responsible for economic growth.[6] Even if the concept of a leading sector is dismissed as ambiguous, the decisions to use existing technology for new purposes had to originate with businessmen who were, in turn, socially conditioned to perceive the specific opportunities for improvement.

The early American development is made more dramatic by the fact that the coming of the new political-business system was accompanied by what now appears to be the most rapid rise in the standard of living of any contemporary nation in the world. It is this phenomenon, recognized in the works of a number of distinguished economists, that so strongly underlines the role structure of entrepreneurship in finance, trade, and service in creating the modern "industrial" world.

A reconsideration of priorities was strongly suggested by Robert Gallman's estimates that in 1840 the United States had a gross national product (GNP) that was, per capita, 40 to 65 percent larger than France and approaching that of Great Britain.[7] Since "value added by all manufacture," manual as well as power, stood at under $250 million in the census of 1840, and steam and iron machinery, aside from steamboats, was just coming into use, clearly some other potent elements had been involved in the rapid advance.

Another economist, Paul A. David, was meanwhile carrying out a detailed study of national income or GNP from 1800 to 1840, the results of which first reached the scholarly public in 1967. The arresting conclusion is that between 1800 and 1840 real per capita domestic product increased between 55 and 62 percent.[8] Since David also finds a gain in the nonagricultural labor force from 17 percent of the total in 1800 to 37 percent in 1840, and a rate of increase in agricultural productivity per worker lower than in nonfarm work, the question must be: what nonagricultural factors were causing this great upswing?

In 1973 a book by the geographer Allan R. Pred organized much of the evidence needed for an answer.[9] Linking information flows to volumes of trade and types of business transactions, Pred for the first time assembled some of the chief dimensions and characteristics of the expanding American business system. His maps and statistics emphasized as never before that upward change in the rate of economic growth depends more on a society that under certain conditions, fosters improvements in the business structure for the utilization of land, labor, capital, and entrepreneurship than it does on any particular local resources. Put another way, neither available resources nor technology can by themselves cause change and growth; they require a social system that produces the necessary knowledge and managerial roles.

THE BUSINESS REVOLUTION

A short historical background is necessary to understand the timing of the Business Revolution in the United States. Prior to national independence, the imperial yoke rested rather lightly on the colonies, yet the fact that they were largely dependent on England for both commercial capital and approval of mercantile practices discouraged American innovation. Trade regulations were designed to keep the colonies as producers of raw material, which they would chiefly have been in any case, and while some types of manufacturing for export (such as finished iron products) were prohibited, it is doubtful if output could have expanded much in the face of the high cost of inland transportation and British competition. Continuous wars at sea in which the colonists were necessarily belligerents may also have been a retarding factor. The chief restraints on Colonial American progress, however, seemed to have involved a lack of capital not tied to Britain, which prevented provincially financed improvements in transportation, and the inadequacy of inland transportation, which fostered the development of isolated urban business communities around the seaports and self-sufficient farms, with small purchasing power, in the hinterland.

Independence presented business challenges and freed pent-up entrepreneurial energies that soon created a business community in the Northeast capable of winning state assistance for commercial development. While some business forms now appeared in America in even more modern guises than in Great Britain, rapid growth, as men like Alexander Hamilton could clearly see, was still held back by lack of capital. In 1790 and 1791, Hamilton, as Secretary of the Treasury, and his supporters in Congress partially met this need through funding the national debt, which was largely held by businessmen, into bonds salable at home and abroad, and through the chartering of the First Bank of the

United States. These two measures created over $50 million worth of high grade securities available as a base for further credit.

But in the long run, more capital was supplied fortuitously by the wars in Europe that were to last, intermittently, from 1793 until 1815. During part of this period the nation became the major neutral ocean carrier, and some American merchants made fortunes of over a million dollars, unheard of from trade in the Colonies. By the time of Jefferson's embargo in 1808, which began a period of interference with ocean shipping, American mercantile houses such as those of Brown, Girard, Astor, or Derby had grown greatly in size; and the specialization of functions had increased strikingly in trade, finance, and handicraft manufacture. Meanwhile, as we will see, promotional policies by government actively furthered these developments.

Specialization was accompanied by far more systematic ways of conducting business. In accounting "the eighteenth century was an era of invention . . . as much as in methods of manufacture."[10] Depletion of capital, inputs, and outputs made their way into the old mercantile bookkeeping. Simultaneously, as the volume and complexity of trade increased, double entry and profit and loss accounts became the rule in large mercantile firms. In Philadelphia in 1796 William Mitchell published the first American text on accounting, which was followed in 1800 by that of Thomas Turner in Portland, Maine.[11] By 1810, Robert Oliver of Baltimore maintained a system of accounts vastly more detailed and meticulous than had been used in earlier decades.[12]

The existence of a number of competing cities within the framework of the same national market appears to have been a major stimulant to business development. At least four of the Northeastern states—Maryland, Pennsylvania, New York, and Massachusetts—felt their general welfare to be dependent on the promotion of their major seaports. Consequently, governments joined in the competition to attract capital and trade to a degree not duplicated abroad. From independence until 1837, at least, the mercantile community of each of the major ports became increasingly afraid of having trade diverted to their rivals, and as a result state legislators became anxious to assist business development in all practical, and some impractical, ways. A common state device for mobilizing private capital and promoting enterprise was the chartered business corporation, the most important organizational innovation of the period.

The states were willing to delegate wide powers to private business corporations, which they claimed would advance the general welfare. In one sense, from Roman times on this had always been the reason for

such delegation of power. The American innovation expanded the definition of general welfare to include practically all local economic growth.
While Colonial governments had chartered political, educational, and
religious corporations, they had maintained grave doubts about charters
for business purposes. Only seven such companies survived from before
the Revolution.[13] In contrast, the legislators of the young states took an
enthusiastic view of corporations for banking, insurance, transportation,
public works, and manufacturing, often subscribing substantial state
funds for corporate stocks, and, in turn, demanding bonuses or selling
state securities to banks, insurance companies, and other profitable beneficiaries of state charters.

Prior to 1800 neither England nor France had satisfactory arrangements for incorporation, yet, all-in-all, the biggest advantage in this
area accruing to business in the United States appears to have come from
incorporation by competing state jurisdictions rather than by a single
unit of national government.[14] The pressure for state development meant
that legal adjustments to the new demands of business firms selling
securities to the public were rather quickly made in the United States
and only slowly brought about in England and France.[15] In 1800, when
neither Britain nor France had more than about a score of the modern
type of corporations, the United States, with only a small fraction of
the population of the two European states, had incorporated over 300
such private enterprises.[16]

The mature corporate form, as Europe was to learn, had a number
of advantages over any partnership. A corporation could be given various
monopoly rights; issue many different types of securities, representing
either equity or debt; set face values on the securities low enough to
encourage wide sale; enjoy eternal life, unless limited by its charter; and
lease other properties or lease itself to other owners. It could also limit
the liability of its stockholders to the assets of the company; operate in
receivership when it could not meet its obligations; be transferred to the
control of its creditors by bankruptcy; and separate managerial control
from ownership.

The early corporation, however, was probably most important as a
device for mobilizing the savings of many small businessmen. One could
not afford, for reason of liability if no other, to join a partnership in a
place that was too remote for any careful supervision of operations. But
with the approval of the state, the granting of monopoly privileges in
some cases, and the requirements for voting and record-keeping, particularly, it might seem safe to buy a few shares in a bank or in a water
or turnpike company located outside one's own locality.

The various possibilities of the corporation were realized more by the process of litigation and judicial decision than through initial definition. It took a generation, for example, to establish limited liability as the rule when there was no contrary provision in the charter, and the right to do business in other states, where not specifically prohibited, was only affirmed by the Supreme Court in 1839.[17] The possibilities of preferred stock and various types of bonds, together with corporate leasing, were not fully realized until a later age. The rise of salaried corporate managers, owning little or no stock, was a gradual evolution from the 1820s on as transportation, insurance, and banking companies grew larger.

MORE SPECIALIZED BUSINESS

Ironically, the first direct beneficiary of the early wave of incorporation was the hard pressed government of the Confederation. Even before the war was over, Philadelphians, in 1780, brought mercantile capital to the aid of the nation by chartering the Pennsylvania Bank, which was superseded a year later by the federally and state-chartered Bank of North America.[18] In contrast to English and European banks that had grown as family partnerships, incorporated American banks could raise their capital from the whole business community through sale of stock and could issue notes bearing the stamp of state government approval. That the Bank of North America was quickly followed by many others, particularly in the flush years from 1793 to 1808, demonstrated the attractiveness and business utility of chartered banks. Since working capital, rather than buildings or machinery, was the largest credit requirement of most early business, these numerous competing banks each making short-term but renewable loans were a strong aid to expansion and growth. Commenting on late-eighteenth-century Britain, Mathias says: "the most important single development lay in the progressive efficiency and expansion of conduits and institutions serving the short term end of the money markets."[19] Much of what appeared as short-term lending on the ledgers of banks was, in fact, continuing and never-demanded investment in enterprises. Such enduring loans facilitated the investment of profits in the expansion of fixed capital. Another source of capital, largely through mortgages, came from the new insurance companies. In the Colonial period the insurance business had first become specialized in Philadelphia, and its rapid spread to other cities was hastened by use of the corporate form. In 1800 thirty-two marine insurance companies were facilitating the boom in ocean shipping. This rapid adoption of the corporation for a wide variety of enterprises in the United States within the course of a single generation must be regarded as one of the most important developments of the Business Revolution.

The division of tasks in early business or office operations was probably as important as the division of labor was in manufacturing plants for raising levels of efficiency. Wholesalers, for example, became more departmentalized within their offices and more specialized in what they bought and sold. Some dealt in foreign imports that were passed on to dealers whose chief connections were with the backcountry; others specialized in facilitating the Southern cotton trade; a few concentrated on still more limited activities such as auctioneering; while many became various types of special commission merchants.[20]

IMPORTANCE OF THE OLD-STYLE MERCHANTS

Because of high profits from the 1793–1808 boom the exporting and importing merchants became the people to approach for all risks that would not be financed by a bank. And even when they were so financed, the local merchants had almost invariably subscribed the capital for the bank. Wholesalers financed the great upswing in handicraft production, as well as the beginnings of mechanized textile manufacture; they provided the goods and buildings needed to establish new retailers in both the city and its surrounding backcountry; they invested in construction and real estate enterprises for both business and residential use and put the profits into new facilities for trade and manufacture; they financed the rapidly growing cotton trade; and at all times they invested heavily in improvements in transportation.[21]

Capital flows and the creation of auxiliary businesses were also stimulated by the trade boom of the 1790s. Issues of government, bank insurance, and transportation company stocks or bonds led some erstwhile merchants to specialize in security brokerage. By the middle of the decade brokers met at fixed locations for trading in both New York and

Philadelphia and later formed exchanges. As time went on some merchants, like the Browns of Baltimore, came to specialize in foreign exchange and stocks, while others, like Stephen Girard of Philadelphia, became private bankers prepared to undertake the initial distribution of securities. By the 1830s note brokers, various mercantile associations, and specialized law firms added to the array of institutions involved in the East coast flows of information, capital, and credit.

THE PRECOCIOUS NORTHEAST COAST

By 1800 the signs of rapid change were obvious in all the big Northern seaports. Business information was being supplied by a score of urban dailies primarily devoted to commercial news and advertising. Printing and publishing became not only one of the principal industries in each large city, but its products formed the central information network of business. Building, representing the largest source of urban employment, was going on everywhere, and profits from construction were being put into expanding ocean and inland trade. Handicraft shops were frequently outgrowing their confines. In order to provide more space in the now crowded business sections the craftsmen's families were moved elsewhere, and the former homes were converted into a mixture of shops for producing and selling.

Rapid commercial development in this period before 1840 was largely confined to the Northeast coast. In 1790 the 100-mile-wide coastal strip extending about 400 miles in a line from Maryland to southern Maine had a population of about 2.5 million people, with under 5 percent living in cities of over 10,000. By 1820 the population in this area had doubled and by 1840 tripled, while that in the cities of over 10,000 rose to 10 and 15 percent respectively. Thus, the total population of major cities increased from 125,000 to roughly one million. This region in which the Business Revolution occurred can be regarded, therefore, as a generating center of activity that was separated from the Southern coast and the trans-Appalachian interior by costs of transportation and by time intervals far exceeding those between neighboring countries in Europe. Along this fertile and accessible coastal plain was a rapidly growing agricultural population, within reach of markets, that supplied the growing cities with laborers as well as food.

Thus, the favorable conditions present in England for the distribution of produce were to some extent duplicated in America; by contrast, the northern coastal plain of France suffered from fewer protected navigable waterways and from over-concentration of business energies in Paris to the exclusion of other urban centers. The coastal plains of Germany and the Low Countries, on the other hand, were not under the control of a single central government. It should also be remembered that from 1793 to 1815, business development in all of northwestern Europe was retarded by war. Compared to the United States of 1830, France and Germany were economically backward nations, not because of lack of resources or business skills, but because of politics, social structure, and geography.

EFFECTS OF FASTER COMMUNICATION

In addition to the American head start arising from the trade boom and consequent specialization of business and labor activities, important further gains came from improvements in transportation and communications. These were aided by continual investment from competitive state governments and by improved mail service supplied from Washington, both chiefly for the benefit of business.

In 1790, after a five-day journey from Philadelphia, a traveler would have gone southward only as far as the head of the Chesapeake Bay, or westward as far as Lancaster, Pennsylvania, or northward to New York and Brooklyn. In 1817, the same traveler would have reached, after five days, either Richmond, Virginia, the cities of mid-Pennsylvania, or New London, Connecticut. By this time, however, a five-day journey from New York would have extended southward as far as Norfolk, Virginia, northwards to Portsmouth, New Hampshire, or westward nearly to Lake Ontario.[22] These simple measures not only help describe the impact of the Business Revolution but also tell the story of the victory of New York over Philadelphia. In the great upsurge of trade, businessmen in the former city could initially reach Europe and populous places in the United States more quickly and, in consequence, the New York port was a better distributing point for the rapid turnover of merchants' inventories. Quicker transport was obviously one of the major factors in gradually reducing the very large amount of working capital required by early enterprise.[23]

Along the Northeast coastal axis itself, improvement in the time of travel up to 1820 was primarily a matter of better highways. In 1818 the statistical analyst Adam Seybert said that the great increase in the number and length of post roads "demonstrated the rapid improvement of our country."[24] Since more than three-quarters of turnpike traffic was on business matters, whether in the form of commercial travelers or in the delivery of newspapers and mail, the economic importance of the reduction in time is obvious. Newspapers devoted 75 to 90 percent of their space to business concerns, and few besides businessmen would send letters costing from $0.25 to $1.00 a page. Thus the flow of information and the speed and efficiency of business transactions were intimately related. It must be remembered in this connection that the buyer had to wait for the transmission of an order for goods as well as for the merchandise to be sent back. The decrease in total time necessary to receive and fill orders led to a much more rapid turnover of inventory or, in other words, more profit from the same quantity of working capital. In 1790, for example, it took a minimum of about two weeks to transmit an order, or to receive other information, between Boston and Philadelphia; by 1836, the mail moved regularly in thirty-six hours.[25]

Before 1835, steam-powered transportation had only a slight effect on the carriage of mail (including newspapers). Total postal carrier movements in that year were 16.9 million miles by stagecoach, 7.8 million on horseback, under a million by steamboat, and about a third of a million by train. Railroads alone could not carry mail continuously between any of the major cities.[26]

For heavy goods the completion of canal systems along the urban axis was highly important. Even in 1840, the necessity of frequent transfers of freight limited the amount of bulky or heavy goods that could be carried on railroads to metropolitan regions. The Erie Canal, (completed in 1825), the Union (Philadelphia to the Susquehanna River; 1828), the Chesapeake and Delaware (1830), and the Delaware and Raritan (1834), provided protected water connections from New London to Baltimore, and inland to Buffalo and the cities in the Susquehanna Valley. While in theory travel to the West either by canal and rail from Philadelphia or by river and canal from New York was now possible, its volume remained small. In 1835 more than four-fifths of all freight revenue on the Erie Canal was from goods shipped within New York

State.[27] Hence, even by the time the panic of 1837 temporarily checked rapid economic development, the new high levels of business activity were still confined to the Northeast coast.

IMPROVED ENTREPRENEURSHIP

All these elements—faster and less expensive transportation, more rapid capital turnover, and the resulting increase in the tempo of business activity—led to the operation of the final, and ultimately most important, factor in the world of business, namely, better-informed entrepreneurial decisions based on faster flows of information including, particularly, more up-to-date knowledge of the state of the market. For overseas information, the daily newspapers were meeting sailing packets outside the harbors and rushing the foreign news to press by racing schooners, while overland mail between major centers was being speeded by relays of horses. There had truly been a revolutionary change in the tempo of activity and in the possible alternatives open to entrepreneurs.[28]

In addition to these feedbacks from trade and transportation, the diversity of knowledge in big urban centers such as New York and Philadelphia led specialists to congregate, talk, and find better ways of doing things. While patent records are unreliable for the period prior to 1837, the four large East coast centers appear to have had per capita rates for patent applications up to eight or nine times as high as the rest of the nation.[29] Large scale urbanization also meant that the capitalist could work with better newspapers, more able lawyers, and more astute financial advisers, and was better able to externalize risks through the use of outside agencies, access to private or commercial bankers, quick transfer of inventory to dealers, or tighter control over suppliers.

EXURBAN MANUFACTURING

Although along the East coast these factors worked to build the major ports into bigger and bigger centers of domestic trade, there were some limitations on their growth and prosperity. Since none of the major cities had fast-flowing rivers within their bounds, mills and factories using waterpower had to be located further upstream. To some extent such locations would also have been dictated by higher urban land values and wages. Thus a fringe of factory industry came, particularly after 1825, to surround the major centers at distances of five to thirty miles. Aside from textiles most of this manufacturing, as well as that in the cities, was by handworkers assisted only by waterpower. In general the old craft processes were still more profitable than experimentation with expensive and unpredictable new machines.[30]

Distance from the markets of the city, however, was a simpler problem to deal with than adequate management. Entrepreneurs needed not only information, but the ability to put it to use, and here again the mercantile community was of primary importance. Management of the industries using power machinery, which by 1840 usually involved large factories only in the case of textiles, became a part of the specialization of mercantile functions. From the pioneer efforts of Almy and Brown of Providence from 1792 on, successful enterprises were based on mercantile experience in finance, supply, and marketing, leaving only plant supervision in the hands of technicians. By 1809, Almy and Brown alone, through aggressive interurban marketing, had underwritten the success of a majority of the spinning mills operating in New England.[31] Thus, in the first three decades of the nineteenth century merchants had organized a modern textile industry with large plants and adequate marketing. This represented an especially important example of alert, experienced, general entrepreneurs with access to working capital, quickly taking advantage of business opportunities to use new technology. The same essential pattern was followed in steam engines, hardware, and a few minor industries that were partially mechanized by 1840.

By then the Business Revolution had taken place in the United States. The nation now had a commercial structure capable of adopting machine technology, whether originating locally or abroad, as fast as it could be developed. American businessmen, as attested to by both natives and foreigners, were particularly attuned to machine processes and were prepared both to innovate in and manage mass production. In all, no matter what the level of value in dollars added by mechanized industry in 1840, the necessary social, structural changes associated with modern industrialism had occurred, and with twenty years of stable government the expansion of manufacturing would follow as a matter of course. In actuality, the census figures show that the decade 1839 to 1849 marked the most rapid rate of increase in value added by manufacture in American history.

While this brief account of the Business Revolution has dealt chiefly with the United States, the logic of the development in America and Britain inspires confidence that further research will reveal much the same patterns in nations that were slower to develop. The American advance was especially rapid because of a social structure permeated by a nearly universal interest in business and because of federal and state governments staffed by men interested in economic development. Also significant in this advance were immigrants who were, perhaps, more likely to innovate than immobile people; a group of entrepreneurs sharpened by the experiences of the Revolutionary War and new national opportunities; and finally, a shared language and trade connections with Britain, the world's business leader. The American experience also illustrates that the ability to produce goods is only a part of the creation of social utility. That such favorable factors need not always be present in the same form or proportions is indicated by the much later case of Japan; yet there, as in America, it was the national culture and business structure rather than resources or technology that initiated the rapid advance.[32]

3

The Competence of
Early Management

H AVING SKETCHED the overall developments of the Business
Revolution in the United States, it is time to examine how
management contributed to or retarded this rapid business and economic growth, to show in more detail how there was economic gain
from specialization of business functions, and why in the process of
change business management faced new problems.

AMERICANS ADAPT TO NEW BUSINESSES

Assuming as axiomatic that men are best at making initial decisions
involving well-known factors, the challenges to specialized management
may be divided into types requiring judgments similar to those of the
old general merchants and those that introduced basically new considerations. In both categories one can also discover decisions that were based
more on familiar perceptions as distinct from those that depended on
previously unexamined situations. For example, the new financial specialties of banking, insurance, and brokerage as well as the subdivisions
of wholesale trade were all familiar parts of the world of the old mer-

chant, as were contracts for shipbuilding and offshore voyages. On the other hand, the construction and operation of canals, turnpikes, and steamboats all involved unfamiliar activities. While some merchants had participated in putting-out operations or been inactive partners in handicraft manufacturing, none had experience with the technology of steam machinery or the problems of managing scores of factory hands. Obviously the traditional type of operations would reflect previous American social and cultural patterns, while the new would constitute a test of the ability of men in the society to adjust to change.

Establishing specialized mercantile functions as separate enterprises appears to have been facilitated by the nature of American society. The business structure was unusually flexible, the jack-of-all-trades tradition stemming from the Colonial period encouraged shifts in careers, and geographic movement made for many new business starts—as well as many failures. In such a mobile society family ties were weaker than in Europe, mature sons and daughters moved rather regularly to new areas, and temporary partnerships were easily entered into and also easily dissolved. Whereas in France, for example, the rule was the family firm staying in the same place generation after generation and managed by relatives, in the United States it was the exception.[1] The same ease of separation and mobility may also be observed in local government and in Protestant religious sects.

Mobility was probably responsible for another aspect of American management. Even in the days of universal small business, proprietors showed a high degree of impersonality in their dealing with both employees and customers. Paternalism was perhaps unnecessary in this land of opportunity; at any rate its practice was limited, and loyalty beyond self-interest was less expected than in cultures like those of Latin America or Japan.[2] This meant that in the United States decisions for expansion, liquidation, or divisions of existing firms were made more strictly on a financial or market-oriented basis.

Ease of physical movement and of entry into small business undoubtedly helped to adjust the entrepreneur to types of business suited to his personality. P. T. Barnum, for example, made ventures in retail trade, with poor results, before he found his metier in promoting amusement, while R. H. Macy failed several times in small towns before finding that his ideas were only suited to retailing in large cities. Yet regardless of suitability of personality, failure was common in America. Nathaniel Griswold of New York said that of a hundred merchants he had known over a fifty-year span, only seven had avoided bankruptcy.[3]

The American characteristics of optimism, ready assumption of risks, and continual movement made for a high degree of flexibility in the small enterprises of the early nineteenth century. Therefore the ease in shifting to greater specialization, in itself, goes far to explain the lead that the nation established in gross national product per capita over all rivals except England—and in the case of that country, the gap was soon closed. This conclusion is reinforced by the fact that European merchants presumably had more experience than American. Yet even in shifting to generally familiar, but slightly different roles, the merchants of the United States may have been more facile if less knowledgeable.

THE MERCHANT'S OFFICE

Let us begin the analysis of adjustment to change with a brief picture of the office and the problems of the old-style merchant. The office was usually run by a single proprietor, but in order to raise additional capital or spread entrepreneurial risks for special projects, partnerships were entered into by signing articles of agreement which allowed each member to speak for the firm and made him personally responsible for all the debts incurred. Sometimes a partnership was either limited to a single venture or formed in order to staff remote offices. In general, where today a firm would set up a subsidiary or contract with a supplier or distributor, it was common then to enter into a partnership. There was no essential difference among Western nations in such early business forms. Merchants in the United States not only ran their counting rooms (business offices) in accordance with British customs, but many of them had been born and trained abroad. Presumably America had no advantage over Europe in mercantile management. To assist him in his office and warehouse the proprietor needed only one or two bookkeeper-clerks and about the same number of porters to move heavy goods around. The critical mercantile need was usually for reliable agents in distant ports, men who were necessarily beyond the reach of control from the home office. Hence partnerships became spread over many small and distant offices, and little experience was acquired in the management of large staffs of employees. The ships, which in the eighteenth century represented a principal form of fixed mercantile investments, required the managing of a score or more of sea-going employees, but by tradition this responsibility was always under the control of the captain or shipmaster. Furthermore, those employed for navigation were doing an auxiliary service that did not directly involve the main activity of buying and selling, and as time went on the management of ship transportation became a specialized business.[4]

The small amount of capital needed to start a mercantile business (the low threshold of entry)—not more than $10,000—kept the business highly competitive and made it appear dangerous and unprofitable to expand by hiring managers and delegating functions. This explains not only the merchants' lack of experience in the management of large offices, but also their interest in investing profits in outside ventures rather than in expansion of the firm. By the 1820s auctioneers and specialized dealers had made general importing and exporting so relatively unprofitable that men like John Jacob Astor, Alexander Brown, or Stephen Girard gradually withdrew from it.

The essentials of business success in general trade with remote areas were twofold: buying, where prices were low, commodities that had a good market in the home or in some other port, and having captains capable of safely bringing their ships and cargoes to the right place at the right time. Aside from luck or lucrative government contracts, neither of which should be slighted, the business called for good judgment regarding the probability of war or peace, the movement of commodity prices in distant markets, the honesty and ability of a small number of captains and supercargoes, and above all else, the shrewd handling of credit. American merchants of the early period had less access to capital than their counterparts in Britain, Holland, France, or Germany, and hence the United States merchant was likely to buy on credit advanced from England and kept rotating by periodic shipments of goods in repayment. The amount of such credit that a merchant could command depended greatly on his reputation for caution, wealth, and probity.

On the marketing side of the business the merchant had to exercise a different type of judgment, one that was common to all types of trade. Practically every domestic retailer or jobber wanted either to exchange goods or be given credit. Cash transactions were few and far between. Much of the merchant's success, therefore, depended on his estimates of the terms he should grant. Around his home city he could keep some track of what his debtors were doing; also, local people were more likely to pay in goods, but even at ports a hundred miles distant he had to rely on the reputation of the applicant, frequently backed by interest bearing notes that would become mortgages on specified real estate if payment was delayed beyond a certain time. Prices were, of course, varied in relation to the amount and type of credit.

COTTON AND LAND

In the rapid specialization of American mercantile activity after 1790 there were some factors that had no counterparts in western Europe, particularly in the fields of cotton exports and land development. The invention of the cotton gin in 1793 by Eli Whitney was the most important exclusively American technological achievement of the first phase of the Business Revolution. Its rapid adoption lowered the price of cotton suitable for spinning far below the price of wool or flax. Furthermore, for many uses cotton was a more desirable fiber. Through the entire period from 1795 to 1860 the United States maintained a near monopoly on the export of short staple cotton. Between 1826 and 1836 these exports rose from $26 million to $71 million annually, providing not only the exchange necessary for buying needed commodities, but supporting the international soundness of the dollar, which aided the states in selling their bonds in foreign markets to finance internal development. The cotton trade created specialized mercantile firms that financed Southern factors who collected the cotton from the planters, advanced the money supplied from the Northern seaports, and shipped the cotton in payment.

A second unique factor, land development, has always had an enormous influence on the entire character of American business enterprise. Throughout our history "real estate" has been the biggest business. In 1972 its intake of $70 billion in fees, commissions, and profits was almost as large as that of the total remainder of retail trade. While all United States land west of the original states was owned by the federal government, the gradual transfer of the farming, mining, or timber sections to private ownership involved countless large and small middlemen. The same process went on with the unused lands belonging to the larger of the original states. In both cases such business participation was invited by official prices often far below market value, and by land grants for military service. Accordingly, it was to be expected that men or firms with capital would buy all they could and resell at a realistic figure, and they did. The more valuable lands were generally disposed of in large tracts either to single enterprisers, such as Tench Coxe in Pennsylvania, or to organizations like the Holland Land Company in New York. Meanwhile, the Continental Congress made a number of enormous wholesale deals covering much of the future state of Ohio.

In a day when there were few other forms of investment, land-selling was a ubiquitous business, in which not only corporations, joint-stock companies, and large partnerships, but practically every business-man and farmer who had any access to capital participated. If a more lively business atmosphere was a cause of the speed of the Business Revolution in America, real estate played an important part.

In addition to being a stimulant to great entrepreneurial energy, land also helped to stimulate rapid diversification by reshaping the law in the interests of active risk-takers. Each of the major seaports became centers for mercantile plans regarding Western development. The most money was to be made from townsite planning or from buying the land adjacent to expanding trade centers. Since it was generally thought that there was more money to be made in this way than from the profits of trade or industry, land speculation undoubtedly drew money from the latter. But in compensation, this activity contributed to the development of banking, credit agencies, mortgage markets, and inland transportation, which in turn increasingly expanded the trader's or manufacturer's national market. Furthermore, this inland market in new areas demanded inexpensive durable goods which could be more readily mass produced than the higher quality items imported from Europe. Hence as merchants organized factory production techniques in the 1830s, American manufacturers, in many cases, were free of any fear of effective foreign competition in the interior markets.

LEGAL SUPPORT FOR THE ENTREPRENEUR

In the United States, law bore a quite different relationship to business than did the legal systems of England, France, or Germany. While legal processes differed between these three nations, they all had prestigious judges, traditional interpretations, and a rigidity toward changes in legal doctrine. In the United States new state constitutions and inexperienced judges threw the common law into confusion. The law came to be whatever smart lawyers and complaisant, poorly paid judges might make it, and the usual type of case concerned land. Such relative anarchy was not an ideal situation for business, but it was fluid, exciting, and offered the possibility of unusual rewards for those attempting new ventures. A law that suggested what one *could* do provided more business incentive than one that chiefly imposed traditional restraints.

Furthermore, the evolution of land law embodied the principles needed by national, interstate business. By the 1820s even Western judges were adopting a conservative attitude toward the sanctity of private property, freedom and security of contracts, and the rights of out-of-state owners. In contrast to England's *Blackstone's Commentaries* (republished in Philadelphia in 1771–72), which emphasized the power of the national state, and to American Revolutionary thought that went in the same direction, Nathan Dane's eight-volume digest in 1823 and James Kent's four volumes published from 1826 to 1830 put limits on all state power in the interests of the individual. Therefore, by the time of the great upsurge from 1825 to 1837, the interpretation of law in the American states seems undoubtedly the most favorable to expanding business of any jurisprudence in the world. Its weakness lay in the courts, in uncertainties produced by local pressures against out-of-state plaintiffs, and in the corruption of incompetent judges, particularly in the newly settled areas.

OFFSHOOTS OF THE MERCANTILE OFFICE

While law and real estate were conducted in much the same way as in earlier generations, trade, finance, and shipping were fields where specialization took off from existing mercantile practice to achieve higher levels of business efficiency. Each of these major branches of business had been a part of the ubiquitous functions of the old-style merchant, and some of the new specialties such as wholesaling, offshore shipping, and brokerage followed the old patterns so closely that setting up separate houses for each was merely a necessary response to the larger size of the market.

In 1815, following three years of war, there existed a pent-up supply of and demand for British textiles. In response to this situation, the device of auction sales at the major seaports was greatly expanded. As the best distributing point, New York City received most of the shipments. To further insure that this booming trade would not be diverted to Philadelphia or Boston, the state of New York in 1817 passed a law more favorable to sales at public auction than the regulations of Massachusetts or Pennsylvania. The auction houses bypassed the old channels of trade and credit in much English goods, but the movement was largely staffed by members of the older general firms. While under favorable circumstances selling by auction could save the producer a large part of his marketing costs, the system inevitably led to wide fluctuations in price and great uncertainties in long-term contracts.

Auction sales were gradually reduced from 1828 on, less because of ups and downs in price (not a new phenomenon in the old-style mercantile system) than because of the rise of more efficient specialized wholesalers. As the total volume of import trade grew, a merchant could concentrate on effective marketing of a special line of goods such as English broadcloth or Irish linen. Domestic distributors would know that this importer could supply a wide variety of types and in large quantity, and as a result, they would not waste time on general merchants with smaller stocks. By the middle 1840s there were nearly sixty different types of specialized importers in New York City, and the resulting economies from their relatively large-scale operations in their selected markets were driving the auctioneers out of business.[5]

Specialized importing was, of course, only one of the divisions in the diversification of marketing processes. Wholesalers and many types of commission merchants bought goods from importers or domestic producers and moved them on to retailers or exporters. Jobbers gave advice, on commission, as to where specific items could best be purchased, note brokers took out-of-town bank notes or commercial obligations and sold them to the banks, while other brokers dealt mainly in basic commodities. To the outsider the system sounds so complex that one would expect higher rather than lower prices to result, but the fact that these intricacies still exist in 1976 indicates that they perform valuable economic services. The overall efficiency, which substantially reduces retail price, comes from faster movement of goods from initial producer to final customer, wider varieties of goods to choose from at each stage, more economical financing of goods in transit, and more information regarding competitive prices.

To knit the system together merchants exchanges were established in the port cities in coffeehouses or other public places up until 1827, at which time New York completed a spacious exchange building. In these meeting places different specialists would come together at appointed hours and locations. Starting in 1790, brokers dealing in securities, which were chiefly bank, turnpike, or canal stocks and government bonds, met away from the other merchants at their own locations in Philadelphia, and shortly later they formed separate groups in New York, Baltimore, and Boston.

Meanwhile shipowning and management were also being detached from the business of the general merchant. Often the separation merely involved one brother staying in some mercantile or manufacturing business while the other supervised a small shipping firm. In the leading port of New York there were no corporations engaged in overseas shipownership, and even big groups owned and operated only three or four vessels.[6]

In 1817 a partnership of five men, three of whom came from England, organized the Black Ball Line for scheduled sailings to Liverpool from New York. For twenty years, until the advent of the steamship, the Black Ball and other scheduled sailing packet lines carried high-priced freight and first class passengers across the Atlantic. Even at their height, however, each firm was a small, highly competitive business run by half a dozen partners and clerks in a single counting room. The efficiencies introduced were an emphasis on punctuality and better understanding of ships—with a former sea captain often in charge of the fleet—and more strictly controlled operations at sea. For low-priced freight, however, the "transient" and private carriers, often with one managing and many inactive owners, were still the rule all over the world.

A ubiquitous problem of the business world at home or abroad, affecting every type of operation from retailing to shipownership, was credit. Men succeeded or failed on the basis of their ability to get credit and their wisdom in granting it. Working capital or trade credit in the United States had several sources, available in varying degrees to different businesses. The well established importers and exporters could operate on advances from England, theoretically liquidated annually, but often in practice accumulating and perhaps being converted into real estate mortgages. Businessmen with some real property, such as a city house or nearby farm, could generally borrow from local banks at sixty to ninety day discounts, and, if the business was judged by the banker to be doing well, the notes would be renewed time and again, becoming part of the capital of the firm. On a more certain long-term basis an entrepreneur could mortgage his real property, often with one of the new insurance companies, with a five- or ten-year renewal date. On the whole, it has been estimated that in the young republic, promising ventures did not starve for lack of credit.

Granting credit to customers was an essential but risky business, one with which merchants had great familiarity. Retailers, in particular, needed credit to carry farmers' accounts until harvest time, and almost all accounts for two or three months, as postponed paydays and seasonal layoffs or stoppages all created uncertainty. Yet there were so many retailers that no big city wholesaler could know about each one. Consequently there was a large element of luck in the number of bad accounts. Informal merchant associations exchanged some credit information from the 1820s on, but it was the pileup of bad accounts resulting from the panic of 1837 that led Arthur Tappan to start his specialized Mercantile Agency for collecting local reports on the reliability of applicants for credit.

In all of this development of trade the United States was not a pioneer. There was probably a higher proportion of foreign-born men in commercial activity than in the general population, and there is little evidence that Americans were by nature particularly good managers. Rather it was the increasing cotton export trade, better inland transportation, a rapidly growing market, flexibility in action, and extreme devotion to business values and needs that moved the nation rapidly ahead. Not only did the Northeast have better geographical features than the big European nations, save for England, but European trade was more important to the United States than our trade was to the Europeans.

INCORPORATED BANKING

In the field of banking the relative scarcity of capital in the United States led to the innovation of widespread incorporated banking. Except for central banks in a few nations, banking was carried on abroad by unregulated proprietors or partners. The typical evolution there started with a merchant or manufacturer who accumulated a surplus that could not safely or profitably be invested in his major type of business. Since real estate investment was difficult in Europe, loaning the money to reliable local businessmen might be the best use for the surplus cash. If the loan had a fixed term, the borrower might deposit money with the lender in preparation for repayment. The lender could then use such deposits to make new loans; the erstwhile merchant had thus become a private banker. As British business prospered in the late eighteenth century, nearly 400 businessmen entered into private banking. Those with a profitable but geographically limited market, such as brewers, were particularly likely to have extra cash that could not be spent on the brewery.

In the eighteenth-century United States there were two forces working strongly against the European pattern: first, there were relatively few old well-established enterprises that were making large profits before 1790; and second, real estate was always an easy and attractive investment. Thus, while some merchants of the Colonial and early national periods made loans and accepted money on deposit, this remained an incidental part of their manifold activities. It was the general shortage of large, privately held liquid funds in the 1780s that led to the American innovation of chartering commercial banking corporations. This organizational innovation not only allowed a bank to gather its initial capital from the stock subscriptions of many businessmen, but also gave the corporation an aura of government approval.

In the new field of chartered or joint stock banking the United States had definite advantages over England and the Continent. Until 1826, English banks, for example, could not function as joint-stock companies or establish branches; in other words, they had to remain as merchant or private banks.[7] Furthermore, until 1815 the demands of all the European governments for wartime financing prevented the rise of an adequate and orderly structure of banks of issue and deposit.[8] In the United States, relatively easy chartering of banks with broad privileges, including note issue, a large federal bank during most of the period, and limited difficulty from excessive government borrowing made it possible to quickly provide the main essentials of a modern banking system.

This almost overnight success of state-chartered banks calls attention to a division that runs through all of business history: the creation of efficient forms for control of economic action as distinct from the effective use of such forms. In this instance, businessmen in the United States led the world in the establishment of new types of financial units, although as managing entrepreneurs they necessarily made many mistakes that stemmed from lack of learning and experience. Merchant training in granting credit was only a partial guide for profitable and safe management of funds based on capital, deposits, specie, and bank notes.

In the organization of two successive Banks of the United States or of other individual banks there was, however, considerable European experience that could be drawn upon. The Swiss were then (as so often) the most advanced operators of unit banking. France and England had central banks of issue. In 1774, private or merchant bankers in Paris established the Caisse d'Escompte. It was ruined within twenty years by forced loans to the government, but Andre Liessé concluded that "in all that concerns proper banking the Caisse was wisely administered."[9]

There is no indication, however, that American bankers studied continental European practice. When American merchants wanted advice they customarily turned to their correspondents in England or Scotland.

There the situation in the late eighteenth century was confused and its lessons not directly applicable to the new United States. The Bank of England held the only legal reserves of specie or government notes in the kingdom. Specie in other banks was generally used as till money. The media for loans were notes of the Bank of England and bills or notes payable by various types of private or merchant banks. The total number of such banks was 386 in 1800, and many had originated as early as the mid-eighteenth century. The prosperous agricultural areas near London were creditors and had a mixed circulation of local and Bank of England notes, while the developing commercial and industrial counties, Lancashire particularly, used mainly bills of exchange on London.[10] The country bankers had agents in London who periodically settled their accounts, but before 1810 or so there appear to have been no specialized note brokers.

All of this must have been known in a general way, at least, to men like Thomas Willing, first president of the Bank of North America, but he denied having any specific instruction on how to run a bank, and the few English texts dealing with finance, such as Sir James Stewart's *Inquiry Into the Principles of Political Economy* (London, 1765), were theoretical rather than practical.[11] In spite of its grandiose title, the Bank of North America was primarily a state-chartered Philadelphia corporation, and its board made up their own rules. They thought of the specie acquired from stock subscriptions as the basis for issuing circulating notes in the form of loans and discounts. At the start deposits were not encouraged. By the 1790s, however, the dozen banks in the Northeastern seaports were operating on what may be called the rudiments of a modern banking system.

Where the system grew slowly was in the recognition that deposits should be the basis for lending, with capital merely a safeguard in times of trouble; that circulation should be by checks drawn on depositors' accounts rather than in the form of printed notes; that a central agency, such as the Bank of the United States, strong enough to secure some degree of uniformity and order was an advantage, if not a necessity; and that efficiency and security both demanded some speedy way of settling accounts between banks. The desirability of deposits was quickly perceived. As early as 1786, Peletiah Webster was urging people to "take a bank credit and draw checks on the bank" rather than ask for notes.[12] By 1791, for example, the Bank of New York had $700,000 in deposits and only $181,000 in circulating notes, a ratio not far out of line with English practice. Whether such deposits had been "lodged" in the bank by one set of individuals while the loans made with the money went mainly to another set, or whether deposits arose largely as the result of money loaned staying in the bank until spent, has not been determined by historians of early banking. The answer may well lie in some variant of the present-day mix of both types of deposit.

From its beginning, the First Bank of the United States, and soon its branches, provided coordinating and monitoring agencies. While the twenty-year charter of the First Bank was not renewed in 1811, a Second Bank was chartered in 1816 for another twenty-year period. Thus from 1790 to 1837 the American banking system only lacked a central coordinating institution for about half a dozen years. The Bank of the United States, even under Nicholas Biddle, was essentially a large branch system operated particularly to assist federal deposit and transfers of funds rather than performing the major central bank function of being a lender of last resort. It did not in 1819, for example, prevent panic in the money market, yet, by the 1820s, the American banking system along the East coast might be favorably compared, in spite of no central guarantor of liquidity, to any in the contemporary world.

Each state-chartered bank held its own reserves against circulation and deposits and had no automatic claim on the reserves of the Bank of the United States. But a generation later Walter Bagehot, the famous British economist, called this arrangement the best.[13] The first statute for "free" or general incorporation of banks was not passed until 1838, and the problems resulting from free banking and no central control belong to a later period. Prior to the mid-1830s the Second Bank, with twenty branches under the able central management of Nicholas Biddle, kept bank notes reasonably sound by periodically sending considerable quantities back to the issuing banks for redemption. In fact, its profits increasingly came from dealings in exchange.

THE EARLY MONEY MARKET

Along the commercially developed East coast, banks could invest in short-term notes that would be automatically redeemed by business transactions, in government bonds, or a few sound urban mortgages, and they only occasionally had to accept large accommodation (unsecured) loans. There was no sharp distinction at this time either in the United States or Europe between investment and commercial banking. Frequently states required banks to subscribe to a large amount of state bonds or give stock to the state in return for a charter or its renewal. Other companies, usually for internal improvements, might secure clauses in their charters permitting banking and note issue. Prior to 1837 state bonds were regarded by bankers as good investments and many issues were contracted for in part or as wholes by banks on the basis of competitive bids. Sometimes merchants, not generally called private bankers until the 1820s, also submitted bids with the intention of distributing the securities chiefly in Europe. In the financing of the War of 1812, Astor as an individual, Stephen Girard as a private banker (operating from the offices of the former Bank of the United States), and David Parish representing British banking interests, bid as a group on one of the federal loans. But investment banking as a specialty became important only in the 1830s and will be discussed in Chapter Seven.

Private banking had undoubtedly developed from merchant lending just as in Europe, but perhaps in few instances under the title of banker before the trade boom of the 1790s. These early enterprises have left few records, and what the private banker could or could not legally do depended on state regulations. In some states, even in the major financial center of Pennsylvania, there was no prohibition before 1814 on the issue of private notes, but even where there was, certificates of deposit, checks, or drafts could perform the same function. Suspension of specie payments during the War of 1812 led to a rapid increase in unchartered banks and at the war's end, to a number of state laws against private note issue or use of the title "banker." The lenders whose business warranted it now became chartered banks, but for those not willing to undertake the lobbying and expense of dealing with a legislature, continuation of their business under some other name than "bank" and the issuance of certificates that were not officially notes continued to an unknown extent, and the state did not interfere with Girard.

All of this testifies to the profitability of commercial lending. There were few state requirements for reserves and those that existed applied to printed notes, not checks or deposits. Entirely unregulated, a private banker could lend as much in certificates of one type or another as the businessmen of the area would accept, and if the paper had little backing in cash or other security the interest received was largely profit. Even the well-run metropolitan banks were uncertain as to how far their loans should exceed cash and invested capital; nor were they in agreement as to what constituted liquid assets. Before 1837, Louisiana and Arkansas both had banks with their investments almost entirely in real estate loans, and backcountry banks, in general, had to rely heavily on earnings from mortgages or crop loans.

Even in this early world of finance there were lenders and other intermediaries under many names. Bill brokers, for example, were middlemen who could match the need for commercial credit to out-of-town merchants with the lending ability and inclinations of the various city banking houses, who appeared about as soon as the multiplication of lenders made the operation economically rewarding. Because of bank issues, note or bill broking had appeared in the United States in the middle 1790s, when it was still in primitive form in England, although bill brokers never assumed as important a role in the early American commercial banking system as they did later in Britain, where banks came to deposit excess funds with the brokers and the latter guaranteed the notes they sold.[14] Reasons for this were no doubt less centralization of the private bill market, as distinct from bank notes, in any single Eastern city than in London and a larger percentage of speculative backcountry personal or even bank notes that no one wanted to guarantee. In addition to intermediaries for domestic personal credit there were dealers in foreign exchange and out-of-town bank notes, who might or might not engage in banking or security brokerage. Building and loan and credit unions had already appeared in the early 1830s.

The one remaining major structural feature of nineteenth century banking, clearing houses for interbank claims, came more slowly in the United States than abroad. The central position of the London banks led in 1773 to clearing through deposits in the Bank of England, but Paris banks did not clear through the Bank of France until 1834. In the United States the large number of country banks close to Boston led the Suffolk Bank in 1822 to offer to clear out-of-town notes for the city banks. But except for a limited system in New Orleans in 1842, major city clearing-houses came only with the great upswing in both the use of checks and the number of banks after 1850. Meanwhile clearing in the big Eastern seaports became more and more cumbersome, with dozens of porters running from bank to bank with ledgers and cash to balance accounts. The low wages paid porters, however, probably made the confusion more obvious than costly.

In all, while United States banking was always troubled by back-country ventures that were largely land banks and hence nonliquid in financial crises, except for the years 1811 to 1816, when there was no Bank of the United States, instability was less of a burden before 1837

than thereafter. If the structure of this period could have been per-
petuated, later scholars such as Rondo Cameron, who suggest that in the
long-run banking was a neutral factor in American economic growth,
might judge it to have been a fairly strong positive force.

BANK MANAGEMENT

Within the new banks policy decisions were more concerned with investment than the details of management. The early bank offices were
similar to those of the merchant—who had, after all, performed the
same functions. The change was in greater specialization. Instead of only
a chief clerk there was a paying teller, a receiving teller, an accountant,
a porter, and above them all, a cashier. At the start the entire board of
directors passed on loans, just as the partners of a mercantile house had
always done, and the president was merely the chairman.

In the bigger banks of the 1820s the president had become a full-
time executive, and he and a small committee of the board, with the help
of the cashier, handled loans. Since there were practically no branch
offices in the North in this period, except those of the Bank of the United
States, everyone in a bank was familiar with the local situation and the
reputation of local borrowers. In contrast, lack of such knowledge in
Britain was a difficulty faced in 1826 when joint stock banks were
allowed to have branches.[15] In both countries the early solution to a lack
of knowledge of applicants was the resort to note brokers specializing
in particular types of risk, and their recommendations made it often
unnecessary to have specialists on the staff of the bank. By 1837 there
were urban markets in commercial paper with quotations carried both
locally and in the *Financial Register of the United States*.[16]

This brief picture of early banking has glossed over some opera-
tional defects. Bank directors were not paid and usually served in order
to secure better personal credit. Tellers, assisted by printed services,
had to become experts on both the value of various bank notes as well as
detectors of even more varieties of counterfeits. In spite of heavy bonding there was a great deal of embezzlement, encouraged no doubt by
inadequate police forces and the uncertain state arrangements for extradi-
tion, yet England also suffered much from both high bonding and the
dishonesty of branch managers and cashiers. In fact, the latter officer

was the linchpin of a well run bank and by 1840 might be paid as much as $10,000 a year. But, in spite of its weaknesses, up to the panic of 1837 American banking probably functioned almost as well as banking in England and, except for some of the small states, better than in the nations of the Continent.

INSURANCE COMPANIES

Casualty insurance was another specialty previously conducted within the old mercantile system. In the eighteenth and earlier centuries merchants had looked over sheets displayed on a table in a coffeehouse and, if so inclined, had signed as underwriters for a share of some maritime risk, such as a round voyage from Philadelphia to London. This was both time-consuming and uncertain for the insurer, who might fail to gain coverage (or in case of loss to collect from the signers). Prior to the mid-eighteenth century most American policies were signed in London, but between then and the formation of the Insurance Company of North America (INA) in 1794, more and more policies were negotiated in certain coffeehouses or taverns of the chief American ports. The INA, with $600,000 subscribed in capital stock, gained quick popularity among shippers. The policy writing required but a single visit and collection on losses was equally facilitated.

Fire insurance on buildings had been written by a Philadelphia joint-stock mutual company from 1752 on, but in the nation as a whole fire insurance was handled in much the same way as marine risks. In 1794, the INA extended its business not only to the insurance of buildings but to goods of all kinds.[17] Life insurance was also sold by many of the early companies, but it was an unimportant part of their business. Only in the mid-nineteenth century, when adverse religious scruples had been partly overcome by more aggressive marketing and more confidence in the insurers had been established, did life policies become popular.

Both fire and marine insurance corporations and their agents spread rapidly after 1800 in the major cities, speeding and stabilizing business operations through more specialized study of risks, easier securing of coverage, and more certain collection in case of loss. Beyond providing a more efficient business service, specialized insurance firms, like banks, provided pools of capital available for mortgages and other types of conservative investment.

By 1819 enough insurance companies had failed because of unpredictably high losses to lead Aetna of Hartford, Connecticut, to offer to act as an agency for reinsurance, providing greater protection from a broader underwriting base with more resources. Stirred by losses of the same period arising from bad investments and the depression of 1818 to 1820, the states started passing regulatory laws limiting the types of securities eligible for insurance company reserves. In spite of growing maturity in cooperation and more regulation, real degrees of risk remained difficult or impossible to calculate accurately, and in conservatively run companies the margins provided against actuarial error accumulated as large reserves.

MANAGING TRANSPORTATION

New problems in management different from those of the merchant's office arose in chartered corporations for inland transportation and in manufacturing plants using new technology for larger scale production. While mercantile partnerships had often participated during the Colonial period in shipbuilding, candle-making, or mining, they had had little experience (aside from shipping) in supervising large numbers of workers at distances too great for personal inspection.

Inland transportation, first on turnpikes and then by canal, posed management problems in construction, collection of tolls, and maintenance. William Bingham, as president of the Philadelphia and Lancaster Turnpike Company, a pioneering organization whose stock was oversubscribed almost fourfold in 1792, first faced the construction of a long, hard-surfaced road. Since such turnpikes were a new development in England and traffic conditions there were very different, Bingham had little accumulated knowledge to guide him. He decided to have the corporation manage construction, rather than using the later railroad practice of dealing with outside contractors, but he did foresee the advantages of both building and managing by dividing the road into sections. Quickly he learned of the difficulties that would harass overland transportation for the next century: uneven, inefficient, and often dishonest construction and lack of proper communication with and coordination of division superintendents. He started by wanting more information than he could reasonably expect, namely, daily written reports from busy supervisors to the board of directors.[18] From the start all of these decisions involved not only the special problems of transportation, but the enduring ones of the sizable, spread-out corporation. Historical perspective shows that Bingham was attempting an unworkable degree of centralized control and expecting more work from both his supervisors and directors than they were likely to perform.

Heavy maintenance because of unreliable contractors and deep winter freezes; the difficulty of finding honest toll collectors, either by contract or company employment; and light traffic during much of the year made most turnpike investments, including the Philadelphia and Lancaster, yield low net returns.[19] Until the mid-1820s, however, a mixture of returns from speculation in adjacent land, state subscriptions to additional stock, and some profitable developments dependent on the turnpike routes kept capital flowing in. From then on as distances increased, railroads and canals became more attractive investments and turnpike companies sold out to the states for low sums. Lack of use subsequently led to inadequate state maintenance.

Some subsidiary enterprises in stagecoach companies, such as the Eastern out of Boston, paid better returns than the roads—forecasting the private car companies of the railroad age. In steamboat operation scheduled line services, except on such heavily traveled waterways as the Delaware and Hudson rivers, or the Long Island Sound, or those that, in the early days, secured temporary regional monopolies, could not overcome competition from boats owned by single proprietors or partnerships and operated on a pragmatic or tramp basis by an owning captain. This is an interesting early example of the fact that in an activity where economies of scale are low, the owner-manager usually has a considerable advantage in diligence, economy, and flexibility over the hired corporate manager. In fact, by the 1840s many steamboats operated at no profit above the wages of the partly-owning captain, but otherwise benefited certain builders and producers who were also part owners.[20]

Canals, posing many of the same problems as turnpikes, but on a larger scale, were another form of social overhead capital that failed to produce sufficiently high earnings to attract continuing private investment. Here again, freezing and flooding made the maintenance of towpaths, banks, and particularly locks a constant financial drain, and lock repairs required skilled labor that was hard to find. A few privately financed canals connecting major waterways such as the Delaware and

Chesapeake or Delaware and Raritan were profitable. Others, such as those reaching into the hinterland to bring coal or other products to a major shipping point showed an over-all profit to the combined enterprises, but with the coming of the railroad canals were shifted to public ownership and management, or abandoned.

Roughly forty years of private turnpike and canal operation had given corporate executives a little experience with hierarchical and spatial difficulties, but since they had not provided the actual transport they were not prepared for the more complex and demanding problems of railroad administration. The real achievement from the standpoint of business efficiency was the entrepreneurial energy that led to the creation through mixed financing of these socially valuable early enterprises.

MERCANTILE INFLUENCES IN MANUFACTURING

American merchants moved readily into the business management of manufacturing, but less easily into dealing with problems arising from machinery. A factory could be placed under a business-oriented mill agent who would hire a supposedly competent mechanic, it could be inspected frequently, and its supply and marketing controlled by old mercantile methods. Often the mill agent was a partner or relative of the merchants. The new problems were finding reliable machines, mechanics, and men who could supervise a large number of workers. The successful pioneers in machine spinning, Almy and Brown of Providence, tried unsuccessfully to copy a British machine and only returned to the experiment when they read in a newspaper advertisement of 1792 that a competent British mechanic, Samuel Slater, was available. In this case Slater turned out to be an able businessman as well, and their partnership ventures flourished, training mechanics who could, in turn, start new mills. Their financing of these early spinning mills (twenty-seven in New England by 1809) represented a mixture of urban merchant capital and credit combined with additional finance by local families who also supplied land and labor.

The largest scale mercantile expansion in this field came in the Boston area when the War of 1812 temporarily reduced British imports. Here merchant capital, business experience, political understanding, and some technical knowledge were all present in the person of Francis Cabot Lowell. The earlier mechanization had been in spinning, but Lowell, on a trip to England just before the War of 1812, memorized the chief features of factory cotton weaving well enough to guide Boston mechanics in the construction of a commercially workable machine. With shipping interrupted by the war, Lowell was able by the force of his own social prestige to assemble a most impressive array of Boston's merchants as investors in the complete textile factory at Waltham. Since in England weaving, dyeing, and finishing involved separate enterprises, Waltham was the first factory in the world to take in cotton bales and turn out inexpensive cloth. To protect his investment Lowell went to Washington and won a clause in the tariff of 1816 placing a high duty on low grade cotton fabrics. The mill prospered, and the allied and related families, referred to as the Boston Associates, successfully established additional large mills for low-priced cotton textiles. By the end of the war some of the many specialized wholesalers in each big city began to concentrate on textile marketing either by purchase or on commission. Thus the old mercantile houses first went into textile manufacturing and then spun off separate partnerships to specialize in the cotton trade and textile marketing.

AMERICANS ADAPT TO MACHINES

Once the construction of simple machinery had been mastered, factories do not appear to have imposed severe strains on management. Businesses in textiles, wood products, and flour, using water-powered machinery made largely of wood, rather routinely expanded and prospered. Guns and various other types of hardware presented more serious technological problems, in the partial solutions of which the government arsenal at Springfield, Massachusetts played a leading role.

In hardware, particularly, Americans showed their tendency to use machinery in place of labor, to be more interested in improving processes than in carefully calculating marginal costs. The experience of Eli Whitney in firearms was a continual example of overconfidence in the economies brought by machines. An excuse that he and others used on the occasion of delay in fulfilling contracts was that the right type of labor was simply not available. Hence in contrast to Japan, which has been seen as relying too much on labor in the nineteenth century, American management may have had its inefficiency in too much use of machinery.[21] The American managerial habit of thinking in terms of machine processes and future markets goes back at least to the beginning of the period of rapid industrialization.

Mechanics who started businesses without mercantile advice or financial and marketing assistance, appear from the scanty records to have done poorly. Two whitesmiths in Taunton, Massachusetts, for example, developed a superior type of pewterware capable of meeting British competition, but with their personal attention devoted to the shop, they soon had to be rescued by a merchant who understood marketing.[22] Even some well-financed ventures by E. I. Du Pont failed to find profitable markets.

OLD ACTIVITIES EXPAND

There were continuing types of activity that grew tremendously but changed relatively little in business structure during the period before 1830. Printing and building construction, for example, among the most important urban industries, were carried on by small firms often financed by their proprietors, who might receive advances from advertisers and customers. One can regard printing and publishing, chiefly of newspapers and notices, as an integral part of the mercantile community, but one requiring too little capital and too much personal skill to make it an attractive area for merchant finance and management. Merchants were, of course, continually financing the construction of all types of building, but the actual work was done by contract with master bricklayers and carpenters operating with a few journeymen and apprentices.

The iron industry and shipbuilding were also partial exceptions to the rule that finance, marketing, and top-management were usually in mercantile hands. In these two relatively large scale, but technologically rather traditional activities, the works manager was more likely to be an owner with practical experience. While shipbuilding, run by a master carpenter bossing a score of highly trained woodworkers, was an old and very successful American business able to compete with similar firms in Europe, iron forging and casting up to the 1830s was a primitive industry turning out goods for local farm equipment and building construction. Prior to 1840 quality iron and special forms were imported from England.

Anthracite coal, made available at Philadelphia first by canal and in the 1830s by railroad, turned out to be an ideal smelting fuel, and when canals were able to bring iron ore and anthracite together, an efficient American iron industry appeared. Development of the inland empire of coal and iron, perhaps the most important on the industrial or technological side of the Revolution, turned the attention of many Philadelphia, Wilmington, and Baltimore businessmen toward the immediate backcountry and made foreign trade seem much less important than it did to the mercantile groups in New York and Boston.

By the 1830s an interior market stretching across the Mississippi River was developing that would have a powerful impact on American business, but discussion of this will be taken up in the next chapter. The present emphasis has been on the maturing business structure and entrepreneurial experience of the Northeast coast that paved the way for rapid industrialization in the decades after 1840.

II

A
National
Market,
1840-1890

4

The Challenges of Space and People

A ROUND 1850 the United States as far west as the Great Plains became a national business system knit together by rail and water, with a rapidly growing population spurred by a high domestic birth-rate and heavy immigration. This enormous rate of growth, which led proud nationalists like Abram S. Hewitt to acclaim iron production as the measure of the height of a civilization, made it difficult, however, to maintain the highest rate of increase in per capita national product or in real personal income.[1] Instead of leading the world in the rate of advance, as in earlier decades, the United States from 1850 on probably lagged behind such leaders as Germany or Japan and possibly France in the rate of per capita increase. All the leading industrial nations save Britain were rapidly increasing their per capita income at rates of around 1.5 to 1.9 percent or more a year, but in this competition, econometrists do not judge the United States to have been the leader.[2]

Between 1840 and 1890 no business system in any other leading nation faced as severe problems as in the United States. Merely to keep per capita gross national product on a par with growth in population, businessmen had to increase total income at a rate nearly 30 percent per decade and had to supply the capital needed for education, new homes, and farm and household equipment. Businessmen had to run fast merely to stand still. In all, population grew five and a half times, while in the other leading nations it no more than doubled. To be sure, much of the American increase came from immigration, which supplied workers without the cost of their upbringing, but the cultural and linguistic differences of the immigrants presented serious managerial problems.

GEOGRAPHICAL SPREAD OF THE MARKET

The sheer size of America, as with Russia, may in the long run have been its most severe problem, but one that was perhaps easier to overcome in a physical sense than in terms of business. In 1840 over half the population of the country lived along the East coast between Maine and Virginia, and few businessmen crossed the Mississippi; America had a tolerably compact population and was fairly well integrated by road and water transportation. By 1890 more than two-thirds of the people lived outside the old middle or northern coastal area, and the outer limits of continuous habitation as well as the market were by then on the Pacific coast. Meanwhile, railroads had made all populated regions accessible, and businessmen seeking a place in the national market had to operate over great distances.

In the early part of this fifty-year period coal and iron were available in sufficient quantities from Maine to Virginia (today's chief American megalopolis), but from the middle 1850s on the sources of these basic materials plus copper, lead, zinc, and oil shifted ever westward, often ending in the inaccessible Rocky Mountains. By the end of the century, for example, copper was being shipped more than 2,000 miles from Arizona to New Jersey for smelting and refining. Put another way, the United States in 1900 had a population and gross national product less than 50 percent larger than Imperial Germany but had to transport ten times as many ton-miles of freight.

Lest these difficulties seem so great that the American business achievement of keeping up with the compact nations of western Europe appears miraculous, it should be added that until after 1890 raw materials in the United States were abundant and of unusually high grade; and agriculture was increasingly productive for meat and staples. In fact, the superficial picture was one of such natural abundance that it would have been hard then (and is still difficult now) to realize that the nation was growing in per capita income no more rapidly than France and less so than Germany.

THE SUDDEN NEED FOR BIG ORGANIZATIONS

The major deterrents to a rapid increase in per capita growth rates were undoubtedly functions of the size of the country and the population growth. But just as part of the earlier advance can be attributed to business, governmental, and sociocultural factors, so part of the failure to achieve a more rapid increase in per capita GNP in the later period must be attributed to these same noneconomic reasons.

Business development in this period divides into two major parts: one in which the operation of the entire network of business units was substantially improved in efficiency, a development also taking place simultaneously in Europe and Japan; and another part in which the greatly increased size of individual firms was a response peculiar to the American situation. This led in turn to new experiments in production and marketing and not always successful developments in management and government regulation. Because the needs and practices of the growing, large organizations were an influence on many other parts of the business system, it seems best to focus initially on the latter of these two developments.

As in the earlier period, change imposed new demands upon the methods of business. But whereas earlier pressures of trade had been met by rapid specialization for which the East coast geography, social structure, and values proved highly favorable, the pressures after 1840 required economies of scale and systems of remote control of decisions, both of which necessitated bigger and more bureaucratic structures, for which Americans were not as well prepared as Europeans. Moreover, the problems of big organizations are often subtle and unrecognized by those involved. For example, in choice of occupations among small firms men have usually to some degree recognized their strengths and weaknesses for meeting the needs of a particular business; however, in big organizations, with hierarchical structures and many levels of specialized employees, the challenges to competency are less obvious. Even

were all outward structures alike, including forms of law and government, the problem of who can best do what would be hard to answer
in new types of situations since each society has its unique ways of
defining roles.[3] A well-known student of international management
remarks that the Industrial Revolution occurred first in England, not
simply because of favorable physical factors, "but because the British
people were inwardly different from those on the Continent."[4]

A general hypothesis may be advanced that the economies of scale
that pay in manufacturing and marketing cause, at some level of increasing size, diseconomies in management. These may be alleviated by
various types of organizational innovation, but the inevitable tendency of such problems to occur has been obvious to most practical
businessmen.

In initially meeting the challenges of increasing size in management,
the United States lacked some of the preparation of Germany, France
or Japan and, to a lesser degree, of England. Neither the Colonies nor
the States had ever developed a specially trained civil service with experience in exercising hierarchical authority and in the operation of a
complex bureaucracy. In America all agencies of government, including
the peacetime army and navy, were small and the state system localized
authority. Therefore, America's businessmen headed into a period of
rapidly growing organizations with fewer guidelines and with a strong
tendency to learn from their own personal experience rather than from
European writing or advice. As Charles Francis Adams saw it, Americans
had a legislative rather than an administrative tradition.[5] This might be
interpreted as meaning a view of situations more focused on immediate
competitive pressures and short-run tactics for meeting them than on
perfecting orderly or routinized ways of doing things. Lack of an elite
public service also deprived big business of an excellent source for the
recruitment of middle managers. In the older nations public administrators initially enjoyed higher prestige than businessmen, and when
brought into the private field they automatically commanded respect
and confidence.[6]

It is one of the great ironies of modern history that a vast continent and a rapidly expanding population forced bigness in many
branches of American business activity on an entrepreneurial group
lacking in personal preparation and unable to draw on any trained
administrative personnel. This meant that until the twentieth century
the supply of competent management remained an unusually scarce or
limiting factor.

SOME BASIC PROBLEMS OF MANAGEMENT

As the need for large-scale administration was forced on entrepreneurs who found no precedents in their own experience, they turned to re-adopting the system of control on a ship and to enlisting the engineers trained by the army, while a few may have looked at similar enterprises abroad. The management of a ship was understood by merchants and perhaps by most Americans; yet the operation of a sailing vessel without engineers or special technicians and involving only immediate, face-to-face contacts was much too simple to provide answers for situations where the quick control of complex, technical, and remote activities came into play. The army system of hierarchy was more or less consciously employed by a number of entrepreneurs, but it was too rigid and elaborate and was only used partially in the early large companies. There is no indication in the sparse literature on this subject that many men went to France, where there were both books on (public) administration and some centuries of experience with big monopolies, or even to England to study business organization; and it is doubtful that the British or French books on industrial management, published in 1831 and 1832, circulated to any extent in the United States or would have been of much use for nonfactory problems.[7]

Since there were no teachers or courses in universities on the problems of business management, there were no American textbooks and probably little or no reading public for such works in any nation. Not until the last quarter of the nineteenth century, when on-the-job training, apprenticeship, and practical experience began to appear inadequate in many types of large companies was there a movement to found business schools and to study administrative procedures as such. By this time, of course, there was a large literature on public administration, particularly in French and German, but practical men of affairs were more artists than scholars and were not inclined to digest theoretical knowledge and apply it to the large corporation. This same aversion was dominant in England as well as the United States.[8]

From the small number of scholarly business histories that cover the nineteenth century, it would appear that trial and error was the general guide, although there was doubtless some exchange of information by personal letters between men in similar types of business.[9] The rise of engineering education, belatedly in the United States and still more so in

England (but well in advance of higher business education), undoubtedly reinforced the simplistic, mechanistic view of the problems of management.[10] Furthermore, while mechanical failure was obvious and had to be remedied quickly, managerial failure was obscure and might persist from generation to generation. Fortunately for all the industrial leaders of the nineteenth century, but particularly for the United States, the vast majority of enterprises remained small and few employees worked in large hierarchical, impersonal organizations. Excluding for the moment transportation and mining, even the relatively large plants in textiles, machinery, iron, and shipbuilding involved operations at a single location, much inside contracting, and numbers of supervisory employees small enough to be on familiar personal terms with both workers and top management. This does not mean that there were no managerial problems in these companies—a strong case can be made for the foreman being the most important man in manufacturing—but, unlike the problems of distance and bureaucracy, the ones in the factory and in supervisor's relations with business proprietors were old and understandable.

American social structure and values continued to function well at the level of the worker and his immediate superior. English visitors at mid-century commented on the democratic and generally easygoing relations of native white male workers with their supervisors.[11] As noted in Chapter Two American individualism did not demand penetrating understanding of man's unique character, nor did the way Americans exercised authority imply social superiority; both operated on a mutual recognition of personal rights and essential equality. Such attitudes made for good cooperation, but possibly less exacting discipline and hard work.[12]

The adverse effects of distance on management, obvious in the case of transportation companies, was shared by others who had to organize and control remote enterprises. In mining, for example, the exploitation of rich ores in a distant region, such as copper in the Upper Peninsular of Michigan, required the construction of several forms of transportation and the ability to finance the period of development involved before there could be net returns. Copper in this particular region was developed by a group of Boston financiers who set up separate corporations for a number of different veins in order to diversify risks; in the case of two of the most successful it took five years and an investment of $170,000 in one case, and more than that time and money in the other, before there were any net earnings.[13] This type of development, repeated again and again across the country, meant that most successful mining companies were large and managed at the top by men who were hundreds to thousands of miles from the actual operations. In other words, economies of scale were demanded by the physical situation whether or not anyone knew how to organize the business.

It is interesting to contrast the copper development in Michigan and later in Montana and Arizona, tied to smelting and refining done on the Atlantic coast, with English mining in Cornwall, where small enterprises sent their ore by boat across the Bristol channel to nearby Swansea in Wales. The latter was almost a community operation compared to the distances and business structures required in the United States.

THE CHALLENGE OF RAILROADS

By far the most severe early pressure on management, however, was experienced in the railroad business. The problems of running the road were obvious, but the drain of managerial ability from other expanding operations was less so. For nearly half a century the railroads were able to recruit as managers a considerable portion of the brightest and most promising young men. Once in the company these men faced the most difficult policy- and decision-making that had ever appeared in business. In fact, very few companies of any type, prior to the moves for diversification in the 1920s, had more intricate operating and financial problems than the big railroads of the latter half of the nineteenth century.

The railroad companies were begun, much as in the case of the factories, by merchants who hired technical men to construct and run the roads, while keeping final managerial power in their own hands. The merchant had been used to running distant ventures by giving them only occasional attention, and he applied the same system to his railroad properties. John Murray Forbes as president of the distant Michigan Central wrote from Boston to his general superintendent, "It is utterly impossible for me to attend systematically to the business of the road. . . . When occasionally I have a leisure hour (perhaps at midnight, as now) I mean to write a private letter with such hasty suggestions as occur to me."[14]

But the railroad was not only the first necessarily big business, it was also an unusually complicated one. The merchant-technologist system had never really worked well even in textile mills, but on roads no more than about fifty miles long, tapping virgin territory, the major problems had been chiefly technological and the lack of adequate top management was less obvious. It was the rapid creation of long lines between 1849 and 1854 that produced a real crisis in railroad management.

The mercantile, banking, and insurance traditions of management practice only partially covered the problems raised by railroads. The older activities were based on business relationships in which technology was at most a minor factor and where those involved in management could be personally supervised by the directors. In contrast, railroads depended basically on tracks, bridges, stations, signals, locomotives, and cars that had to operate reliably, continuously, and on schedule, with each unit in the hands of a different employee upon whose competence and cooperation the system depended. Horrendous accidents could, and did, occur from temporary lapses in diligence by a single operator. Furthermore, these men were not working from a central business office. They reported for work at their appropriate yards or stations, where they might seldom or never be seen by the top echelon of operating management and were, of course, for staff executives merely so many necessary pawns in games of law, accounting, and finance.

The problem of administering railroads had, at least, three distinct aspects: first, continuous large-scale finance and planning of expanding enterprises sustained by expectations of profit; second, costs of acquisition of property and construction; and third, efficient operation of the road. In addition, many novel legal problems had to be dealt with, but these were less critical than the three main activities. Of these, construction and operation led early entrepreneurs to think more about technological processes than ever before. Only in the second generation did emphasis return to competitive strategy.

FINANCE AND CONSTRUCTION OF RAILROADS

As might be expected, finance was handled by merchants and bankers more efficiently than the new and untried aspects of the venture, and this was also true in England and on the Continent. While all of the new financial techniques other than state assistance were probably first introduced in England, it is hard to know how much of this knowledge was brought to the United States by traveling financiers and how much originated from meeting similar situations.

Alfred D. Chandler, Jr., is no doubt correct in saying that in general Americans did not borrow ideas regarding management, but taught themselves—although he obviously is thinking more of construction and operation than the field of finance, where correspondence across the ocean was continuous and intimate.[15] In any case, to remain competitive with their neighbors the American states moved into financing railroads just as they had canals, first by subscribing to railroad common stock, then to preferred, and finally, in the great boom from 1850 to 1854, by guaranteeing railroad mortgage bonds. In contrast, Parliament made few advances to railroads and used up much of the companies' time and resources in securing corporate charters. The English government, that is, continued the general laissez-faire attitude of the eighteenth century and also exacted a concealed tax on these ventures in the form of the costs of parliamentary delay and perhaps even corruption.[16]

As railroad indebtedness soared in relation to total real capital and earning power, railroad financiers all over the Western world introduced other new forms of securities such as bonds convertible at a price into stock, equipment, and other forms of trusteed bonds (see Chapter Seven), and debentures that merely had priority over the claims of stockholders. Everywhere, except perhaps in Germany, a mixture of overoptimism, dishonesty, and excessive construction costs made the total initial railroad capitalization extremely high.

Part of the high cost came from honest errors in estimating costs that had no precedents. Every area of technology seemed to have its own problems. In seeking to foresee such difficulties, technical men during the half century after 1825, in the absence of written sources, traveled, observed, and talked to others who had some experience or who could show machines in actual operation. Self-styled engineers met at railroad and technological gatherings not only all over the eastern and southern United States, but in Britain as well. Since the early booms in English railroad construction preceded those in the United States by only a few years, there was a considerable interchange of useful experience. The rest of Europe lagged in railroad construction before 1842, and the French sent early commissions to England and the United States to study developments.[17] In spite of "the universal language of the machine," however, language was a high barrier to interchange of information with the Continent.

In Britain and the United States, the first nations to complete long lines, construction was done by contracts wih specialized companies. In the United States, particularly, scarcity of capital led to payment for construction in stocks and bonds of the future railroad, occasionally to an extent that transferred control of the railroad to the chief stockholders of the construction company—who were frequently the initial promoters of the entire enterprise. Put another way, there was often more profit to be made in the long run from acquiring railroad stock or bonds in payment for high construction costs than by subscribing to such stocks and bonds on the market. Many state laws prohibiting the selling of railroad stocks at less than par accentuated this practice, as well as that of passing on shares to banks as security for loans of only a small part of the face value of the stock. An additional temptation to profit from building rather than operation came from state and federal land grants. Before the Civil War some 25 million acres of the Mississippi valley were conveyed by the federal government to the states and by the latter to railroad companies. From 1862 to 1871, the federal government made grants to potential transcontinental railroads of which around 140 million acres were ultimately validated. The land was often transferred on the basis of venal inspectors certifying sections of mere grading as "completed" track. John W. Brooks wrote of the St. Joseph and Denver: "I suppose it is clear that the road is being built for the profit of building. . . . I should count on such people selling lands and getting the road only half done and leaving the landholders to finish it to get something out of their swindle."[18] Even when companies were honestly and conservatively financed, construction costs in any new area were, and remained for half a century, an unknown quantity. Problems from swamps, rocks, mountains, drilling equipment, and a dozen minor causes could never be accurately estimated in advance, even when construction engineers had had a generation of experience.

One of the profits from construction that was regarded as ethical was the advance purchase of land by directors or other insiders at points where stations, repair shops, or extensive yards were to be constructed. A somewhat similar source of legal profit came from building bridges in advance and leasing them to the railroad. It was rumored that Cornelius Vanderbilt, for example, owned most of the bridges used by the New York Central Railroad.

MANAGING RAILROADS

From 1849 to 1860, Henry Varnum Poor, editor of *The American Railroad Journal*, published in New York City, was the most continuous and constructive critic of railroad practices. Quickly building an international reputation during the great railroad financial boom from 1850 to 1854, he was entertained by leading English financiers and had a chance to study both British and European systems. Of these he thought the Prussian was the best managed, but that their state ownership would not be acceptable in America. In the course of a dozen years of editorials he touched on every major weakness of the large, bureaucratic corporation in ways quite suggestive of the views of critics in the late twentieth century.[19]

Looking at the presidents and directors of railroads he saw, as the great merchant-financier Nathan Appleton of Boston had a decade earlier, the dangers inherent in the divorce of ownership and control. Directors in a large corporation with widely held stock neither represented nor were accountable to the mass of stockholders. Rather, directors were chiefly promoters who expected to profit from security manipulation or from subsidiary enterprises in land, equipment, and supplies. In small partnerships, the traditional business model of Europe and America, there was nothing unethical about selling to your own firm because, in part, you were openly selling to yourself, whereas a director buying his own products with the stockholder's money should obviously not determine how much he should pay himself. Yet, a man such as the highly respected Erastus Corning took no salary as president of the New York Central, while his mercantile house supplied the road.[20]

Perhaps the fiduciary or trusteeship obligations in managing other people's money were more respected in England and continental Europe than in the United States, but the scandals were so numerous everywhere in the 1840s and 1850s that comparative judgment seems impossible. Obviously, as Poor emphasized, the difficulty was inherent in the situation and continues to be so.

But securing a reasonably honest and attentive top management, and there were such, as for example on the Pennsylvania in the 1850s, was less than half the battle of building and effectively running a railroad. The directors and their elected president, vice-president, and treasurer were primarily financial officers; operating management rested with a general superintendent. Financiers were numerous, but good superintendents very scarce and really able ones close to nonexistent in the early days. Consequently the good ones shifted often from road to road at rising salaries.

The railroad needed far stricter discipline from its employees, often combined with technical skill, than any previous type of business. It was not hard to map out proper systems of control on paper, as Benjamin H. Latrobe demonstrated in the Baltimore and Ohio rule book of 1847, or Daniel C. McCallum in his principles of management published in the 1850s in the *American Railroad Journal*. (Alfred Chandler says that McCallum designed a railroad management plan the way he would build a bridge.)[21] Human beings, however, could not be cut to scale and rigid resistance to pressure was not necessarily a business asset. McCallum's faith in systems and complete information reminds one of the faith of some men in the 1950s and 1960s in computers as the answer to the difficulties of management. The real problem was not the drawing up of a rational plan, but rather the finding of a system acceptable and rewarding to the men involved.

Aside from hard drinking and an easygoing attitude toward work, which, whether the rule or not, were also probably present in England, there were particular American cultural and social characteristics inimical to strict observance of impersonal authority. All that has been said in earlier chapters about the national complex of equalitarianism, individualism expressed as rights to be respected, resistance to arbitrary or ascribed positions of power, and unfamiliarity with complex structures of command worked against acceptance of the prescribed rules of the big corporation, and particularly against the minute controls demanded by railroads.[22]

The roads, like the Erie under McCallum, where discipline and order were the strictest, were the ones most plagued by work stoppages or strikes. When a dispute led to the formation of the National Protective Association of Locomotive Engineers, the call to the organizational meeting asked, "Can we longer submit to the tyrannical will of a few men?"[23] Henry Poor saw such problems as solvable through better executive leadership, incentive pay, and some flexibility; he was more worried in the long run about loss of initiative in management from the deadening effect of rigid systems.[24]

In financial results, at least, the drains of prescribed tasks and bureaucratic structure on initiative were probably more serious on middle management than on operating personnel. Most of the latter did varied tasks such as running trains, repairing equipment, or talking to customers. The men whose task, however, was to see that the orders of the general superintendent were passed on to those who would execute them, and who expected promotion more on personal influence and seniority than on any measure of performance, constituted the soft inner layer of all bureaucratic structures. In finding it "difficult to believe that any man on a salary would do more work than was absolutely necessary to collect his regular wages" and that "incentive was even less when a man was in the pay of a large organization," Poor was unconsciously emphasizing the individualistic, materialistic orientation of Americans in contrast to the incentive of working for the welfare of the nation or to fulfill one's duty in an accepted authoritarian order.[25] All bureaucracies, of course, suffered somewhat from lack of incentive, but probably in no other nation was the contrast with outside profit-making activities so odious to the bureaucrat and so unrewarding both internally and externally.

In all the developing nations various palliatives for the adverse effects of bigness were proposed and given some trial. From 1854 on Poor advocated leasing the operation of a road to prime and subcontractors, called inside contracting, in order to spread the incentive of profit throughout the ranks. The fact that small roads made better profits than large pointed in this general direction of closer contact between operatives and profit makers. The practice, however, did not work well in the nations such as England and France that tried it during the 1840s or 1850s. President Samuel M. Felton of the Philadelphia, Wilmington and Baltimore, which had introduced the most complete contracting system of any American railroad, found a number of serious disadvantages such as poor coordination, dishonesty, and inefficiency among contractors, too many subcontractors, and too little community of interest. Beyond these specific problems was the fact that in highly competitive situations like that of the eastern trunklines, and unlike the sheltered position of the Philadelphia, Wilmington and Baltimore, railroads had to be operated as whole systems, making profits where possible and keeping a place in the market on traffic where profit was temporarily impossible. Obviously this could only be managed through central controls and planning.[26]

Defeated in making contracting a panacea by the very element of bigness that seemed to make it desirable, Poor turned to publicity as a solution. Here again he was an early participant in a continuing struggle between the large corporation and the investing or consuming public. Since in 1975 relatively little can be learned from the more detailed reports required by the Interstate Commerce Commision (ICC), or for corporations in general by the Federal Trade and Securities Exchange

Commissions, it is clear that little was accomplished in the mid-nineteenth century. There was an inherent difficulty in forcing publicity by state laws or commissions that both Poor and, twenty years later, Charles Francis Adams overlooked; there was, and is, no way to prevent deliberate or systemic distortions arising from methods of accounting. Consequently, while there is a long history of state legislation to compel annual reports or other forms of publicity before the ICC Act of 1887, there seems little value to the student of business in tracing these unsuccessful efforts. Frustrated in both his plans for contracting and publicity, Poor thought the "railroads . . . will drag along . . . and become worse managed and less productive year by year."[27]

In spite of this gloomy forecast improvement did come, but from external forces other than regulation. A strong and immediate external force was the Civil War, which by checking new construction, providing government traffic, and inflating prices put the debt-ridden roads on a firmer footing. One might say the burden of past errors was significantly lightened, and meanwhile managers had come to assess traffic possibilities and construction costs more expertly. As in all industries with a rapidly improving common technology and an expanding market, unit costs continuously fell. Railroads in 1890 could transport passengers or products at a small fraction of the costs of 1860. Working against this salutary trend, however, was a period of competitive over-building in the 1880s that again burdened many roads with heavy indebtedness and made their widely fluctuating and cheap common stocks attractive to speculators.

In contrast to the untrained pioneers necessarily drawn to promote newer types of big business, in the last quarter of the nineteenth century, most chief executives had had a lifetime of experience in railroading, and it was on the basis of such observation and correspondence among themselves more than on knowledge of foreign business practices that they set up new methods of management. Robert Harris, as president of the Burlington, sent a copy of a French railroad management system to his directors in 1877, but subsequent correspondence does not indicate that it made much impression.[28] As the *Baltimore Patriot* had observed, to directors "a book or treatise upon the management of railroads would be an intolerable bore."[29]

The chief American innovation, largely a product of early experience with relatively distant operations on turnpikes and canals, was the divisional system that, in turn, initiated on railroads a sharper distinction between the functions of staff and line. While finance, legal advice, decisions on buying and allocating cars and motive power, and major contracting were kept in the head office, it was found expedient on the Pennsylvania and other trunk lines (except for the New York Central) to set up a series of operating divisions of about 100 miles each. The division superintendents reported to a general superintendent and were responsible for results on their part of the road, including, in the period before 1870, solicitation of traffic. This meant the superintendents had to deal with head office departments regarding revenue, equipment, and maintenance, but were responsible for good day-to-day functioning on the road. This basic division between "staff," which is supposed to be made up of experts in accounting, law, and technology, and "line," which does the actual operating, has never been satisfactorily bridged. It was mitigated on the railroads by careful definition of duties, but as Leland Jenks says of Pennsylvania, the model railroad of 1880, "inside criticism . . . deplored the prevalence of *ad hoc* idiosyncratic solutions to generic problems . . . the prevalent lack of continuity in positions and methods."[30]

By this time the troubles of the big roads were leading to the clear formulation of some basic principles of accounting and management. In the first British railway acts of the 1820s double entry bookkeeping was required, which Nicholas A. Stacey calls the debut of modern accounting. Companies in the United States followed English practices of including the charging of replacements against profits as the means of depreciation. Obviously this gave a false picture of depreciation on a newly completed and equipped road, but the practice was not altered until the twentieth century. While few companies furnished useful annual balance sheets, American management came to use auditing internally to check the comparative results of divisional operation. Historically such checking was not new. Comparative audit of departmental financial performance was practised in the seventeenth-century French tobacco monopoly, and in early nineteenth century Britain, but appears to have developed on American railroads in the 1860s on the basis of experience.[31]

Similarly, the desirability of clear lines of communication and control could scarcely be overlooked, even if seldom achieved on the railroads. Just as the divisional system was an American innovation, George F. Perkins may have been one of the pioneers in advocating in 1881 that responsible decisions be made at the lowest practical level by men having some contact with the actual customers[32]—a marketing principle simple in statement but complex in its actual application. Divisional freight agents, for example, were generally given a certain degree of control over rates and tried to build traffic at their own stations, sometimes frustrating larger plans of the road by taking business away from an apparent competitor that was secretly controlled by the agents' own managers.

MANAGING OTHER BIG BUSINESSES

Before 1890 big companies (aside from railroads) were limited to utilities and to a few processors or manufacturers, while on the fringe of bigness there were some retail distributors. Banks and insurance companies were growing rapidly toward the end of the period but had not come to employ as many people as the giant companies in transportation, utilities, and primary processing. Yet, as will be seen in the two following chapters, the national business structure in finance and marketing was maturing, and far larger enterprises could be promoted in the 1880s than a half century earlier. The slow spread of steam power over about seventy years may be contrasted with the rapid promotion of electric power, light, and communication in the single decade of the eighties.

Each type of big company involved particular characteristics of management, and a few examples will have to suffice. Gas and electrical utilities had a mixture of the problems of railroads in dealing on the retail level with thousands of customers, large and small, free and captive. Also, as in the case of the railroads, their monopoly position led to state regulation, and the community required continuous service. The effects on managers were inevitably similar, although since utilities were generally local enterprises, it was potentially easier for them to acquire good management. For the executive who saw business as a game of shrewdness and wit, more money was to be made by selling land and franchises to utility companies and merging them into chains than by managing them efficiently. Some men like Samuel Insull of Chicago did both. In all, few organizational innovations emerged from utility management.

In food processing such as flour milling and meat packing, large companies developed before 1890, but usually still under the influence of the charismatic and resourceful entrepreneurs who had built them up. Such men, both in the United States and abroad, usually exploiting hitherto unrealized economies, could violate the principles of sound management with impunity and still achieve good results competitively. The principal weakness of this style of leadership based on loyalty to an able man was the same as that of the family firm: there was little rational planning for succession, and it was unusual for a son or other relative to have the ability of the old master. When faced with need for a rational system of management run by average executives, the erstwhile one-man firm both in the United States and abroad usually has had a decade or more of trouble.[33]

One of the most spectacular examples of a one-man enterprise was the Carnegie Steel Company. Andrew Carnegie's relationship to basic steel fabrication was much the same as that of the old merchants to the processing of raw materials—both exercised a form of absentee control —however, the scale and complexity of the Carnegie operation were far greater, because of new technology and the large numbers of customers in railroads, building, and naval construction. Essentially a marketer, Carnegie delegated supervision of manufacture to men like Captain Jones, Charles Schwab, and Henry C. Frick, while he traveled around America and Europe selling steel products to railroads and governments. His relation to the business can scarcely be seen as systematically organized. Until 1892 the firm was a partnership controlled by Carnegie, who, from wherever he happened to be, read reports and issued orders. In 1901, when a syndicate led by J. P. Morgan merged the Carnegie properties with others in the United States Steel Company, Carnegie sold out. The new monster, the largest corporation in the world, was over-capitalized, lacked proper coordination, and functioned poorly.

The largest industrial enterprise in the United States before 1890, the Standard Oil Company, represented the unusual case of an organization inspired and led by one exceptionally gifted entrepreneur, John D. Rockefeller, who appreciated the advantages of sharing authority with able executives. In fact, the major criticism of Standard Oil in the 1880s is that it was too decentralized and uncoordinated. Ralph and Muriel Hidy think Rockefeller's greatest contribution was the idea of combination and the ability to persuade strong men to work together.[34] By the 1880s the Standard Oil Companies, New Jersey and New York, had been joined through the advice of lawyer S. C. T. Dodd into the first industrial trust. It was a loosely coordinated collection of many producing, refining, and marketing organizations whose majority stock was voted from 1881 on by nine trustees. The trustees who happened to be present on any given day constituted an executive committee and made decisions, usually based on recommendations from below. In fact, the company had reached its monopolistic position by becoming an association of pre-

viously independent refiners in which there was much individual autonomy. Its structure represents an unplanned precursor of the present
multidivisional form of organization. There were numerous staff and
line committees, and, until 1890, cooperation between the dual Cleveland
and New York headquarters was often slow and inefficient.

There had really been two stages in the administrative growth of
the company: an early one up to around 1878, when the personal drive
and efficiency of Rockefeller and, to a lesser extent Henry M. Flagler,
built a refining and marketing system that was able either to drive out
local competitors in the most strategically located distributing areas or
to bring them into the company; and a second stage from then on, when
the market position of the trust was so strong that it could stand its
somewhat slow and cumbersome management. In any case, Standard Oil,
even in 1911 when it was broken up by the Supreme Court, was far
from being a good model for textbooks on business administration.

Aside from finance and railroads, management during the 1870s
and 1880s was generally thought of by theorists in America and abroad
as synonymous with the running of manufacturing plants. The phrase
"systematic management," becoming popular in the eighties, meant
careful analyses of the cost of various operations in the plant, the proper
routing of materials to be processed, and efficient supervision of workers
and machines. Young Frederick W. Taylor in the steel industry was to
greatly stimulate such analysis in the generation after 1890, but meanwhile systematic management was probably more popular in the engineering journals, read only by specialists, than it was in the thinking of
top executives.

Frustrating to all attempts to shape managerial practice by analyzing
collective experience was the widely held business belief that each company's situation and problems were unique.[36] This meant that "experience" was personal rather than industrywide and hence noncumulative
from one man or generation to the next. Except for routine technical
problems, neither historical nor statistical analysis of management
policies was undertaken on an industry-wide basis, and moves in this
direction by perceptive entrepreneurs were blocked by irrational desires
for secrecy—desires so strong that they often blocked the proper flow
of information within a single organization.

But in spite of the most inspired and rational efforts, the problems
created by distance, size, and bureaucracy were bound to persist in varying degrees because they involved, even in 1975, what appeared to be
insoluble problems. Technology can partly overcome distance but only
at high cost. Size forces impersonality and lack of interpretive communi-

cation. Bureaucracy is the necessary form of organization but it cannot overcome weaknesses that seem inherent in routinizing the work of human beings and asking that they both compete with each other for promotion yet cooperate for the welfare of the company. Management has progressed by a better understanding of the nature of the problems involved rather than by the discovery of their general or basic solution.

But while there have been negative effects in both costs and efficiency caused by distance, there have simultaneously been positive benefits from a domestic market with several times the buying power of any in foreign nations. It allowed, for example, for specialization in the manufacture of expensive tools and equipment that in turn permitted higher levels of mechanization and productivity per worker. "By the end of the nineteenth century specialization had been carried to a point where some firms were just making chucks for lathes."[37] In the big market companies could afford more expense for the development of new products, such as the introduction of structural steel for building purposes by the Carnegie Company.

The relatively unified character of the big market made it difficult to protect little regional enclaves against national competition, as was often done in France and Germany. This meant that except for patent protection there was little security save in either efficient specialization or in the marketing advantages conveyed by size. These physical facts were reflected in managerial thought. Whereas most observers have seen European executives as primarily cost-conscious, Americans have thought more in terms of achievement and expansion. The European attitude has led to caution and meticulous supervision of operations, the American to more optimistic risk-taking and emphasis on increased production, with confidence that if sales were large enough costs could be brought into line. Such an approach was probably an aid to business in a period of low cost land and raw materials and reasonably inexpensive labor; whether it can continue to be so in the late twentieth century is open to question.

5

Adaptive Americans

WHILE American managers experienced unusual difficulties in the special fields dominated by large enterprises, in the broad general areas of business they adopted both European methods and inventions rapidly and successfully, and in the process, made their full share of the Western world's innovations in the use of machines and commercial practices.[1] As was to be expected in a rapidly industrializing nation, the number of business firms grew faster than the population, but in contrast to most of Europe the number of farms also increased at nearly the same rate as the total number of people. Consequently, in spite of the upswing of commerce and industry, by 1890 there were still 4.5 million farms and only about 1.5 million other types of business firms. While the spirit of the people of the United States on farms as well as in cities was perhaps more businesslike than in the urban British Isles, nearly a two-thirds majority of Americans were still rural. The United States, however, was only slightly more rural than Germany and slightly less so than France.

Business followed, or even preceded, population moving across the continent, so that a frontier town a decade old might have an occupational structure not greatly different from a nonindustrial town of similar size on the Eastern seaboard.[2] The great majority of American businessmen were storekeepers, millers, blacksmiths, and various other types of specialized artisans, and for them, aside from buying and pricing, managerial problems were practically nonexistent. The strong pressure for growth and adaptation fell more on the medium-sized firm in trade, finance, and manufacturing, the group that people often have tacitly in mind when speaking of American business.

THE SPREAD OF FACTORIES

The replacing of skilled labor operations by factory machinery has generally been regarded as the most important economic feature of the half century after 1840. Textile mills, averaging sixty workers each, were the chief factories in 1840. By 1890 a score of industries had built up production complexes so large that in order to promote efficient management they were subdivided into separate plants. Essentially industrialism had matured, although better mechanization and routinization of work, sometimes with continuous-flow or assembly lines, would continue to alter manufacturing processes.

The early changes had many aspects. Railroad junctions where competitive rates were available made attractive sites for factories. If there had been an artisan shop at the junction it might expand and mechanize, but samples suggest that capital generally came from outside and was invested in a wholly new plant. Initially small enterprises might evolve in several ways. They might specialize on an intermediate product or process and develop a relatively secure market by supplying manufacturers at the next stage of production. On this basis family firms existed for generations without undergoing any rapid changes in size. Profitable local enterprises might merge with or be bought by competitors and made into larger multiplant companies selling in a regional or national market. Still others, and these were numerous, failed to meet increasing competition and went out of business. In such cases the building might be sold for other purposes and the used machinery marketed to an expanding competitor, but the returns from such liquidations were usually small, and hence banks did not favor mortgages on manufacturing plants.

Before the 1880s most metal fabricators used all-purpose machine tools for cutting, boring, or finishing, although the latter was often done by hand. The Brown & Sharpe Manufacturing Company of Providence, Rhode Island, for example, made tools for other factories but also manufactured in their own plant for outside companies such as Wilcox and Gibbs Sewing Machine. Bicycle manufacture was another example of fabrication in plants working largely on other goods, with only final assemblage or finishing by the company imprinting its label. Thus medium-sized manufacturing involved a host of contractual relations that facilitated the rapid utilization of new technical knowledge. It is worth noting that the more progressive Midwestern shops often adopted European improvements not yet taken up in the more conservative East.

In all, value added by manufacture, increasingly mechanized, was the fastest growing part of the national product, increasing, at about the same price level, from a mere $240 million in 1839 to $4.1 billion in 1899. Striking as such figures appear, on a per capita basis they are less than those for Germany and Japan. On a share or percentage basis of American national product all aspects of business were growing compared to agriculture, but income from the latter was also advancing in absolute figures.

THE PRESSURE OF DECLINING PRICES

The period between 1840 and 1890 was one of fairly severe price fluctuations that necessitated wise inventory decisions. The Warren and Person wholesale price index stood at 84 in 1850, 93 in 1860 (having touched 111 in 1857), and 193 at its high in 1864; then from 135 in 1870, it sank back to 82 in 1890, a movement in sharp contrast to the secular uptrend of the twentieth century. While the long downslide after the Civil War benefitted a few producers whose selling prices were fairly rigid (such as the marketers of the five-cent glass of beer or soda), on the whole it put continuous pressure for economy and rapid turnover on most types of business. During this time there were also three severe periods of depression, from 1839 to 1843, 1857 to 1862, and 1873 to 1878, and two milder ones, from 1865 to 1867 and 1883 to 1885. Taken together with an ever-expanding market brought about by better transportation and more productive technology in manufacturing, these features made for a highly competitive era full of pitfalls for the average entrepreneur.

In England, for example, the whole period between 1873 and 1896 is often spoken of as the Great Depression, a point of view that may, one can guess, have helped spread a pessimism that inhibited entrepreneurial and organizational innovation. But, while France, Germany, and Japan were also subject to price declines, the latter two had a varied prosperity somewhat resembling the changing conditions in the United States.

The rapid expansion in American settlements and population, which were deterrents to growth in income per capita, were benefits to many marginal businessmen, who might fail in one location and move to a new one where competition was temporarily less severe. Migration also took away skilled labor, and as labor markets remained fairly local, manufacturers were led to invest more than their European counterparts in machines to supply the growing market for products. This led to a recurring situation wherein the newest entrants to the market had a technological advantage, and to an appearance of much new machinery in the United States that was often commented on by foreign visitors.

COMPETITIVE PRESSURES AND THE LAW

When a company had an advantage because of its size (economy of scale) either in manufacturing or marketing, the spread of ever-cheaper transportation, chiefly by rail, often enabled it to bring severe competitive pressure on smaller local producers. Because of the geographical size of the national market this competiton was probably more severe than in France or Germany. To remain in business the local enterprise had either to improve efficiency, sell out to the bigger competitor, or enter into some type of protective association. In a few lines of production or distribution there was no solution except to shut down. A small country ironworks or poorly equipped shoe manufacturer could not compete with mass production. A small town wholesaler could not carry as varied a stock as one in a large city. Such operations might also be too small to interest a larger firm in their acquisition. Yet, in many cases, the demise of the small enterprise occurred because of either a poor location in relation to transportation, the desire of the owner-operator to retire from business, or the opportunity to become a highly paid employee of some larger company. The attrition was a gradual one, and each decade hundreds of thousands of new small enterprises appeared with enough efficiency to supply local markets or larger companies.

In manufacturing this group of efficient, medium-sized firms were the ones that could often secure good terms for merger with a larger competitor. The process of consolidation seldom led to national monopoly, but usually to the creation of strong regional firms capable of competing successfully with their outside rivals in areas where the local enterprise had an advantage in marketing. There were, therefore, home-market areas where the local firm was dominant, and other parts of the surrounding market where a dozen or more firms might be competitive.

Trade associations go back at least to medieval guilds and master's associations, but they appeared in their modern form in both Europe and America with the rise of mechanized production and transportation to larger markets. Everywhere cooperative organization was a normal response to harmful competition, and associations were formed to control prices and quota production, but nowhere else as successfully as in Germany. Here the principal banks that took an active role in industrial finance and management led the way in bringing efficient competitors into cartels to control prices and production. The German cartel movement started in the 1860s with price-fixing, but by the depression of the later 1870s, it was clear that, to be effective, the association must exercise some control over production and distribution. In the three decades after 1870, about 350 cartels were formed, of which some 250 were still operative in 1900. The dropouts represented not only companies made obsolete by changing types of production, but also a lively movement toward consolidation of cartel members into large unified companies.[3]

In the United States such associations had appeared in river steamboating before 1820, but in contrast to other nations including Britain, the American (state) courts had interpreted price-fixing agreements as conspiracies in restraint of trade. The difference in the interpretation of the common law probably mirrors the greater value placed on the freedom of the individual entrepreneur in the United States. Repeated throughout the century in decisions by state courts, the conspiracy doctrine deprived price-fixing or production quotas of legal force.

In the 1870s and 1880s some American producers of only slightly differentiated commodities, such as bourbon whiskey, tried to make agreements work by selling through a common agency, or "pooling" their output. But pools were never in operation for more than a year or two before some cheaters were detected selling outside the pool. A sign that the pool price was too high, this would lead to negotiations for a new agreement that would, in turn, last only as long as everyone was satisfied.

The way around the conspiracy doctrine was merger into a single concern. As we have seen (Chapter Five) lawyer S. C. T. Dodd of Standard Oil, by expanding the doctrine of trusteeship to cover the centralized voting of the stock of many companies, offered competitors a simple method for merging. A committee representing the different competing firms would be appointed to place values on the various stocks. The trustees elected by all the stockholders, voting in proportion to the estimated worth of their assets, would then receive the various stocks and issue uniform trustee certificates for the proper amounts.

Consolidation offered several advantages. The less efficient plants could be sold for other purposes and the more efficient run at full capacity, deliveries could be made from the facilities nearest the customer, and local plant management could be reduced in size by centralizing finance, sales, and staff work. But in practice voluntary consolidation had two strong disadvantages: if competition was greatly lessened the incentive to efficiency and technological improvement also declined; and the initial valuations on which the trust certificates were based were almost uniformly excessive. From 1880 to 1900 the history of voluntary trusts was a poor one from the standpoint of return to the stockholders.

Consolidations brought about by the ability of one firm, favored by location, entrepreneurship, or new technology, to force smaller operators out of business—as with Standard Oil or American Sugar Refining—had better records for earnings and efficiency. In addition, during a period where managerial ability was a very scarce factor, the abler executives of the acquired companies could be absorbed by the dominant firm. But for the same reasons, the growing concern was likely to be able to build a national monopoly, and this, in turn, led (as will be seen in Chapter Eight) to new laws and judicial interpretations against such a monopoly that differed from those in the rest of the world.

Railroads had, on the whole, more success than manufacturers with pooling. The system operated by apportioning through-freight between major points at uniform rates based on past records, and then having companies that exceeded their quota pay penalty rates into a pool for annual division. Since it was easier for competitors to keep track of freight trains than of barrels of whiskey, for example, railroad pools worked tolerably well.[4] The leaders of the industry would have liked the federal government to have legalized pooling, but instead the Interstate Commerce Act of 1887 set up a commission to prohibit pooling, prevent abuses in rates, and maintain fair conditions of competition.[5]

FAVORABLE LAWS AND INTERPRETATIONS

While in their interpretation of contracts to abridge competition the state, and ultimately the federal, courts may have appeared to oppose business, this was far from the general rule. Strong managements and their able lawyers steadily reshaped the common law to conform to the needs of nineteenth-century American business. In this respect the Anglo-American type of judge-made law was less rigid than the Roman type of codified law prevailing upon the continent of Europe.

Up to perhaps about 1840, the aid offered by competing states had been a benefit to business, but as more enterprises came to operate across state lines, differing jurisdictions caused problems for management; to this extent the national codes of Europe were an advantage. But the tendency from 1840 to 1890 was for state laws and their judicial interpretation to become increasingly uniform. Judges and lawyers read the same legal texts and responded to much the same business pressures. Bankruptcy, contract, and negotiable instrument laws essential for business operation became reliably similar. Incorporation merely by filing a request conforming to conditions established by state law became possible for all types of business companies in practically all the states between 1837 and 1875. Often passed as reforms to limit the broad power that could be conferred in special incorporation acts, general laws had the net effect of making incorporation much easier and more popular.

In 1840 corporations were largely confined to banking, transportation, and public utilities; by 1890, most sizable businesses had found it best to incorporate. There were, however, two disadvantages: corporations were slower-moving than partnerships because they needed the approval of important decisions by a board of directors; and limited liability weakened the confidence that the outsider could have in the responsibility of the chief managers. Investment bankers, for example, thought it wise to operate in partnerships. For small enterprises run by the head of a family, incorporation might merely add to paper work without providing any compensating advantage. Therefore, corporations have never made up more than a small minority of all American enterprises.

England, which had, as we have seen, lagged behind the American states in the use of the corporation, rapidly caught up in the joint stock banking act of 1826 and the general companies acts from 1844 to 1856, but in France and Germany incorporation continued to be difficult. In spite of drastic changes in government, in France the continued need for action by the Council of State made incorporation as a *societe anonyme* difficult until the general incorporation act of 1867, which provided charters on request for all but insurance and a few other types of companies. Before 1850, only Prussia (1843) and a few other German states had any provision for business incorporation, and until 1860 only Hamburg and Bremen had general laws. In the great business upsurge following the victory in the Franco-Prussian War, general acts were passed for the new German Empire as a whole.[6]

In all, by 1872 incorporation for most purposes was possible by application under general acts in all four of the leading Western industrial nations. But Britain had made use of this flexible means for mobilizing capital for more than twenty years longer than the two continental powers, while some American states had preceded England by three decades, and by half a century in frequent use of the specially chartered corporation. Corporate regulations illustrated the difference between the rather extreme laissez-faire, somewhat anarchic state system of late-nineteenth-century America, and the centralized statism of Germany. Laws passed in Germany in 1884 controlled corporate practice to a degree that would not appear in the United States until 1933 and 1934.

IMPROVED COMMUNICATION

Alfred D. Chandler, Jr., has called the two decades before the Civil War the time of the genesis of modern management.[7] By 1850 communication by telegraph and shipment by rail were producing a new business tempo and a need to consider nationwide as well as Northeast-coast market conditions. As we have seen in Chapter Five, railroads were leading the way in creating more complex and specialized hierarchies within large firms. But equally significant was the higher efficiency and lower risk brought about by the multiplication of what may be called auxiliary enterprises.

The twenty years after 1845 were a period of spectacular improvement in business communication in the Western world. By 1850, foreign news in daily papers, collected by press associations from incoming steamers, provided the basis for much better-informed decisions by traders. But meanwhile the physical transport of messages was being superseded by electricity. The telegraph, for which Professor Samuel F. B. Morse of New York University had perfected a transmitter better than its German predecessors, was, to his surprise, turned down by the federal government. The telegraph's resulting spread at the hands of numerous private promoters, mostly licensed by Morse—but some under competing patents—was fast but inefficient. Cheaply constructed, over-capitalized lines gave poor service, and the confused system called for either government purchase or consolidation by a strong private company. In accordance with mid-century American attitudes and in contrast to those in Europe, the latter happened. By 1867, Western Union Telegraph had gained a virtual monopoly by taking over its last big competitor, American Telegraph. Prior to this takeover, Western Union, with government subsidy, had strung wires to San Francisco (1861), and American, with the help of a British syndicate, had laid the first Atlantic cable (1866). The monopolistic company of 1867 was grossly overcapitalized and remained a prime target for stock market speculators and new competitors. By 1888, Western Union entered into a general agreement with its smaller but strong rival, Postal, that ended the telegraph wars, partly because the telephone was superseding communication by Morse code.

The patent on a telephone receiver and transmitter in 1876 by Alexander Graham Bell, a Scotch-Canadian teaching in Boston, illustrates the uncertainties of marketing inventions. It seemed commercially practical and was put in commercial development by Boston financiers. This group decided to manufacture the phones through their own company, eventually called Western Electric, and only lease them on an annual basis to users. This wise business decision initiated a practice later followed by International Business Machines (IBM) and other marketers of patented equipment. Usually, lack of familiarity by manufacturers with a complex rented device greatly reduced the chance of their finding a way of circumventing the patent.

Immediately, however, as one would expect, the Bell Telephone group had a powerful rival in Western Union. At the start the Bell directors would have sold all the telephone rights to the telegraph company, but a committee of the latter reported that the invention was not worth the $100,000 asked. Quickly realizing its mistake, Western Union commissioned Thomas A. Edison to construct a better phone, which he promptly did, although probably with some infringements of Bell's patents. At all events the Bell company, now more confident of a market, bought off the financially hard-pressed Western Union for $325,000, plus 20 percent of phone rentals for the next seventeen years, and put the Edison, rather than the Bell phone into production.[8]

The other important office or communication aids to business were the typewriter and cash register. In one sense these can be seen as part of the American tendency to substitute machines for labor as rapidly as possible. The invention of both certainly stems from an interest in tinkering with machines that was perhaps most widespread in the United States. The typewriter evolved gradually in the mid-nineteenth century, although the commercial model that the Remington Arms company marketed in the 1870s was patented by C. Latham Sholes in 1868. Together with carbon paper, which was developed in America at the same time, the typewriter made multiple copies feasible and divorced calligraphic accuracy from penmanship. Business offices, correctly fearing the impression of impersonality, were slow to adopt the typewriter, but it came into use in big offices by 1880.[9]

The cash register, patented in 1879 by James Ritty, a prosperous Ohio saloon owner, was essentially a device for circumventing employee thefts and giving management a correct record of sales. For five years neither Ritty nor other local businessmen saw any great value in the device. It took an imaginative entrepreneur, John Henry Patterson, who bought control of the patent for $6,500 in 1884, and put the kind of drive for which Americans became famous behind its marketing, to spread the device throughout retail business.[10]

In the long view it does not seem accidental that the United States, which had the greatest problems of communicating and marketing over great distances, should have been the pioneer in adopting new technology in business communication. This surmise is strengthened by the fact that America, aided by the later innovations of IBM and Xerox, continued to lead the world in this type of technology in the 1970s.

The use of connecting railroads and the long periods required for goods in transit, both necessitated by the vastness of America, led to two other new business facilities. Starting in the late 1830s, the transshipment of goods from stage to rail and from line to line was facilitated for a fee by smart New England transportation employees, some of whom soon formed full-time express companies. It is interesting that in Great Britain, with its shorter hauls and heavier traffic, the railroads themselves did the work of the express companies at a saving to the shipper and a profit to the railroad.[11] The other device, pioneered as far as I know in the United States, was the private freight car—owned either by freight companies that supplied the railroads with cars or by producers big enough to ship in multicar lots. This development saved the financially hard-pressed railroads the cost of the rolling stock and assured the shipper of prompt switching of his clearly marked cars. By the 1880s a considerable percentage of all cars traveling the trunk lines between Chicago and the East were privately owned, including many refrigerator cars belonging to the meat packers.

AUXILIARY AIDS

Other aids to business were of a type essential in all nations: agencies for supplying advice on legal, engineering, and accounting problems; trade journals and business magazines; and mercantile credit bureaus. As separate agencies these various enterprises generally appeared in the British Isles in the post-Napoleonic period and in the United States in the 1830s. In most cases, aside from accounting, there was no need for consciously copying British practice. The services were obviously required by all expanding business and would be provided either through internal or external hiring. Much of the advantage of paying for the cost of location in a big city accrued from the ability of the firm to externalize these services and secure the best, paying for them only when needed.

One such special service, too costly for any company of the day to supply for itself, was nationwide credit information on mercantile buyers. That the United States led in creating this addition to the business structure was another result of distance. No one in the East coast cities could know about the financial reliability of the hundreds of wholesalers in the interior. Impressed by New York merchants' uncollectable accounts, Lewis Tappan, in 1841, opened the first mercantile credit agency, which later came to be R. G. Dun & Company. Tappan collected his information through correspondents, chiefly lawyers, in all the important trading centers and sold it to subscribers. Starting with Boston in 1843, branches were opened in the principal cities of the United States and in 1857 in London and Montreal; by 1890 Dun & Company had 126 offices.[12] In 1880 the company was already supplying information on nearly 800,000 firms. From 1855 on the original firm had competition from Bradstreet's Improved Commercial Agency, and by 1880 from a number of specialized or regional agencies. Nevertheless, the two early rivals continued to dominate the field and merged in 1941 as Dun & Bradstreet.[13]

In contrast to such new auxiliary services, created in the formative period of the 1840s and 1850s, law offices were as old as trade itself. The change of the 1840s was the growing importance to the legal profession of general business clients, who now came to rank along with or in some offices above those whose problems related to land titles. The railroads were among the earliest firms to find it economical to have salaried legal departments, where lawyers could be kept busy with state relations, land acquisition and sale, damage suits, and corporate problems. Because of the routine character of most in-company work and the custom of fixed salaries, the ablest lawyers preferred to form partnerships of men skilled in each different branch of the law and sell their advice to companies that needed such help. Hence by 1890, the United States had a business-oriented bar with the largest metropolitan legal partnerships rivaling the biggest manufacturing or railroad corporations in business influence. The bench had moved in the same direction, but, because of the political nature of appointments, there were many judges with small-town backgrounds who were not altogether in tune with the most advanced business attitudes.[14]

During this period engineering advice was generally secured, either on a fee basis or by salary for a fixed period, from individuals who had made some reputation as constructors of public or private works. Neither management nor engineering advice was available from concerns especially created for such a purpose. Advertising services, however, were offered from the 1850s on by specialized agents such as George P. Rowell in Boston and later N. W. Ayer in Philadelphia. The latter led the way in making the agent the representative of the advertiser rather than the media, although he often sold his client space that he had purchased wholesale in advance. Soon there were a number of competitors in the field, and by the 1880s the agencies were designing national campaigns for their customers. The agents, particularly Ayer, also began to provide necessary information in manuals and annual lists of newspapers with estimates of their circulation.[15]

ACCOUNTING

In contrast to trade information, law, engineering, and advertising, bookkeeping or accounting generally remained until after mid-century a function performed within the firm. Outside or "merchant accountants"

were generally used in eighteenth-century England and Scotland only
for special purposes such as liquidations, inheritance, or trusteeships.
Usually the accountant had an additional business or profession. The
English Companies Act of 1862, which provided that dividends could
only be paid from income, joined the many bankruptcy statutes in
making British accounting a full-time activity.

While old-style bookkeeping had by 1800 partially absorbed the
ideas of capital as an entity separate from earnings, or profit and loss,
and the use of periodic balances, there had been more of an eighteenth-
century revolution in theory than in practice. With a few exceptions
among the leading merchants of the major ports, proprietors kept their
books much as they had since the Renaissance. The corporation was the
agent of change that gradually introduced the elements of modern
accounting, and since the United States had the largest number of corporations some of its bookkeepers were moved to keep abreast of English
practice and continental theory.

In all nations the history of accounting from 1820 onward is one of
advancing theory and lagging practice. One reason for the latter is that
there may never be a single answer to the question, "what is the best
system of accounting?" The reply has to be: "best for answering *what*
questions?—future earning prospects, present value, operating efficiency?" With present-day computers firms may run a number of
systems each designed to clarify the overall meaning of certain data,
but in earlier years this was both beyond entrepreneurial perception and
would have been judged too expensive.

In continental Europe methods of accounting were rather precisely
prescribed by law, although theoretical writing by Frenchmen, Germans,
Netherlanders, and Swiss was in the mid-nineteenth century well in
advance of the laws. What A. C. Littleton has called the first truly
theoretical book was published in London in 1818 by F. W. Cronhelm.
Systematic accounts were required in the English railroad acts of the
1820s.[16] Meanwhile the United States proceeded on a laissez-faire basis
with systematic accounting (or its absence), depending upon the desires
of management.

Three principles, however, emerged willy-nilly from the nature of
corporations: 1) periodic balances; 2) seeing the firm as an entity separate
from its owners; and 3) recognition of accounting as a statistical, mathematical mirror of what was physically taking place. Larger-scale manufacturing companies in the 1870s also placed more emphasis on
knowledge of costs than had been thought necessary in mercantile firms.
In the Pabst Brewing Company, for example, the seventies and eighties

were a period of increasingly detailed costing, although modern accountants would no doubt say that expenses were still put together in too
aggregated a form on the head office books, that depreciation was entirely
unsystematic, and that advance calculations of cost were not made.[17]
Pabst's policies were apparently similar to those of other companies of
the period.

The first American book to argue for logical theory rather than
traditional or practical rules was Thomas Jones' *Principles* (1841), but
modern approaches can scarcely be said to have been clarified before
the 1880s. Meanwhile the same theoretical progress was taking place on
the Continent. In 1870, J. G. Courcelles-Seneiul in *Cours de Compatibilité*
gave clear expression to the entity theory, as did I. N. Brenkman in the
Netherlands a dozen years later. Both serve as bridges from old
fashioned double-entry bookkeeping to modern accounting.[18] But, as
usual, foreign knowledge reached America largely by way of Britain.
There the Companies Acts of 1844 and 1845 required annual audits but
left their character in the hands of the stockholders. The British Bankruptcy Act of 1849 provided for legal review of the accuracy of accounts.
These and subsequent laws transformed bookkeepers into accountants.
In 1854 the Accounting Society of Scotland became the first regional
association. A generation later urban societies in England sponsored a
journal, *The Accountant* (1874–), and in 1880 formed by government
action the Institute of Chartered Public Accounts in England and Wales.
By 1882 the Institute was admitting new members only on the basis
of examinations.[19]

The American railroad scandals of 1854, involving millions of
dollars in fraudulent securities, led more American stockholders to
demand audits by outsiders or "public" accountants. Aside from the
railroads, however, the practice did not spread much until the late
1870s, when the English began sending auditors from firms such as
Price, Waterhouse to examine the books of American companies in which
they had major investments. By the 1880s some of these English and
Scottish firms opened New York branches, and in 1886 joined with local
practitioners in forming the American Association of Public Accountants.
Its original membership of thirty-one, however, had only grown to
forty-five ten years later. All but a few companies in the United States
valued secrecy more than disclosure, and there were no federal laws
requiring audits.[20]

SOURCES OF INFORMATION

Prior to 1840 stockbuyers and entrepreneurs had been able to get digested statistics and business information from *DeBow's Review*, *Hunt's Merchants' Magazine*, and numerous government reports. By the mid-forties more specialized periodicals were beginning to appear. In one respect, France was a pioneer in serial publications useful to business, but the *Compte rendu* of the Bank of France (1819–) and the later *Revue de droit commercial et industriél* (1837–) were of limited utility to the ordinary businessman. The English *Bankers, Insurance and Agents Magazine* (1844–) was a more direct predecessor of the specialized business periodical or trade journal. New Yorkers quickly produced a *Banker's Magazine* (1846–) and three years later an *American Railroad Journal* (Chapter Five.) English and American publication multiplied at much the same rate; for example, in the year 1866 an *Engineering Journal* appeared in London and an *Engineering and Mining Journal* in New York.

In spite of more printed information, the age of learning by travel persisted. Technicians made regional and international trips to observe new ways of doing things, conventions of specialists met, and the old trade fairs grew into elaborate international expositions, such as the Crystal Palace in London in 1851, the Centennial at Philadelphia in 1876, and the Paris World's Fair of 1878. About Germany Jurgen Kocka writes:

> Of the methods by which this knowledge was transmitted, the most important was the foreign journeys of the future or already practicing entrepreneur. . . . Up to 1870 almost every third entrepreneur in the Rhineland and Westphalia had been on business or study trips abroad.[21]

American trade associations, unable to control prices or production, became devices for exchanging information and developing uniform practices. The tariff and tax battles of the Civil War period gave a strong impetus to the formation of more national associations to represent their respective industries before Congress. Brewers, for example, who had never assembled beyond their local city areas, now formed an American Brewers Association. Iron- and steel-makers and wool growers, already well-organized, had association secretaries, James M. Swank and John L. Hayes, who developed many of the techniques later called public relations. Swank, for example, as editor of the *Bulletin* of the Iron and Steel Association in the years after the war, published statistical analyses showing how the whole economy benefitted from the tariff protection granted his industry, and beyond that made the *Bulletin* a standard source for industrial information.[22] Collectively, such men and their backers in Congress formed a powerful business lobby that reinforced the natural bent of many senators and representatives who were themselves interested in business needing government favors.[23]

Unlike the Germans, American entrepreneurs of this period were generally not conscious of lagging behind foreign practice and also saw little need for more education. Businessmen tended to regard even high school as a considerable waste of time, especially when the necessary studies of bookkeeping and applied mathematics could be learned in evening schools. Beyond the fact that a college brought money to a town, only engineering and law justified higher education, and even law could be learned while clerking in an office. It is an interesting contrast that, whereas the United States since the Colonial period had had private business schools or "colleges" offering brief courses in the needs of the office, Germany, while lacking such schools, had state supported technical institutes at the secondary as well as the college level from 1820 on. By the late nineteenth century this difference may have contributed to America's being more of a leader in business forms and Germany more in technology.

The new development in American higher education from 1850 on was largely in practical engineering. Until Abbott Lawrence's moderate gift to Harvard in 1847 for a scientific course, Rensselaer Polytechnic Institute had been the only college of engineering or applied science, aside from those in the government military services. By 1870 the United States had nearly a dozen engineering schools, but the level of scientific, as distinct from directly applied, instruction was not high.

Perhaps because they wanted to catch up technologically to the earlier industrial leaders or perhaps for reasons of national character and traditions, the Germans placed emphasis on advanced scientific study. Business employment was not highly esteemed, but university-trained scientists might pursue their studies into fields with practical applications and join companies using chemistry or physics without much loss in status. Neither England nor the United States had any such flow of scientists from universities to industry, and the chemical companies of both nations tended to remain guided by men with only practical experience.

NATIONWIDE MARKETING

While American marketing in general was modeled on that of England and the Continent, the great distances and continuous migration unique to the United States were part of a complex that gradually differentiated some American business practices from those of Europe. The traveling salesman and the city hotel, for example, came to play such special American roles. The traveling man had been important from the beginning of the great upswing in business at the end of the eighteenth century, but in England and Europe his sales territories were generally small and he covered much of them without leaving home for more than a day. In contrast, American salesmen took extended trips by stage, boat, and rail, and were often gone from home for weeks or months. In fact, the distances were so great and the travel time involved so long and expensive that before the spread of the railroad net in the 1850s very few companies tried to cover distant parts of the nation. With faster connections the salesman could plan to spend nights in a chain of cities, for which he required hotels. Hence the American hotel with its increasing size and luxury from 1840 to 1890 should be seen primarily as an extension of business marketing. Besides housing salesmen, the hotel performed additional functions closely related to business—such as attracting political, social, and business meetings to the city. These gatherings also benefitted the city merchants and advertised the town as a good place to have an enterprise. Together with the local newspaper, and somewhat later the local chamber of commerce, the hotel was a major device for the promotion of community business. Of course, there were some manufacturers selling to a national market who did not want new growth that might lead to shortages of labor and higher taxes, but in most business areas they were a small minority.

Many aspects of hotel living were so colorful that they led to the national legends of the hotel keeper, the editor, and the salesman—particularly the latter. It should be remembered, however, that they all represented marketing costs that were less necessary in more compact economies. That is, they all appeared as plus elements in the gross national product, but they were a burden on the consumer's real standard of living.

Aside from these unique American features, the period from 1840 to 1890 marks the maturity and peak of the traditional types of marketing. While each Western nation had its own terms and some differences in function, for various types of middlemen, more perhaps than in any other field, America continued the customary practices, and there was very little change in these forms prior to the mid-nineteenth century. Innovations, such as chain stores and wholesaling by factory branches, based on new means of production, communication, and transportation, began about that time but developed relatively slowly before 1890.

The increasing volume of trade that had created specialized firms for the many functions of the old-style general merchant continued to operate in the same direction. Not only were domestic wholesalers separated from importers, but dry-goods wholesalers split into ever more minute specialties such as dress goods, sheetings, novelties, or millinery. In 1850, New York City had 740 importers in eighteen special fields, 139 in dry goods alone.[24] Commission houses, jobbers, salesmen, and various other facilitators of trade spread correspondingly. In 1861, outside the special field of railroad supply, where users were in direct contact with manufacturers, about 95 percent of all manufactured goods as well as practically all food products not consumed where they were grown passed through the hands of wholesalers.[25]

During these decades there was a marketing frontier, more important to the business and economic life of the nation than the frontier of westward-moving population—although the two were seldom far apart. Early in the century wholesale outlets were appearing in the West, and by 1840, Cleveland, Detroit, Cincinnati, Louisville, and St. Louis were all wholesale centers, soon to be joined and overshadowed by Chicago.[26] The Midwestern wholesalers, like Easterners of an earlier day, had to deal in a wide variety of products. The specialized shoe wholesaler in Boston, for example, would sell to a full-line apparel house in Cleveland and it, in turn, would market by salesmen to general stores in its area. An innovation, said to have been brought from England in 1845, was to supply the salesmen with samples as well as catalogues.

This overly simple description fails to do justice to the complexity of marketing in many lines by the 1880s. As a general principle, the more uniform the goods in type or quality, the simpler the marketing process; the more complex and varied the products, the more middlemen would be needed to collect the special items from hundreds of small manufacturers or importers and see that they reached the wholesalers, who could then move them toward retail distribution.

Credit problems further complicated the process. In this period mobile capital or credit was still largely in the hands of the old mercantile firms, and they and individual capitalists rather than banks financed manufacturers. Once the goods had been produced, however, and were moving toward the ultimate user, bank credit became available. Hence jobbers, commission merchants, and other agents might borrow to finance the movement of goods through stages of the distribution process. Not least of all in this chain of credit-users were the great numbers of general store keepers who could only collect from some customers when they sold their crops and consequently had in the meantime to have credit from the wholesaler.

Since the United States was chiefly an exporter of raw materials or semimanufactures on order, little attention was paid to overseas marketing. There was no effort, such as that of Germany, to train salesmen for trade in foreign nations. Only an occasional manufacturer, such as John D. Rockefeller in Standard Oil, Edward Clark in Singer sewing machines, or James H. Patterson in cash registers, tried to sell in European markets.

This situation is not surprising considering the size and rate of growth of the American domestic market. In almost every line the rewards seemed greatest for successful marketing at home. A company that could reach most of this market more cheaply than its competitors was on the road to wealth. Yet, in spite of the apparent complexity of the sales structure, the size of the market made it difficult to bypass a given stage. Wholesalers, jobbers, and commission merchants were experts who knew their fields better than anyone in a production plant. To duplicate their complex but efficient operations the producer would have to hire a staff which, in turn, would have to establish contacts, decide questions regarding credit, and do other tasks not familiar to their superiors in the home office. Right down to the present day it does not pay to "internalize" these unrelated activities unless there is some major compensation in special, more direct promotion.

Aside from the fact that increasing urbanization made buyers easier to reach, the chief business reasons for direct distribution might all be grouped under efforts to specialize the product and build it a market separate from its erstwhile competitors. Nationally advertised brand names—pioneered, for example, in drugs and soaps—might force all general wholesalers to stock the product and in a few cases warrant special trips by factory salesmen to retailers. The establishment of regional factory sales branches by a few big firms also helped to assure the consumer of good service from local sellers. This shift toward branches did not have to be made all at once. The Pabst Brewing Company, for example, used independent wholesalers, factory branches, and controlled retailers simultaneously, depending on the size and remoteness of the market.[27]

When the product was a complex patented device, such as the Singer sewing machine, provision of service and repairs added to the value of direct factory salesmen. When such devices or even unpatented machine parts were being supplied to another manufacturer there was often little need for middlemen.

In economists' language these were examples of forward integration by manufacturers. Another threat to the middleman was from backward integration by retailers. Chain stores, such as the Great Atlantic and Pacific Tea Company, spreading rapidly in the 1870s, might buy much of their goods directly from the processors. Big department stores, which appeared after 1850, might even contract to have goods especially made for them and sell from catalogues, as did the still relatively small mail-order houses of Montgomery Ward in the 1870s and Sears Roebuck in the next decade.

THE START OF A NEW BUSINESS ERA

In one sense the great increase in the different kinds of articles to be sold and the more complicated means of selling them in a big national market introduced no elements that management had not previously faced in principle in earlier years; the shift was in the relative importance of the various problems and the increased knowledge applicable to them. In the earliest days of machine technology, production had generally presented the most troublesome problems, especially if much of marketing and finance was handled by an allied mercantile firm. Now production in many lines was routinized and the novel problems more often arose from meeting competition in the market. How much should be risked on sales efforts? Would nationwide newspaper or magazine advertising pay? Which territories were most endangered by competitors? In a longer historical view business was moving from a temporary preoccupation with technology back to the age-old problems of the market.

But, as of 1890, these new problems were still at an early stage. National advertising was just building up to a significant volume, and many conservative firms regarded it as closely akin to fraud. Few companies sold consumer products so complicated that they needed special agents or servicemen. Therefore, it is better to analyze the challenges of the great national market to management in the following generation.

The big changes of the years 1840 to 1890 had been in the productivity of machinery and in the increasing speed and volume of business transactions and information. In 1840, even along the Northeast coast, information moved little faster than the horse, or than it had between the central Italian cities of the Roman Empire. The nearest ports of Europe were still two or three weeks away. Aside from the newspapers and "prices current," businessmen had little or nothing in the way of literature concerning their specialties. By 1890, save for travel by air, the modern sources of rapid and voluminous information had all appeared. Telephone, telegraph, and cable connected the business centers of the nation with each other and with those in Europe. Each important type of activity had, at least, one trade periodical; general business magazines and newspapers had multiplied; and the ticker reported to subscribers the minute to minute sales on markets.

The increasing speed and volume of information as well as the knowledge needed for more complex technology undoubtedly favored the medium to large business firm that could institutionally separate the intake and digestion of information from the demands of daily activities. The problem for the larger firm was delegation of the task of first reading and then transferring the right knowledge to the ultimate decision-maker —or, in modern business language, the transfer from staff to line. The problem has continued to grow and the perfect answer is still to be found.

6

Real Estate and Finance

AMERICANS of the nineteenth century were intensely proud of being different from Europeans. People, geography, and ways of doing things were thought to be uniquely American and better than in the old world. Yet, as emphasized in the preceding chapter, most business and technological knowledge became available almost simultaneously in all the industrial nations; if there was a two- or three-year national lead or lag it was generally connected not with lack of knowledge but with some local conditions. Since Europe had many varied business systems, in comparison to only one in the United States, and since in 1850 England was still the most advanced business nation, the United States was only occasionally a leader in innovation.

In two respects, however, the differences in America were so great that some business processes went on, not necessarily in a more advanced, but in a quite different way from their European counterparts. These were: the great American business of real estate in new, fast-growing areas; and some of the aspects of banking and finance in up to forty states where there was very little central government assistance or regulation.

EASTERN REAL ESTATE

In many respects land and townsite developments were inextricably tied to credit, so that the two types of business interacted strongly upon each other. Real estate dealings in turn may be divided into trading and mortgaging in old established centers, a business engaged in all over the world, and negotiating for virgin or slightly improved land in large quantities, which was a business no longer indigenous to Japan or Western Europe.

Throughout the world buying property or mortgage-lending in solidly established cities seemed a safe way for prosperous citizens to invest their money. It required little day-to-day management and, particularly in the growing United States, improved land always promised to go up in value. Because urban growth necessarily involved changing the functions of already bulit-up areas, increases in price were unpredictable; a good neighborhood for living or shopping might deteriorate into one fit only for slums or warehouses. Consequently, even urban real estate investment was a business based on predictions whose demands for knowledge far exceeded the information available to the ordinary purchaser. But, on the whole, urban property rose in value, and compared to unimproved land, common stock, or even railroad bonds, must have seemed conservatively safe.

Big general entrepreneurs such as the old merchants had always combined relatively well-informed and strategic urban land buying with their other activities. In New York City in 1850, for example, Moses Beach, editor of the *New York Sun*, estimated that there were twenty-three local men worth over $500,000, of whom eight had made their money and kept it chiefly in real estate. Since the next biggest category was merchants, numbering seven, and since merchants were generally heavily involved in land operations, it seems safe to say that even in New York City, real estate was the chief business of the rich.

BUSINESS IN WESTERN LAND

Some of the wealthy men of the East coast were ready to enter into the development of new Western cities. Those that grew rapidly, like Chicago, had local representatives of Eastern investors sending back deeds and mortgages in return for capital. English and other European money might have moved into Eastern cities for such investment had American financiers established a London market in bonds representing consolidated mortgages. Undoubtedly this failure in business organization prior to the 1880s somewhat retarded the growth of the United States.

Continual investment in Western lands opened for sale by state or federal governments was an American business that had no western European counterpart. Since success depended on the wise selection of Western agents by Eastern capitalists, good selection of properties to claim, and sale at just the right time, it did not readily lend itself to big bureaucratic operations. One of the more successful mid-century operators, for example, was James S. Easley, a Virginia merchant who owned a small local chain of general stores and initially put only $50,000 into Iowa lands.[1]

It was a highly complicated business in which many different types of people and organizations participated. The consumers were both genuine farmers as well as squatter-claim-sellers, with no firm line dividing them. Claim sellers, under the Preemption Act of 1841 or the later Homestead Act of 1862, settled briefly on a tract of land that was or would soon be opened for sale and, as soon as possible, secured a government title that they had often already consigned to a land operator. Since the process could be completed two or more times a year and (illegally) on more than one tract, the claim seller might do a substantial business with local or Eastern land operators who would hold the land a year or more while awaiting a price increase.

The practice by state and federal governments of rewarding military service with land warrants made both additional complications and opportunities for land operators, particularly in the late 1840s and 1850s. Starting in 1788, Revolutionary veterans had received a bonus in the form of land warrants. Since most ex-soldiers wanted to return to their homes, and warrants were generally held to be transferable, markets for them soon appeared in the big cities. During the period before 1862, surveyed tracts of federal land were initially offered for sale at public auctions at which warrants were unacceptable. This forced warrant holders to choose from the land still left on the books after the auction. In normal or depressed times the residual land still offered a wide choice, but during boom times the auction might exhaust the supply. Partly to meet this problem, from 1830 on state or federal warrants were made exchangeable for treasury scrip that was valid at any sale but had only half the face value of the warrant.

The peak of warrant trading came between the end of the Mexican War and the pre-Civil War depression. At this time Iowa, the most fertile of American states, was being opened for sale, and Congress was issuing warrants in larger quantities than ever before. Two weeks' service or having been in a single battle with Indians qualified an ex-soldier for such benefits. Of a total of nearly 70 million acres covered by federal warrants from 1788 on, 34 million were allotted in the act of 1855. During this period there was an informal brokers' market in warrants, with regular quotations carried in New York's *Thompson's Bank Note and Commercial Reporter*, which was presumably followed by all speculative interests.

Men like Easley established regular accounts with brokers who bought warrants, made personal trips to the areas open for sale, and tried to forecast the growth of towns and transportation. The few sample studies that have been done indicate that these types of estimates were of more importance to the prospective buyer than soil quality or timber.[2] County treasurers and recorders, if reliable businessmen, made ideal buying agents. Yet, Robert P. Swierenga holds that deciding when and to whom to sell were more important than wise buying. Or, in general terms marketing was more important than arranging for supply. This often meant heavy reliance on the judgment of Western agents. To hold good land empty for any long period involved not only loss in taxes and interest on the money invested, but policing to keep off squatters.[3]

The Civil War temporarily interfered with the trade, but Easley was able to send orders and cash through the battle lines and, although he lost money, his land business survived. Land taken from Confederate owners by the states for tax liens was often recovered, and the postwar boom again made business highly profitable. The heavy demand for loans to improve virgin land and the continuous transfer of titles differed so radically from lending on real property in Europe that the practice of government-owned mortgage banks such as the Crédit Foncier had no application to the United States. By 1870 special companies located in the West, like J. B. Watkins Land Mortgage Company of Lawrence, Kansas, were bringing Western mortgages to the Eastern money centers for sale. By the mid-eighties some of these companies were offering guaranteed mortgages or issuing debenture bonds secured by portfolios of mortgages. But the local companies were not strong enough to withstand the long drought, from 1887 to 1896, on the Great Plains. Their failure cut off the substantial flow of private Eastern capital into Western mortgages from then until after 1900.[4]

FINANCING WESTERN DEVELOPMENT

The fact that cattle from the enormous unfenced ranges of the Southwest could, by 1870, be driven to railroads and shipped to Midwestern packing houses created a new attraction for investors. Cattle companies laid claim to moderate acreages of federal lands bordering on water supplies and grazed their herds on the open range. Their securities sold well in the East and in Great Britain, where some of the companies were initially organized. Between the problems of managing at a distance, cattle stealing, and uncertain rainfall, very few of these companies made satisfactory long-run returns; and in the continuous drought from 1887 to 1896, most of them disappeared. Scottish mortgage companies, however, carefully selecting their risks throughout the West, did better. By 1889 the Alliance Trust of Scotland had over $4 million in interest-paying farm and ranch mortgages in the United States.[5]

Aside from the federal government, the two most important land sellers during this period were the states and the railroads of the far West. Congress gave the states lands for railroads, claims to swamplands, and special land warrants to promote agricultural colleges. The grants for railroads and swamplands in the 1850s chiefly benefitted the Mississippi valley states, but the education act of 1863 gave claims to all the states on the basis of their federal representation. Very large federal grants were made to the transcontinental railroads, which ultimately qualified them for nearly 140 million acres. With all of these agencies claiming and selling land it is not surprising that farmers who freely acquired land by five-year residence under the provisions of the Homestead Act of 1862 were only a small minority and were generally not located on the most desirable properties. Like much of the West, the prairies and plains were a frontier of business enterprise, before the acreage was converted into family farms.

At all periods the Western real estate development went on with little direct aid from American chartered banks.[6] Hampered by state usury laws, these banks could not get the going rates of interest by selling mortgages directly to early settlers, who were consequently forced to rely on loans from individual capitalists, private bankers, or land companies, often negotiated at 20 to 40 percent interest by roundabout means of transferring titles. The National Banking Acts of 1863 and 1864, which prohibited members of the system from lending with land as security, therefore, ruled against a practice that, as far as unimproved property was concerned, was not important.

For those with good credit resources, townsite planning and development probably continued to be more profitable than speculation in newly opened lands. The two, of course, might be combined, but usually the initial virgin-land operator was in and out again before a town could grow and create major new values. Geographical features such as trans-shipment points or exceptionally good landing places on rivers or the Great Lakes and the forecast of future advantages such as railroads led to the formation of companies to promote towns. A general store, a mill, a church, and a school would form the nucleus of a settlement, and if it grew, land acquired for $1.25 an acre might sell for $500 in half-acre town lots. But the process involved both considerable investment, a waiting period, and a high risk that the location was wrong. The men who could engage in such investment most safely were railroad directors who knew the future route of the road and the location of the stations.

Once established, each town became an informal business organization seeking collective gain from attracting new enterprises, becoming a county seat, acquiring a bank, a hotel, a newspaper, factories, wholesalers, and possibly a college. The towns that succeeded in the competitive race, often by making cash bids for county seats or railroad stations, came to promote further growth through some type of businessmen's organization called a commercial club or ultimately a chamber of commerce.

This competitive rise of new towns or cities upon previously virgin land was peculiarly American and most important in the fertile and open Mississippi and Ohio valleys. It gave to businessmen in these rising towns boisterous, competitive, defensive attitudes that were lacking on the old East coast or in Europe. Even in England, where population shifts related to business were probably greater than in France and Germany, there was a general atmosphere or assumption of town stability and few dreams of unlimited growth. Local areas in France were particularly stable in population and also more self-sufficient, resisting rather than welcoming upsetting change; in contrast, fast-growing, Midwestern cities aspired to be the Athens of America or the hub of the nation and often planned developments far beyond possible realization.

BANKING TROUBLES

Rapid growth in population and continual settlement of new areas at long distances from major metropolitan centers produced unique problems and some unusual attempts at solutions in American finance. Physical expansion created a greater scarcity of capital in relation to pressing needs than existed in Great Britain or northwestern Europe, while distance made it difficult to distribute what money or credit there was to the places where it was most wanted. This problem, in turn, inspired entrepreneurs who were seeking credit to favor devices of questionable stability, and those who regarded themselves as the pillars of finance to feel frustrated by the lack of any overall system of security.

Although not as advanced as Scotland in some practices, England was by all odds the area whose financial customs were best-known; yet there the situation was so different in almost every important respect that it could not provide politically or practically acceptable guidance for the construction of an American system. The basic difference was that England represented a rich nation with short distances and a high density of population. By 1840 it had a strong central bank with branches that issued notes; an undisputed financial center where notes were cleared and commercial bills redeemed; a shared knowledge of the important firms of the nation that allowed note brokers to specialize on certain trades and buy the trade bills for resale to banks; and a surplus of capital seeking foreign investment. The "discount houses" that dealt in buying, selling, and often guaranteeing commercial paper were of the highest financial standing and favored by the Bank of England.[7] After 1844 new issues of country bank notes were forbidden, and issues by the new joint stock banks discouraged; in other words, England was moving, as was France, toward a single circulating currency under the control of a central bank and its branches. In the most advanced American banks, the principles followed by the managements were much like those in similar offices in England, but the great majority of the 2,000 banks of one type or another in the pre-Civil War United States were in small towns or cities, run by men little versed in banking and operating in communities sorely in need of credit.

As long as the Second Bank of the United States and its branches had dominated the situation and banking activity had been largely controlled from the Eastern seaboard, the nation had had a banking system almost as mature as those of the world's leaders, such as Scotland or Switzerland. A decade after the end of centralized influence, one can not speak of a national "system" at all, and banking practice varied widely between parts of the nation.

The chief forces of destruction were the failure to recharter the Second Bank of the United States, the panic and long depression from 1837 to 1843 (during which nearly half the banks founded after 1830 failed), and the inevitable confusions of differing state laws.[8] The nation was faced with the problems of building a new business structure in the field of banking and in devising managerial procedures for its operation that would work in the peculiar American situation. While no satisfactory overall structure was devised within the century, increased specialization of financial functions and their management, together with better understanding of banking risks, somewhat improved the chaotic situation of the 1840s.

The troubles, of course, were most severe in the backcountry areas. As a result of losses to depositors and note holders several Southern and Midwestern states prohibited chartered banks, whereas others passed "Free Banking Acts," presumably providing safeguards against weak currency but in reality making note issue under the guise of "banking" extremely easy.

To start a bank under the "free" laws it was only necessary to borrow money to buy state bonds, which served as security for the bank notes, and loan the notes to the directors, who would use them to profit from local development. As might be surmised the circulating currency of the nation was thrown into confusion, with hundreds of genuine notes of varying value and an even greater number of counterfeits circulating. As a result, dealing in domestic exchange became more complex, speculative, and potentially profitable than in foreign.[9]

To carry on the national economy, business had to find new financial methods. Some of the difficulties in exchange were avoided by backcountry banks keeping deposits in the port cities, particularly New York, that could be drawn on to buy goods for their local customers. The metropolitan banks invested these deposits, that were sure to be drawn upon at certain times of the year, in call loans to stockbrokers and other very short-term paper. Consequently any sudden demand for money in the backcountry adversely affected the stock market, and in an already tight situation might lead to a panic.

Other businessmen who both profited from and helped ease the confused currency situation were the note brokers and exchange dealers who now developed into private bankers. Partnerships such as E. W. Clark and Company, Drexel and Company, or Corcoran and Riggs expanded into major business enterprises with offices, usually run by partners, in the chief financial centers. They moved specie and acceptable notes, either bank or commercial, to the places they were needed, while other private bankers, by issuing personal notes or certificates of deposit, provided currency for areas like Wisconsin, which did not allow banks.[10]

Many of the private bankers had been general merchants and were related to each other. These new family businesses had many problems in common with their previous mercantile experiences, which had depended so much on judgment of credit risks and of the movement of markets. As in England, each of the private banking houses tended to familiarize themselves with special types of paper, but the diverse and smaller American markets and the higher degrees of risk prevented the specialization represented by English discount houses and banks.

There were two major aspects of the domestic exchange business: first, the exchange of specie and sound bank notes between regions— a relatively low risk, low profit operation; and second, the buying or transferring of obligations to pay of all other types—operations of such highly variable risk and profit that personal bills were usually handled on commission rather than by purchase. To make possible the flow of cash or credit across state lines there came to be a fairly satisfactory standardization of negotiable instrument laws in the 1840s, making collection problems by out-of-state creditors relatively secure from the legal standpoint. Up to the Civil War this interstate business remained largely in the hands of some 600 private bankers. By 1890, aided as we shall see by unwise federal legislation in the 1860s, there were over 4,000 private banks.

As in western Europe the structure of commercial banking in the United States underwent important changes between 1840 and 1890, but since the relations between American bankers and those of France, Holland, and Germany were almost entirely in the private investment sector, foreign practices appear to have had little influence on the management of chartered commercial banks in the United States.

In all of this discussion an exception must be made for the finance of the Old South. Here, after some disastrous experiments with land banks in the 1830s, banking became largely geared to the movement of staple crops, financed locally by relatively sound branch banking systems that were, in turn, middlemen for factors drawing on northern metropolitan credit. While some of the orderly branch systems shine by contrast with the weaker varieties of Northern banking, it must be remembered that the risks, confined largely to staple crops, were more uniform, repetitive, and better understood. The Civil War, of course, largely demolished the old order, and in the later nineteenth century small banks with inadequate capital grew up in much of the South.

In the Middle West a promising beginning in organizing chartered banks into systematic structures was made in the 1840s and 1850s in Indiana, Ohio, and Iowa, and on a slightly different basis in Missouri. In these states privately owned banks submitted to overall control and regulation by a state "bank" that held common reserves and supplied part of the capital. The central bank had a board partly appointed by the state but chiefly made up of representatives from each of the cooperating banks. Alongside these well-organized states were others in which free banking acts (general incorporation laws for banks) produced currency mills. In Illinois in 1860, for example, in seventy-four chartered banks deposits averaged only 8 percent of note circulation. The lack of deposits in the American West should not be confused with the slow growth of the practice of deposit in France and Germany, where deposits were also small in relation to loans or circulation. In the two foreign nations people still hoarded savings, but bank circulation was backed by paid-in capital and adequate species, whereas in at least sixty of the Illinois banks the capital was in promissory notes and the currency was loaned to the chief stockholders.[11]

CONFUSED FEDERAL ACTION

In any case, the Western state developments in banking structure were interrupted and thrown into confusion by the National Currency Act of 1863 (renamed the National Bank Act in 1874) and the amendment to it in 1865. The first law, by allowing banks to issue national notes up to 90 percent of the amount of federal bonds held, set up "free banking" for the nation as a whole; the amendment put a prohibitive tax on state bank notes. The difficulties with both actions arose from an ambiguity in aims. The laws were not designed to suit bankers or to create an interrelated system, but rather to finance the war by selling government bonds to banks, which required a minimum of $50,000 worth to qualify for a charter and the privilege of note issue. While national banks were in effect given the exclusive right to issue notes backed by federal bonds, the practices of these banks were regulated by the government in negative rather than in positive ways. For example, no system as such was set up for flexible control of note issues or the marshaling of ultimate reserves in crises, while the banks were forbidden to lend on mortgages. Consequently, in contrast to France and Germany, where mortgage banking was done by government agencies such as the Crédit Foncier, in the United States it was largely forced into the hands of note brokers, private bankers, savings societies, and insurance companies. In addition, since the practice of using checks against deposits was still largely confined to metropolitan areas, the fast-growing backcountry, lacking national banks, was left without sufficient currency. It took over twenty years for Western-state banking to rebuild outside the national banking system on a check and deposit basis. Interest rates on loans differing by as much as 2 percent between East and West, illustrated the failure of the "system" to evenly distribute capital.[12]

INNOVATIONS IN BANKING

Meanwhile a new type of banking institution had been spreading in the metropolitan centers: the trust company. Started in the 1820s to administer estates for women, orphans, or others who needed help, usually by an insurance company, lawyer, or private banker, they began in the 1850s to become important as legal trustees for corporate bond issues and in addition began to receive deposits and do a regular banking business. Unrestrained by state or national banking laws until late in the century, they had greater freedom than chartered banks to invest in stocks and bonds. The spread of trust companies throughout the nation was limited by the fact that trusteeships, in general, originated in large volume only in the cities that were centers for security-selling syndicates or private inheritance of old wealth. Trusteeships combined both functions by becoming intermediate agencies mobilizing trusteed savings for transfer to houses selling securities.

In this rather dismal period a structural innovation of basic importance was the introduction of clearing houses with new functions. Scottish banks had operated clearing systems in the eighteenth century, and by 1773 the Bank of England was clearing for the banks allowed to deposit in it.[13] Systems for local clearing were delayed in the Northern metropolitan centers of America by lack of branches of a central bank or any completely dominant money market, as well as by the uneven character of local banks. A clearing house was a self-regulatory agency which some weak banks feared. New York City did not establish a clearing house until 1853, and Boston and Philadelphia only followed in the later fifties. The new aspect of American clearing houses was their use to support the liquidity of metropolitan banking communities in times of crisis, the way central banks did in England and France and, after 1875, in Germany. Temporary liquidity was achieved by issuing clearing house certificates backed by all the member banks and accepted in lieu of specie. The New York City banks alone devised this innovation during the crisis of 1857, but by the panic of 1873 the clearing houses of the other major financial centers had adopted the practice. Fritz Redlich regards the use of the clearing house loan certificate as "probably first in importance" among innovations in the half-century between the National Banking and the Federal Reserve Acts.[14]

In spite of this new aid in emergencies and more specialization of functions between mortgage lending, note brokerage, and security marketing, it is hard to say whether there had been much progress in the overall business structure of banking in the half-century after 1840. Except for the special field of investment banking, to be discussed presently, the more obvious needs for organizational innovation had not been met. Aside from clearing houses, the improvements were in a better understanding by bank managers of procedures and risks; but these were internal rather than interorganizational innovations.

BANK MANAGEMENT

In understanding the routine problems of banking, the leaders of the East coast metropolitan banks in the generation after 1850 were abreast of British knowledge and probably ahead of that in most of continental Europe. But this enlightenment was not widespread. One reason was that many interior bankers lacked the type of short-term commercial loans that made up the core of British and big American metropolitan bank portfolios. Because there was plenty of short-term, well-secured commercial paper only in the major centers, most American banks lacked the regular services of the British type of note brokers. Elsewhere bankers had to gauge the risks of unsecured "accommodation" loans signed by a borrower and a guarantor, crop liens, eight-month notes against inventories, and various types of mortgages—far too big a task for a small banking office.

As time went on, the resources of a bank, aside from its relatively small capital, came to be increasingly in the form of demand deposits, so that the great majority of country and small city banks, chartered or private, were having to some extent "to borrow short and lend long," to tie up obligations in the form of deposits that could be called for at any time, in investments that could not be liquidated quickly. Since the bankers of Europe did not operate under such heavy demands for long-term local credit, it is impossible to determine whether they would have been better at handling these risks. The situation inevitably encouraged overlending in periods of optimism and resulted in many bank failures in depressions. There may actually have been less liquidity as time went on and railroad bonds and six-month notes of backcountry borrowers replaced some of the short-term loans.

The idea that demand deposits were both a liability of the bank and a substitute (by check) for note circulation was peculiarly slow to spread in the entire Western world. The early nineteenth century conception was that deposits were a stable type of transfer from customers to the bank against which it was unnecessary to keep reserves in specie. Sound ultimate reserves and the ability to redeem circulating notes were generally confused with true liquidity.

Not until 1855 did deposits for the country as a whole equal note circulation, and only the lessons of the panic of 1857 taught even some East coast bankers that deposits were volatile liabilities. By the late 1850s it was thought in advanced banking circles that 20 percent in specie should be held in reserve against both circulating notes and deposits, but only a few saw higher reserves as a way of attracting depositors.

In the larger centers the daily decisions regarding investments and reserves were no longer a matter for action by the board of directors. Either the cashier alone, reporting only once a month or so to the board, the cashier and a full-time president, or the cashier and a small committee of board members ran the bank's finances. More and more the stock of these big city banks came to be widely held and their administrators became professional managers. Yet the advantage of wielding the resources of a strong bank was so great that many men of wealth and power were willing to serve as bank presidents, and the more these men did so, the higher rose the prestige of the office.

INVESTMENT BANKING

Investment banking—in the modern sense of underwriting whole issues of corporate securities—did not appear in the United States until after the Civil War, although some of the elements that were to lead to the mature practices had been present from the beginning of independent American governments. The marketing of securities in Europe long antedates the use of the corporation for private business purposes, and the four early means of flotation all developed in connection with government finance. Subscription books could be opened at some central point for subscriptions on set terms and closed when the loan was completely subscribed. A loan as a whole, or some part of it, might be marketed by private bankers on a commission basis, referred to as "negotiation." Individuals might contract for parts of a loan. And finally, a government might ask for competitive bids for various amounts and distribute the obligations to the highest bidders until the loan was completely placed.

These same techniques were transferred to the finance of private corporations, with the obvious limitation that the securities of a small enterprise selling only locally could not enlist the services of contractors or negotiators. The early American states and the public utility corporations used simple subscription books, with the new chartered banks often being among the chief subscribers. As we have seen (Chapter Four) the War of 1812 forced the federal government to contract loans to John Jacob Astor, Stephen Girard, David Parish, and Hope and Company.

This latter event illustrates the overall function of investment banking: to transfer substantial amounts of capital from areas in which it is in surplus to places where it is needed. On this basis American private and, later, investment bankers served up to 1890 as middlemen first between the states and then the railroads, who were consuming the capital, and the British and continental financiers who were supplying it. Although there were pockets of available savings in the old cities of the East, no large venture such as a long state canal or, later, a trunkline railroad could be easily financed without recourse to a foreign money market.

In the period up to 1836, it appeared likely that the Bank of the United States and the big commercial banks might take over large-scale security marketing and develop into larger banks, such as the later German and Japanese ones, companies that conducted all the functions of banking as well as some supervision of the directions of economic development. In almost all American banks there were some accommodation loans that really represented capital investment in the borrowing enterprises; conversely some water, canal, or railroad companies had note-issuing privileges written into their charters. But the demise of the Second Bank of the United States and the poverty of the local money markets from 1837 to 1843 put the security business much more firmly in the hands of private bankers with European connections.

By 1870 these men, following British and continental practices, gradually evolved the mechanisms which were common all over the Western world.[15] From 1840, aside from national government issues, railroad securities became the major type to be marketed. To facilitate finance, American railroads after 1836 copied the English practice of issuing preferred nonvoting stock, especially in return for state investments, but ultimately the mortgage bond became the major type used for general sale. After 1850 large land grants, first to the Western states for railroads and then, after 1862, directly to the companies made mortgages secured by land or equipment particularly appropriate, whereas English bonds were only first liens against income, and early continental railroad bonds were largely government-guaranteed.

In the 1850s a lively trade in such American bonds developed between private banking houses in New York, Philadelphia, and Boston and those in Europe, but the American firms were negotiating sales for the railroads on commission rather than underwriting entire issues and selling through syndicates. The Civil War temporarily cut the United States off from British finance and suggested the possibilities in better methods for the local marketing of securities.

A Philadelphia private banker, Jay Cooke, demonstrated that an aggressive marketing network embracing many firms with, of course, the advantage in this case of patriotic appeal, could sell hundreds of millions in war bonds by personal approaches to prosperous citizens and local banks. In 1870, Cooke applied the same type of operation on a smaller scale by forming a syndicate to underwrite (guarantee the borrower his money) and sell $2 million in Pennsylvania Railroad bonds. While some federal refunding issues were so large that they were contracted for in parts, syndicate underwriting gradually became the rule for big private issues.

Since some of the corporations needing public financing had come, as we have seen, to be bigger than in Europe, American investment bankers became increasingly important in national financial affairs. That much of the money had to come from abroad, however, limited leadership in the formation of syndicates to about a dozen American firms that had strong foreign connections, or even foreign branches. Of this group Drexel, Morgan and Company of New York and Philadelphia and its head, J. Pierpont Morgan, became the most active in giving lasting form to the emerging structural relationships.

Morgan's first step in the direction of taking a continuing interest in the customer who had been financed, as did the *Kreditbanken* (general banks) in Germany, came in 1879. In that year he secretly marketed abroad about $20 million in New York Central & Hudson River Railroad stock for the personal account of William H. Vanderbilt and took a seat on the road's board of directors, where he voted the proxies on many of the shares he had sold. The result of this tie between banker and client in both continental Europe and the United States was that the banker assumed responsibility for representing the people to whom he had sold securities and expected the client to do all further public financing through his house.

This adoption of the German innovation in structural relations that made the investment banker the financial conscience of his client, while confined in both nations to the relatively small number of enterprises that needed continual public financing (less than a tenth of one percent of the total), had a number of important aspects. In 1882 a United States federal court decision made it easy for a railroad to go into receivership with its own officers as receivers. While the purpose of the move was to hold creditors at bay until a new financial structure had been worked out, it also made the investment banking house, representing the first mortgage bondholders, the most important influence in shaping the new capital structure. Since railroads operating about one-third of the total U.S. mileage went into receivership for varying periods between 1873 and 1897, and since even the strong ones that did not welcomed investment bankers to their boards, by 1890 it was becoming doubtful whether railroads were, in fact, controlled by their operators or by their bankers.

In at least two instances in the 1880s, Morgan removed railroad presidents who had tried to shop around for subsequent financing, and the other big houses tacitly agreed to the principle.[16] While it is easy to exaggerate the degree of banker control, especially in financially strong companies, at the minimum it meant that plans for improvement or expansion needing major public financing became subject to banker veto. While the investment banking group, even including the lesser houses that were more sales outlets or brokers than they were bankers, was small enough so that personal friendships and family relationships tended to build cliques, the most obvious division was based on the sources of foreign funds. Drexel, Morgan and the majority group of houses sold abroad chiefly in the British, French, and Dutch markets, while the minority, led by houses such as Kuhn Loeb, and J. & W. Seligman, drew on German and central European resources. Some of the banks in both groups had important branch partnerships in their foreign sales territories. Only on a few occasions did the dozen leading houses act in concert.

In contrast to Germany, therefore, where some eight big "general" banks and a dozen slightly smaller ones all with close ties to the *Reichsbank*, carried on all types of operations and were in close touch with government policy, in the "specialized" banking of the United States, those chiefly involved in syndicate underwriting were in practice separated from banks whose emphasis was on deposits and commercial loans, and there was no governmental development pressure. While the investment banks received some deposits, mainly from the firms they financed, and made a few large-scale business loans, they were partnerships whose portfolios were free from either state or federal government regulation or influence. In contrast, the investments of national banks were restricted by law to certain types of bonds, and they were forbidden before 1922 to have any branches and after that only in their city of residence. They were not, however, forbidden to sell stocks or bonds to their customers, and some of the city banks became frequent members of marketing syndicates. By the time state banking recovered from the blow struck by the National Bank Act Amendment of 1865, it had lost the chance for much of a role in the security selling business.

The American type of functional division also prevailed in English and French banking, but the situation of these international lending or investing nations was so different from that of the capital-demanding United States that close analogies are impossible. Starting with the Crédit Mobilier in France in 1852, there was a rise of joint stock finance companies, which today might be called development banks, that sold their own stock and invested in transportation and industry either locally or abroad, or lent money to foreign governments.[17] The same type of companies appeared very rapidly in England following the limited liability (for corporate stockholders) acts of 1855 and 1856.

These new enterprises grew up alongside the old private banking houses such as the Rothschilds in both nations, the Barings or Morgans in England, and the Lafittes, Andres, or Blounts in France.[18] The basis for peaceful coexistence appears to have been that the old houses could attract syndicate leadership of the relatively secure, large ventures and include the finance companies on the selling end. The new companies overexpanded, and many of them failed in the Anglo-French crisis of 1866. The exact equivalent of these firms never appeared in the United States, because when, in the twentieth century, the nation became fully self-sufficient in capital supply and also a substantial foreign investor, the domestic investment bankers and their affiliated bank, trust, and insurance companies controlled the market.[19]

In both the Second Empire and the Third Republic, the French government was far more active in using the flow of investment to foreign nations as a diplomatic tool than was the case in England or even Germany.[20] Consequently the French investment bankers and finance companies marketed many of the bonds of the governments of less-developed nations and took relatively few American railroad bonds.

CONTINUING INADEQUACIES

In addition to the trust companies that could legally buy most of the offerings of the strong investment banking firms, mutual life insurance companies from 1840 on were piling up reserves which with few state restrictions could be invested at the discretion of their trustees. The founding of Equitable Life in 1859 by Henry B. Hyde, an inspired marketer, symbolizes the beginning of rapid growth, but the great upswing in both mutual and stock company insurance reserves that was to attract investment bankers to their boards of directors came after 1890.

In the period ending in that year the United States had had to solve the unique problem of acquiring capital for the development of the West involving unprecedentedly large-scale ventures in transportation. While local banks, through accommodation loans automatically renewed, extended the use of local credit, a central banking system might have aided in both better allocation of total national savings and in providing more reliable liquidity. In the middle of the period the National Bank Act Amendment of 1865 forced a major readjustment in banking that reduced the flexibility of the structure and left much backcountry finance in the hands of small private bankers, and note and mortgage brokers who, before the 1880s, at least, were not capable of effectively mobilizing Eastern or European capital.

Although manufacturing growth had to be largely self-financing, the investment bankers did well in attracting Eastern and foreign capital into railroad transportation. Had the Civil War not diverted them for a decade, largely to government finance, progress might have been faster. In this respect there is an analogy to the retardation of France resulting from the much shorter and less destructive Franco-Prussian War.

Yet, in spite of the fact that capital accumulation and distribution and the creation of essential credit went on tolerably well, it cannot be said that the United States, with its weak central government, many states, and strong demands for local control of banking had been able to provide a good financial system. In 1890 this still remained to be accomplished, and the same local rivalries and fears of the power of metropolitan finance were to continue.

III

Adjusting
to
Bigness,
1890-1930

7

Marketing and Manufacturing

ALTHOUGH there are no reliable figures for the comparable industrial nations, it seems almost certain that the marketing of factory-made consumer goods became most important in the United States during the late nineteenth century. With new technology being adopted almost too readily, the uniquely American problem was, therefore, domestic marketing of machine-made family and household equipment in the face of the heavy costs of selling and transportation. Technology, of course, continually interacted with both these problems. From 1890 on, synthetic materials, electricity, electronics, and the automobile all changed the things to be sold and the ways and means of moving and marketing them.

THE EXPANSION OF CONSUMER TRADES

The broad impact of automobiles and the new electrical consumer durables did not become obvious, however, until after World War I. Expenditures for "consumer durables," as defined by the census, made up less than 4 percent of GNP in 1899 and only 4.1 percent ten years later; but by 1929 the figure had risen to more than 6 percent of GNP and about 10 percent of private income. Robert E. Gallman and E. S. Howle, using a different definition, set the figure at 9 percent of GNP between 1899 and 1918, and 10 percent from then through 1929.[1] Further differences in calculation would arise if a large part of the immense annual cost of electrical installation, a considerable part of highway expenditure, and many other new conveniences were to be counted as costs of consumer durables.

Meanwhile, the increase in the use of prepared foods and ready-made clothing, and the steady fall in the percentage of partly self-sufficient farm population were expanding wholesale and retail trade at a rate slightly higher than the total value added to materials by manufacturing. In people employed, the contrast was more striking, with those working in trade growing from 1899 to 1929 at a rate of 160 percent as against 100 percent for those in manufacturing—illustrating the well-established assumption that as industrial society matures employment in the trade and service sectors rises the most rapidly. Both the trade and manufacturing sectors were still growing in relation to agriculture, but the true gain of the trade sector was significantly larger than shown in the census, since many large manufacturing firms carried on extensive marketing activities within the company, occasionally reaching all the way to the retailer or even the ultimate consumer.

A high level of income per capita, which the United States still had in comparison with Europe, produced greater demand for consumer goods prepared in factories, even though these items often cost more than "natural" commodities. The high income level also offered a good market for increasingly expensive varieties and fancier types of goods. This, in turn, led to the development of more specialized retailers and wholesalers and to new means of marketing. Hence the wealth of the nation made it the world leader in entering the new phase of business.

In the transition, the period after 1890 may be seen as a time of fruition of innovations that were made in preceding decades and only then began to have an effect. These include the electrical devices of telephone, light, and power machinery; the automobile and interurban highways; oil as a major source of energy; better alloys and specialized tools; an easier capital market helped by the huge reserves of insurance companies; a mature system of investment banking; trade, employer, and civic associations; chain stores and mail-order houses; more specialized wholesale and retail distributors; nationwide advertising by new devices; direct factory marketing of branded products to retailers; and increasing federal and state regulation of business practices.

A WORLD VIEW OF MARKETING

Innovations that were chiefly American in origin usually arose because of the size and dispersed character of the market. In contrast to their dominance in earlier periods, large marketing or selling firms in the United States were by 1900 weaker in relation to producers than in England, France, Japan, or Germany. In England, particularly, the export merchants had a powerful influence on what was manufactured, and merchandising in general was more specialized. In Germany the banking influence was strongly behind the manufacture of products that could have either military use or export sale. Careful studies were made of the needs of foreign markets and sales literature was printed in appropriate languages, but by 1914 Germany was only beginning to overcome the British head start in international political, financial, and marketing controls. Japan, in its early *zaibatsu* combinations of government finance, marketing, and manufacture, also represented authoritative planning to capture markets. France, more than the other large producers, still had its marketing operations geared to the discriminating demands of the *haute bourgeoisie*. The quality and distinctiveness of products were regarded as more important than mass production and lower costs. To supply this market,, manufacturers employed costly hand labor and limited runs on machines. They made little use of the emerging American concept that producers, by advertising and selling, could alter consumer tastes.[2]

In contrast, a producer in the United States made an article as cheaply as possible, using all the methods of machine mass-production known to him, and expected that if his price was low jobbers and wholesalers would dispose of the product. There was relatively little systematic feedback from merchants or consumers to manufacturers on matters of style or quality. But by the 1920s manufacturers were beginning to undertake studies themselves of how to increase mass sales. Only a handful of firms, however, gave much attention to export markets.

It may be too bold a generalization to say that only stable population and technological excellence permitted France to keep up with, or perhaps exceed, the United States from 1900 to 1929 in the rate of growth of income per capita. Certainly America's bold and developing marketing processes must be given great credit for neutralizing the heavy burdens of distance, together with low density and a high rate of increase in population.

INNOVATIONS IN MARKETING

A worldwide stimulant to marketing, but one particularly affecting the United States, was the reduction in household self-sufficiency—in other words, more of the family income passing through commercial markets. A declining percentage of the total population were engaged in farming or living in rural communities where fruits and vegetables were grown on home plots, and where labor and its products were exchanged without statistical record. The population in places of more than 1,000 people (places we may safely consider as somewhat cut off from self-sufficiency) grew from 40 percent of the total population in 1890 to 60 percent in 1930. During the same period the percentage of women in the labor force rose from less than 17 percent to 22 percent, and if the decline in domestic service could be accurately included, the number of women who worked outside the home and bought more in stores probably increased as substantially as town population.

However, some innovations, such as the department store, were not connected with either mass production or national markets. Before mid-century such stores, in dry goods and apparel, had appeared first in France and then in England and the United States; but this big city marketing device grew rather slowly in the following decades. By 1890 department stores offering charge accounts, such as John Wanamaker of Philadelphia and New York, or Marshall Field in Chicago, had strong positions in the retailing of semidurables, dry goods, and apparel. In order to increase the variety of merchandise without trying to buy unfamiliar specialties, many of these firms leased departments to outside contractors. This practice, common before 1900, has never altogether disappeared.

All of these big city stores, with their elaborate buildings on high-priced land and with proportionate wage costs double those of unit stores, had severe business problems in meeting the prices of specialized retailers. The latter were often quite efficient family enterprises with low or nonexistent wage costs and managerial overhead. While the management of a department store could insure more specialized knowledge, the organization had to be quite elaborate. Under the general manager (who might be the owner) there were normally: the store manager, with superintendents for, at least, service, store supplies, traffic, protection, and maintenance; the merchandise manager, with a buyer for each special department; the accounts manager (later the comptroller), with assistants for credit and payroll; and the publicity or advertising manager, with specialized assistants for different functions. With all of these people to pay, department stores had recourse to demanding special discounts from manufacturers or wholesalers based on the threat of withdrawing their trade, or even of producing for themselves—a risky business for a single store.

Another approach to overcoming initial diseconomies from an increased scale of operations was that taken by R. H. Macy in New York. Located in the biggest city, he was able by 1890 to keep prices low through rapid stock turnover, shrewd buying, and selling only for cash. But as Macy discovered later, this policy could not attract the necessary volume of trade in a medium-sized city. F. W. Woolworth in five-and-ten-cent stores had been able to make a profit from a large chain of stores selling variety goods on a cash basis, even in small cities, by hiring young inexperienced clerks and making special arrangements with manufacturers. In 1902, J. C. Penney started in the Midwest a chain of cash department stores partly owned by local managers but serviced by central staff and buying departments.

In groceries and allied products chain organizations were very old, going back to the Colonial period, when a three- or four-store local chain supervised by the owner could show savings in systematic arrangement, purchasing, and accounting. The success of the Great Atlantic and Pacific Tea Company stores in the 1870s and 1880s (with no store west of Kansas City) brought a number of imitators. In 1900 there were approximately sixty chains of all types, with 2,500 outlets. These figures rose by 1928 to 600 firms with 150,000 outlets, but chains still made up only a tenth of all retail stores, although they did a fifth of the dollar volume of business.

As can easily be imagined, the major business problem of the chain store, whether in variety goods or groceries, was supervision. In theory chains had the advantages of able executive planning, better locations, tighter control of inventory, faster stock turnover, and specialization of functions such as display and accounting. In practice the major problem was to secure reliable store managers and clerks. Dishonesty was endemic, as it was in other nations as well, and a fair amount of pilfering was often overlooked in return for low nonunion wages. The supervisory personnel probably had more ability than in the case of the unit store, but less incentive to work hard for long hours. In 1923, Melvin Copeland wrote that the higher wage costs of chains just about ate up the savings gained from not delivering or granting credit.[3]

Thus, only efficient chains or the very big stores in major cities could compete in price with the specialized retailer. Some stores that catered to customers on the basis of fine quality and convenience, however, often did well without close regard for price; examples were B. Altman and Bonwit Teller in New York, and later, Nieman Marcus and Sakowitz in Dallas and Houston. Some of these luxury stores were only expanded dry goods and apparel shops making no effort to stock hardware, toys, or furniture; some specialized exclusively in women's or men's wear. Others, like their counterparts in Europe, were simply large-scale specialty shops charging high prices for luxury goods.

A few low-price department stores, such as Macy's, tried to sell by mail, but all eventually gave it up as a steady practice. The difficulty was basic: ordering by mail appealed chiefly to country people who did not have easy access to, and were relatively unfamiliar with, the big stores in the large cities. Only by investing in extensive coverage of rural regions over the course of one or two decades were Montgomery Ward, from the 1870s on, and Sears Roebuck, from the 1880s, plus a few more specialized sellers, able to build secure positions as exclusively mail-order houses.

Two federal services—rural free delivery in 1896 and parcel post in 1912—greatly aided the distribution of mail-order catalogues and goods. Even though the rural population that the catalogues were reaching grew relatively slowly in both numbers and income, the successful penetration by mail-order firms of rural markets increased enormously between 1895 and World War I. In 1905 and 1906, Ward and Sears, respectively, began to open branch distributing centers, which were similar to private wholesale houses. Part of the sales increase resulted from the gradual extension of installment selling. For example, at Sears (for which there is a good scholarly history), pianos, furniture, and other durables were being sold on credit by 1900 and automobiles were added in 1910; the possibilities of deferred payment, however, were not advertised in the catalogue. Publicity for installment credit in the 1913 catalogue brought an increase in piano sales, for example, from $350,000 in the prosperous year 1912 to over $1 million in the depression year of 1914.[4]

But after World War I both the big general mail-order houses were forced to adjust to economic and demographic change. Rural population began to decline, while automobiles made it possible for farmers to shop in the larger market centers, and many rural and urban customers preferred to go to stores and see the actual goods rather than use a catalogue. As a result, the mail-order companies started opening retail stores in cities. Adjustment, however, was not simple; management built around distribution by mail was unfamiliar with the problems of department stores. The ultimate solution, achieved over the course of a decade, was divisional separation (see Chapter Ten), with new head office managers and a high degree of autonomy for those in charge of the stores. On this basis both chains, but particularly Sears, successfully adjusted to the decline of rural purchasing.

The supermarket and the shopping center, both largely dependent on motor transport, did not become important until after 1930, but both represented a further adjustment of marketing to demography and transportation.

WHOLESALE MARKETING

The stronghold of wholesale trade was the small town or rural area. Consequently, the rise of urban population reinforced the tendency toward innovations in retail selling in order to bypass middlemen. On the other hand, the wholesaler was often able to reinforce his position by developing groups of associated retailers, such as Rexall in drugs or United Stores in groceries. A major force that, in spite of factory marketing and chain distribution, kept wholesale trade a growing sector of the economy through the first three quarters of the twentieth century was the increasing complexity of finished goods and components resulting from technological progress. Even in industries dominated by three or four manufacturing firms there could be a big and varied business in replacing components or substituting special makes, and such a business was best handled by a local wholesaler who could stock all lines.

One of the most important means for the local wholesaler to hold on to his trade was through close knowledge of the credit standing of his customers and by a willingness to buy from the manufacturer and assume the risks of collection from retailers. Furthermore, it was a business of low profit on volume of turnover (in groceries, for example, around half of one percent), and a manufacturer would, on the basis of proper accounting, probably lose money trying to take over such distribution.[5] In fact, manufacturers recognized this, but some saw a compensating advantage in "missionary" efforts through factory salesmen and directly assisted retailer advertising.

Marketing special types of consumer goods, such as sewing machines, types of hardware, or some petroleum products overlapped industrial supply and might lead either to complete factory selling and service to retailers or to selling to other factories directly and to consumers through wholesalers. Many companies in books and household equipment tried house-to-house selling, but very few made this means pay.

In the late 1880s, companies increased the advertising of brand names or trademarks in an effort to force all wholesalers to stock their line. Not always completely successful in this strategy, a few firms sent their own salesmen to retailers, a costly process requiring a big line of goods, such as Proctor and Gamble in drugs and cosmetics, or high-priced durables, such as pianos or automobiles. In some cases, such as prepared cereals, the salesmen were merely "missionaries" trying to achieve more "intensive" penetration of their market area by inducing retailers to ask wholesalers for the brand. This did not require a new department within the company or a very large new staff—it was in effect a form of advertising.

Bypassing middlemen obviously required internalizing the same functions within the firm, which, in turn, required hiring new types of managers. The vertically integrated company that carried out all business processes, from buying raw materials to supplying the retailer, often found that initially, at least, its costs ran higher than they would have if some of the stages had been left to outside specialists. Quite a few companies retreated from various stages of such integration after an unprofitable trial.

In this changing world of marketing the reverse process could take place; a wholesaler might invest in manufacturing to dispose of surplus raw materials—as for example, the Dairymen's League, a selling cooperative, going into butter, cheese, and other products in the early 1920s in order to market surplus milk. Insofar as these products could be shipped longer distances than fresh milk, the League was also extending the area of its market.

FACTORY CONTROLS OF RETAILING

The marketing of the automobile, the most exciting consumer durable, may serve as an example of an industry moving in the period of three hectic decades from considerable emphasis on technology and production, as cars penetrated a virgin market, to a major interest in the promotion of sales, as technology became routinized and the market tended toward saturation by the 1920s. Early in the century the eighty or more firms that at any single time put their names on the cars, assembled them from the parts of dozens or hundreds of suppliers and sent the finished product to wholesalers. The wholesalers sold retail in the urban area around them and granted the right to sell to exclusive agencies in outlying districts, often paying cash to the manufacturer and financing the retail outlets. In the second decade the larger companies were still working through wholesalers in low sales areas but had superseded them by factory branches directly supplying retail dealers in the major urban markets. About the middle of the decade Ford set up regional assembly plants and eliminated all wholesalers. By the 1920s this was the pattern for marketing the more successful of the remaining thirty-odd "makes."

In this decade General Motors led the way in establishing such strict control over dealers that to some analysts they seemed to be company agents selling on commission. In 1923 the Chevrolet Division started to demand uniform accounting practices by dealers and hired accountants to set up "bogeys," or acceptable results for every part of the dealer's business. His prices offered for used cars and their turnover were scrutinized, and he was required to give good service to his customers for both new and used cars. In return General Motors gave him a 24 percent markup (higher than for goods in most chain or department stores) and financed 90 percent of his new car inventory, while also retaining title to each car. After 1925 his car insurance was taken care of by General Exchange Insurance Corporation at low rates. At the same time General Motors supported sales by massive advertising and annual model changes.[6]

The oil companies marketing through wholly owned gasoline stations rented to the retailer is the other most striking early illustration of what in later decades was to be called franchising. The practice raised the question of whether the retailers were independent businessmen or factory agents. There were several factors favoring an emphasis on independence: retailers could make their own profits, which for the successful could be very large; they hired their own employees; conducted their own customer relations; and lost their franchises if they did not succeed. These all add up to the dealer being a risk-taking businessman, dependent for success on his entrepreneurial ability, and merely regulated by a large corporation in some of the same ways that the Interstate Commerce Commission regulated railroads and interstate trucking.

The most profitable marketing arrangements depended greatly

on the type of products—whether a line was varied and supplied only occasional needs (as with hardware), more uniform (as with shoes), expensive (as with durables), or cheap, varied, and in continual demand (as with food products). Location, for example, was comparatively unimportant in high-priced durables or semidurables. The seller had a territorial franchise for his brand and, based on advertising or experience, the customer decided on the brand in advance and then went to wherever the agency was located.[7] In contrast, location might be a major factor in the success of a drug or grocery store.

MARKETING PRODUCERS' GOODS

Industrial goods, those sold from firm to firm in the processes of production, presented quite different and almost as varied marketing problems as consumer goods. Factory installations of some advanced machinery had to be sold by technically trained salesmen, more and more of them graduate engineers by the 1920s.[8] But some small standard machines like hand printing presses or lathes were sold through jobbers, who assumed the credit risks, or by manufacturers' agents, who did not. The factory might also establish branches to take orders and supply parts. If machines were very expensive or protected by patents a manufacturer with enough capital or credit could speed distribution by leasing instead of selling. In an industry of rapidly changing technology this also gave the manufacturer control over the rate at which improvements were introduced. Another way of speeding the distribution of expensive machines was for the producer to take partial payment in the stock of the buying company. All methods of marketing industrial goods were influenced by the aim of smoothing the extreme variations in sales, i.e., between times of expansion, when many companies wanted new equipment, and times of contraction, when few if any did. This kept some wholesalers, who would accumulate stock in bad times, alive even in trades with generally rather direct transactions.

In supplies of materials for eventual sale or use in operations, as distinct from plant installations, the purchasing agent of the buyer would shop around among specialized wholesalers, brokers, or commission merchants. The latter two categories were much the same, each trade having its own language, but they usually handled undifferentiated products, such as "gray goods" in cottons, whereas the specialized wholesaler handled manufactures where size, type, and make were considerations.

In this maze of company interconnections many fabricators, as late as the 1920s, did not know within a 50 percent margin the real costs of various products.[9] Consequently, some sellers pushed the wrong lines, some buyers got bargains, and many new producers found weak spots in old industries. This lack of proper accounting stretched all the way from the very small supplier who found he could undercut a big firm on the cost of some cheap but essential part, to men like W. C. Durant, who bought automobile accessory and assembly firms from 1908 to 1920 with no proper regard for their true profitability.

Part of the uncertainty of costs and price competition within a trade came from the discretion given to salesmen regarding discounts and terms of credit. While, in 1920, 2 percent was a common discount for cash with a net price usually based on thirty days, in hardware, electrical goods, apparel, and many other lines no two buyers necessarily paid the same net. Salesmen were often allowed to sell to dealers from catalogue prices on as many as five different rates of discount, and marketing studies around 1920 showed little correlation between the size of the order or credit of the customer and the discount granted. Even disregarding corruption between buyer and salesman, a wide range of discounts, up to 20 or 30 percent of price, might reflect either effective sales resistance or desire by the agent to meet a sales quota. These differences in price only slightly connected with the market exceeded the average rate of profit of almost any merchant. They also call attention to the vital importance of an honest and efficient sales organization whose work affected profits far more than could small improvements in plant efficiency.[10]

ADVERTISING

One control over selling that remained effectively in the hands of top management was allotment and distribution of money for advertising. While the producers of trademarked or branded consumer goods became the chief spenders, the pull of the market created by advertising affected spending at various middle levels. Advertising in the form of eight to ten line items was as old as American newspapers. The early ads were usually in the form of announcements of the availability of bulk or "generic" goods, as from the cargo of a newly arrived ship. Before the mid-nineteenth century newspaper advertisements seldom attempted to build steady patronage for a shop or a brand.

The opening of a national market by rail carried with it the possibility of equally wide distribution through advertising in daily and weekly papers all over the country. Such coverage required either the establishment of a special department in the producing firm or hiring the services of an outside agent. As in most specialized functions, the latter offered the easiest initial solution, and, as we have seen, advertising agents began to appear. By the 1870s patent medicines used the largest amount of space—much of it in religious weeklies—and N. W. Ayer of Philadelphia (see Chapter Six) was publishing an annual guide to newspapers.[11] In the 1880s, national magazine advertising began to assume importance, and, in the absence of real competition from other agents, J. Walter Thompson of New York City acquired a commanding position in the field.

By 1890, however, the agency business as a whole was still small. The old newspaper agencies such as Ayer or Rowell were, in fact, industry middlemen. They bought space in advance at wholesale rates from newspapers, selling them type and other printer's supplies in exchange. The agents subsequently retailed the space to clients, influenced no doubt more by their profits as space sellers than by any careful plan of campaign. Market testing amounted to asking a few questions of dealers in the commodity, while copy was prepared by the advertiser. Not until 1891 and 1892, respectively, did Rowell and Ayer have full-time copywriters, and only in the mid-nineties did Ayer invade Thompson's preserve in the magazine field.[12]

A great upsurge in daily newspaper and even more in magazine publishing came between 1890 and 1910. Doubling each decade, the consumption of print paper rose from 350,000 tons a year in 1890 to 1.5 million tons in 1910. Meanwhile, monthly magazine circulations rose from 18 million in 1890 to 64 million in 1905, with some periodicals such as Ladies' Home Journal, published by Curtis Publishing Company of Philadelphia, selling over a million copies a month. By 1929, however, the runaway leader had become The Saturday Evening Post, also published by Curtis, with a weekly circulation close to 3 million and advertising revenues around $50 million.[13]

The agencies, of course, expanded and specialized to meet the demands of annual advertising outlays by clients. These rose rapidly up to the early 1900s and then at a more gradual pace, with total advertising outlays running about 4 percent of GNP.[14] By 1922 expenditures by the top ten advertisers ranged from $118,000 a year to $1.2 million.

In the sharp upswing around 1900, the changes within agencies were similar to those caused in mercantile houses by the expansion of trade that occurred between 1793 and 1808. Specialized departments were set up for selling, designing, and market research, and artists and psychologists were added to staffs. In 1903, Walter Dill Scott of Northwestern University published his first book on the psychology of advertising. While the impact of psychology on campaign planning was probably slight, it helped the move from the meaningless jingles of the eighties and nineties toward deeper emotional appeals through the use of pictures and the invocation of status symbols. This is well-illustrated by Packard Motors' picture of people in evening clothes entering a limousine and the caption, "a man is known by the car he keeps."

Divorcing the subsidiary business of printer's supplies, the remodeled agencies became more purely auxiliary service organizations for their clients. Space was bought only for the individual user rather than in bulk, and the Ayer Newspaper Directory ceased to carry advertising. In 1913 agency men in Chicago and New York cooperated in establishing an Audit Bureau of Circulation to prevent fraudulent publisher's claims.

Trolleys, subways, and suburban trains produced a new agency business in advertising cards above car windows, while the automobile changed outdoor advertising from an occasional sign painted on a barn or a rock to roadside billboards systematically placed by specialized firms. Illuminated signs in major cities appeared at the same time but were limited to a very few central locations, such as Times Square in New York.

All of these developments were common throughout the Western world. The United States, with its big domestic market led in volume and ingenuity of magazine advertising, even carrying paid articles such as North German Lloyd Steamship Company's thirty-two page "To Far Away Vacation Lands" in *Harper's Monthly* for May, 1896.[15] In newspapers the international differences were more in custom than volume; English papers, for example, still carried front-page advertising, which Americans had dropped. But in outdoor display Europe was ahead of the United States and remained so. While the slower spread of the automobile may have made for somewhat less open country billboard advertising, the outdoor posters of Europe were often minor works of art and appeared more thickly in railroad stations and other public places than did their counterparts in the United States. Again, as in the case of magazines, each nation adjusted advertising to its own culture and opportunities.

Throughout the period companies selling consumer goods in highly competitive lines led in advertising expenditures: Proctor and Gamble in soaps and cosmetics; Swift and Cudahy in meat packing; Packard and General Motors in automobiles. Some makers of household equipment, such as Simmons mattresses, and of food products, such as Postum and other packaged cereals, were among the leaders in the 1920s. Unquestionably some of the "saturation" campaigns produced new consumer wants and in this way readjusted markets for goods bought with "discretionary" income. But even markets for basic necessities could be altered. Advertising could lead to a life sustained more by meat and Coca Cola than by unadvertised farm products.

PUBLIC RELATIONS

It was but a short step from advertising the products of a company to building good will toward the producer as a business corporation. Those most in need of such general good will were companies subject to or threatened by government regulation, and, therefore, the railroads led the way.[16] In the late nineteenth century free passes were given to influential citizens, and favorable articles were planted in newspapers and magazines; by 1906, a sophisticated Eastern press agent, Ivy L. Lee, was working exclusively for the Pennsylvania Railroad.[17] World War I, however, educated big business in general to the use of public relations. The effectiveness of war propaganda convinced many that public opinion could easily be manipulated, while an excess profits tax, continued to 1922, made "good-will" advertising seem like a profitable pretax outlay. Following the war, men like Lee and Edward Bernays, now adopting the title "public relations councilors," persuaded cigarette companies, fruit marketing cooperatives, and other businesses to try to increase the consumer demand for their *type* of product without too much emphasis on any specific brand.

Gradually big companies internalized parts of both advertising and public relations activities. Advertising or publicity departments, or more usually a single man and his secretary, go back to 1890. These slim organizations might deal directly with some local publishers, but normally worked out national programs through an outside agency. The values of internalization were in better planning and expenditures in conference with chief executives and monitoring the results achieved by the agency. Around 1900 advertising executives had low standing in most companies and were regarded as more in the category of fixers and lobbyists than of sound solid businessmen, an attitude that lasted in France until, at least, 1930. By the 1920s, however, and chiefly in America, the heads of big departments handling both advertising and public relations were often at the vice-presidential level. Outside the company they commanded among agency men the respect that comes from fear. By this time the agencies were numerous and more competitive than the steadily big advertisers, and to lose one such account might wipe out any profit for the year, as well as the job of the account executive responsible.

SOME EFFECTS OF TECHNOLOGY ON THE MARKET

In an industrial nation the production and distribution of goods make up two necessary and fairly equal sides of the same coin. Within the limits of existing technology what can be cheaply distributed can be produced, but the reverse is not necessarily true. In modern capitalist nations, therefore, the marketers, often within manufacturing companies, have had to be accorded the final judgment. Both production and selling, in turn, rest on an infrastructure of building construction, finance, and transportation that plays a vital part in what is or is not profitable to make and sell.

This perspective is necessary in viewing the rise after 1890 of a few score of companies in each of the leading Western nations and Japan at strategic stages of manufacturing. In this field the United States played an ambiguous role. The big domestic market encouraged successful producers of goods to combine in order to achieve some internal economies and improve their marketing potential, a process which created a few of the world's largest manufacturing firms. Yet, on the whole, big business was less integrated than in either Germany or Japan, and in 1905 only about fifty American companies were larger on the average than those of similar rank in Britain.[18] While most very large American and British companies specialized on one or two stages of the complicated processes of large-scale production and received banking advice primarily on policies that involved marketing new securities, the great combines of Germany and Japan included production, marketing, banking, and finance under the same group of executives.[19]

Americans had traditional objections to bigness and monopoly that often led writers to picture such growth as contrary to the public welfare. They also failed to distinguish between growth in size required by improved technology and growth by mergers to make speculative profits or to dominate markets.

The demands of technology for increasing size were largely confined to certain branches of manufacturing. In steel, for example, British mills were too small, and the United States led the world in economies of scale. A mill in the first decade of the century could cost $50 million and by 1928, a wide sheet rolling mill, $250 million. But such spectacular needs for large-scale plant production were confined to a very few industries. The United States, because of its size, was often a pioneer in economies of scale in manufacturing, and as such it bore the burdens of the inevitable mistakes or false moves made by the international leader. As David Landes notes: "Where the gap between leader and follower is not too large . . . the advantage lies with the late comer."[20]

In general, however, technological trends made it economical to limit the size of individual plants. Electric motors, which in 1919 accounted for 55 percent of manufacturing horsepower, and more specialized tools, worked in the direction of higher efficiency for the small plant, while motor trucks made it no longer necessary to ship manufactured articles in carload lots. Thus, multiplant structure was usually preferable to increasing size in one location. Yet economies from relatively small-scale manufacture could not overcome the tendency of companies in industries with large investments in fixed capital to try to forestall cutthroat competition by some kind of controls over the market.

THE EXPANDING WORLD OF BUSINESS

While the putting together through holding companies and mergers of firms with large slices of their respective markets was rapid from 1897 to 1904, mergers were slowed down thereafter by a combination of government hostility, poor financial performance, and the fact that the giants had occupied the areas of high-fixed capital that allowed such unwieldy combinations to promise advantages. From 1904 to 1929 these few hundred large industrial, utility, and transportation corporations gradually raised their total sales in relation to the GNP, but they became still less significant in relative number because of the rapid proliferation of small and medium-sized business firms. Even if the big companies in manufacturing were the final assemblers of over 40 percent of the factory product, it must be remembered that, in general, marketing adds more to the consumer price than does fabrication (not including the cost of the raw and partly finished materials), and that services involving no manufacturing were a rapidly growing sector of the economy.

The population of business firms may be categorized either by the number of employees hired by each, in which case the norm has always been less than four; by size of sales, which can only be learned from sampling studies, but the norm was almost certainly under $50,000 a year in 1929; or by type of activity, where the norm has always been retail trade.[21] In 1890, there were probably less than 1.5 million firms in business, and in 1930 there were 3 million—nearly half in retail trade —but meanwhile much home fabricating for sale had been dropped from the census. At the latter date only about one-sixth of the businesses were incorporated. Therefore, any discussion of typical American entrepreneurs or managers should deal largely with the problems of small retailers, but unfortunately most of the exact data are on samples of those who went bankrupt. Consequently a detailed history of the forces influencing management and the market cannot be written, nor can the information even be assembled currently except from bits of special research. Sample studies made in earlier periods, however, can suggest some generalizations.

In very small enterprises entries and exits were numerous, running perhaps as high as 200,000 dropouts a year by the late 1920s but with a higher number of new starts. At the lowest levels, as in earlier times, Americans alternated between earning wages and self-employment. The very small capital needed for a start in retailing could come from savings, advances by family or friends, credit from suppliers, occasionally from a mortgage—where some remodeling or special equipment was needed— but very seldom from banks or finance companies. Except for a few special features of each different type of activity, the same generalizations would apply to very small service, brokerage, or manufacturing enterprises. A surprising number of proprietors lacked experience with or competence in the field of enterprise they attempted to enter. According to Dun & Bradstreet, which usually had only the more stable two-thirds on their records, 26 percent of failures were from such causes.

Over the period from 1890 to 1930, there appears to have been little change in the life span of small companies. Mortality was around 50 percent in the first two years. In general, there was no proper planning or calculation of future risks, and location was likely to be dictated by the residence of the entrepreneur or the chance for a low rental. But while perhaps two-thirds had less than ten years of life, the minority did well enough to continue, and a few not only survived but expanded in scale or range of activities. A successful retailer might add some whole-saling, particularly in less built-up areas, or a lawyer might expand into real estate and insurance. Of all types of activity open to the small entrepreneur real estate continued to be the most profitable.

As long as an enterprise needed only family labor it usually had about a 15 percent wage advantage over a bigger company run by hired management, and if business details such as accounts, credit, and inventory control were reasonably well attended to, perhaps an exceptional combination of skills, the small enterpriser could meet the competition of larger sellers.[22]

In all, the patterns of small and medium-sized business did not change greatly from those of the mid-nineteenth century. The managerial and policy problems of brokers, wholesalers, and other middlemen and small bankers were essentially the same, although the markets in which they operated were larger and more complex. Medium-sized manufacturers still specialized in light products poorly adapted to large-scale production—those protected by patents, or ones in which personal marketing played an important part. Such companies avoided competition as much as possible, seeking to supply a market sufficiently small and specialized to discourage newcomers.[23] Often it was much more expensive for a big company to set up a department to manufacture a component than to buy it from a specialized shop. Consequently most of the higher priced consumer durables were assembled from the products of many companies. The 100,000 or so medium-sized firms, employing from twenty to even 1,000 employees, although seldom more than 500, were the nation's largest employers. If one thinks in terms of a norm for American business, it would be a company of this size in trade or service.

Building construction, America's continual leader in capital formation, remained by 1929 in the hands of over 300,000 independent contractors. Specialization in certain parts of construction had become the rule in urban areas, and an initial contract made with a general operator would be subcontracted to plumbers, roofers, or masons. In a few big cities the overall contracts for skyscrapers, running into the millions, were handled by relatively large firms with hundreds of employees. These enterprises required all the managerial skills of finance, organization, and proper delegation of authority, but the average contractor was a man of action directly supervising construction while his wife or a secretary and a part-time bookkeeper kept the records and answered calls in the office.

In all, except for the problems of the big company which concerned, at the most, only 4 or 5 percent of American businessmen, the remainder of enterprise changed only gradually. Changes did occur in facilities for communication, more rapid delivery and turnover, and somewhat greater need for specialized knowledge, but in the business of all the industrial nations, continuity was the rule.

8

The Growing Importance of Business Services

S ERVICES needed in the conduct of business had been growing since the beginning of the Business Revolution and by the early twentieth century had developed most of their present forms. The required services varied from the essential, such as financial or legal help, to the useful but not necessary, such as membership in a trade association; and between those that could be well-performed within the firm, those that required some outside organization, and those that gained from a combined effort.

TRADE ASSOCIATIONS

As noted in Chapter Six, attempts to restrict competition had been unenforcible because of judicial opinions that price-fixing agreements were conspiracies in restraint of trade. When there were only a limited number of enterprises in a field, associations occasionally took on what were probably illegal functions without too much danger from the costly process of testing in the courts. For example, in 1890, an association of all but five or six of the window glass manufacturers joined with the

Window Glass Workers of America in a "rather effective control over the industry," but the situation had broken down by 1900.[1] With a small number of competitors it was also possible to rely more on verbal or gentlemen's agreements made at association meetings.

Large-scale voluntary agreements, even with legal approval, might have been unworkable in any case because of the size and diversity of the American market. A new, less rigorous method of price stabilization was urged in 1911 by A. J. Eddy, a Chicago lawyer, who persuaded some 120 associations to have their members post their prices and discounts in the various association offices. This policy probably had some stabilizing effect, but little enough so that it was upheld by the United States Supreme Court in 1923 as not necessarily a conspiracy to raise prices. The policy was also endorsed by the then-Secretary of Commerce, Herbert C. Hoover. Yet the Federal Trade Commission from the time of its creation in 1914 rather steadily opposed trade association activities that might lead to more uniform pricing. Such contradictions in views among various authorities, state and local, legislative and legal, have been continuing hazards of American business.

The chief lawful function of trade associations with hundreds or thousands of members, however, was still that of supplying information, to the members on one side and to political bodies on the other. A big association would usually sponsor a trade journal, which by publishing statistics on volume of turnover or production, exits and entries of firms, or noting cases of exceptional success could give the medium-sized concern a considerable advantage over working in the dark, guided only by gossip and rumors. Trade associations were used by the government in World War I to estimate possible maximum output in many industries. In 1925 there were around 1,000 such associations of one type or another in America, in contrast to some 3,000 in Germany. The influence of any of them on either prices or competition in the United States has been impossible to determine.

SPECIAL TYPES OF ASSOCIATIONS

The operation of taverns, restaurants, inns, or hotels must be among the oldest of all service activities of a nonprofessional type. As we have seen (Chapter Six) the great distances in the United States made hotels essential for commercial travelers and other visiting businessmen. By the latter half of the nineteenth century big city hotel builders were seeking to outdo one another in lavishness and size. By 1890 the old "American" plan of charging by the day for room and board had given way to the "European" plan of a la carte restaurants and separate charges for rooms. This change, occurring in the course of a single generation, had somewhat divided hotel managers between country and city types, but both agreed that protection against "deadbeats" or fraudulent guests was their major common problem. To gain stricter criminal statutes, in most of the states, the proprietors formed hotel associations, and in 1910 some joined in an American Hotel Protective Association.[2]

Associations for the general promotion of the business of a city were another type, not related to any particular commodity market. In 1912 the Department of Commerce listed 2,960 such local organizations, 183 state or territorial, and 243 national. Of these, 414 called themselves chambers of commerce, 490 boards of trade, and 868 commercial clubs.[3] Rotary, Kiwanis, and Lions, often referred to as service clubs, starting with Rotary in 1905, were local business associations with limited memberships which allowed for more intimacy than in a chamber of commerce. Any of these local or state organizations might take an active part in securing political reforms and tax or other concessions that would make their area attractive to entrepreneurs locating new businesses.

Management associations of various sorts had their origin in the National Association of Employment Managers, which by a number of mergers and changes between 1914 and 1923 became the American Management Association publishing the *American Management Review*. By 1930 its membership included 1,500 firms and 100 professors, not an imposing percentage of the 100,000 medium-to-large firms. One suspects that membership was largely limited to companies big enough to spare the time of some executives to read the *Review* and attend meetings.

In all these types of associations it is hard to separate their business utility from their appeal through sociability and the value to professional managers of knowing people in other companies that might offer better jobs. But on occasion the man who went to enjoy himself on an expense account at a convention might pick up useful business knowledge. Whether any or all of these characteristics were more true of the United States than of similar western European associations remains to be investigated.

THE SALE OF INFORMATION

Firms selling information and advice were directly concerned with the problems of the individual business. Among the oldest of these in all nations were law partnerships. By 1900 the largest law offices in the major cities, particularly Chicago, Philadelphia, and New York rivaled the big business companies in income and prestige. As trustees for many substantial fortunes, they might have great influence in corporate affairs, often through seats on the boards of directors of major companies. About 1900 a New York lawyer boasted of speaking for a billion dollars in capital. Since partners gave advice to government as well as to business and served temporarily in government posts, their influence in politics was usually considerably greater than that of other business leaders.

Furthermore, they sold their advice in a market relatively free from price competition. Customers were attracted by the firm's reputation and influence, not by quoted rates, and fees were based on the sums of money involved more than on the work done. With able lawyers in state and nation making the law ever more elaborate, statutes and precedents had become so complex by 1900 that even if a company had its own legal department capable of handling normal types of litigation, for unusual problems (such as government actions) the executives would still turn to outside specialists.

By 1900 consulting firms of various types were appearing in all advanced nations. In France and Germany, for example, firms specializing in accounting, engineering, and law had been in existence for many years, but only in the United States was there much expansion into specialties such as employee problems, management, or public relations. As with the law, many American firms had their own staff for routine operations but needed specialists for emergencies.

THE GROWING NECESSITY OF ACCOUNTING

In this period the most important development in the sale of knowledge in the United States was the refined and, in part, enforced use of accounting. While by 1890 accounting theory was fairly abreast of the basic problems of the corporation, commercial use of such knowledge lagged far behind. Few large firms received the full services available from public accountants, and smaller firms still kept books using methods inherited from earlier generations.

During the next forty years two separate developments coincided: better internal accounts were used for detecting departmental weaknesses and guiding future plans; and specialized public accountants were used both to instruct management and to assure stockholders of the honesty or reliability of the figures supplied by their company. The public accounting firms, such as Price, Waterhouse or Arthur Young, having the largest concentrations of highly trained specialists, were generally responsible for both the improvements in knowledge and practice. There were few professors of accounting in the academic world before 1910.

Companies that relied on their own bookkeepers made slow progress in making accounting a tool for business decisions. For example, although 1897 to 1920 was a period of accelerating price increases, few medium-sized firms (and not all large ones) adjusted their inventories and fixed capital to price changes, nor did many adopt realistic write-offs for depreciation. A general lack of accounts for depreciation, systematic allocation of overhead, or adjustment for price changes made balance sheets unrealistic during the inflation of 1897–1920, thus illustrating the fact that accounting had developed in the late nineteenth century when the previous or "historic" cost of assets was generally higher than that of replacement.

During the early twentieth century cost accounting, applied first to the field of factory operation, took on its modern form. Traditional practice had been merely to spread variable costs over the items produced in a plant and thereby get a rough basis for pricing. In 1906, John Whitmore, an American, applied the idea of proper or standard costs based on calculations made in advance. This marked the beginning of a shift from cost accounting being a record of past experience to its becoming a tool for managerial planning and testing. By 1920 the new conception of standard costs was being used in manufacturing but had made little impression on the main body of business operations. Large hotels, wholesalers, department stores, and even railroads made little effort to standardize and check the validity of their costing.[4]

In the long run the United States suffered in relation to other large nations from the fact that control of accounting fell under forty-odd state jurisdictions. To create some acceptable standards public accounting firms formed membership associations in the 1890s in five industrial states to work for laws requiring examination for the title of certified public accountant. New York passed such a law in 1896, followed by Pennsylvania in 1899 and most of the other important business states shortly thereafter. In 1900 there were perhaps 300 public accountants in the three largest cities, and there must have been quite a few more west of Chicago. In the first decade of the century some firms even with closely held stock hired public accountants for the value of the trade information they could supply. For example, when it first hired Price, Waterhouse in 1904, the Pabst Brewing Company was pleased to learn that its freight and manufacturing costs were lower than in other breweries doing a similar type of business.[5] But it was hard to convince many practical businessmen that they needed to pay high prices for better information from their own books; also, right into the 1920s many kept "private books" which they wanted no one but themselves to see. In spite of all the talk about the openness of the new competition, many if not a majority of businessmen thought competitors would gain from accurate knowledge of financial operations, and that outside accountants were not to be trusted.

Considering the relatively small number of companies with publicly held stock (and thus with some demand on them for releasing information), public accounting would have gained slowly but for the help of the federal government. In 1909 an excise tax of 1 percent on corporation income above $5,000 forced the complying companies to produce accounts. Those who hoped to have the law declared unconstitutional and were willing to risk the maximum fine of $10,000 were forced into compliance by the Supreme Court decision of Flint vs. Stone and Tracy (1911). Meanwhile the Sixteenth Amendment legalizing personal income taxes was moving through the states fast enough to permit such an act by Congress in 1913. Again, although the rates were low, with graduated increases only over $20,000 (the equivalent of nearly $100,000 in 1975) and a maximum of 7 percent, the wealthy had to have accurate accounts.

In 1914 the Federal Reserve Board demanded that balance sheets presented in connection with loans on commercial paper be certified by public accountants. This led to the formation of a distinguished committee of the American Association of Public Accountants, which consulted with the Reserve Board and the Federal Trade Commission on approved methods of audit. A resulting "Approved Methods for Preparation of Balance Sheet Statements" was published in the *Federal Reserve Bulletin* in 1917, and the principles stated came to be regarded as minimum requirements.

While these governmental actions led to the broader use of public accountants, it was the wartime tax laws of 1917 and 1918 imposing an excess profits levy that made CPAs almost a necessity for medium-to-large-sized companies. Those profiting from the war, as many firms did, had to have able accountants in their own departments or hire their services from outside firms.[6]

For accountants themselves the new requirements produced a flood of literature from 1917 to 1929. It seems safe to say that more books on accounting appeared in these dozen years than in the entire previous history of the nation.[7] The trend of the theorists was to emphasize sampling and appraisal of the systems of financial control rather than the English careful auditing of records. But theory was well in advance of practice. Prior to 1929, at least, management was not ready to receive lectures from auditors, and sampling was adopted only because it saved expense.

By making balance sheets prepared by public accountants the basis for large bank loans or corporate mergers, a great responsibility was placed on these visitors to company offices—visitors who could only work from the material supplied, plus, at the most, verification of deposits in banks. Soon, a number of cases of accountants having been fraudulently misled arose, and the courts began a possibly endless process of defining the liability of accounting firms. The first case of major importance led to a New York state decision in 1931, known as the Ultramares Case, which followed nineteenth-century British precedents. The court held that third parties could not recover from an accountant in instances where he had been merely negligent, but that they could recover if there had been fraud and the accountant had been "grossly negligent."[8] Obviously there was much defining still to be done.

Increasing the reliability of the profession as a whole depended largely on state laws, better academic education, and national supervision by strong voluntary associations. By 1924 all the states had laws defining the CPA title and implying, at least, the requirement of an examination. In 1924 the United States Supreme Court upheld the right of the Alabama Board of Public Accountancy to deny the title to a man who had not met the state requirements.

In 1900 there had been no college majors in accounting; by 1916 some sixteen were available, and from then on, all of the increasing number of schools of business had such departments. In 1905 the *Journal of Accountancy* gave both academic scholars and professionals a chance to spread their views and freed them from total reliance on *The* (British) *Accountant*. The growth of this new academic field produced a large number of professors of accounting anxious to improve the standing of CPAs and to increase the amount of knowledge necessary to pass state examinations. Both objectives, widely shared among practitioners, could be advanced through better organization, which was badly needed.

By 1915 state accountancy laws were in great confusion. In some states certification was a matter of political influence, and even where there were strict laws requiring an examination, administration of the law varied widely. This situation reinforced the scholarly demand for corrective action by some type of national association, which by winning the endorsement of the important federal agencies could demonstrate to general business the advantage of using qualified practitioners. But the existing Association of Public Accountants lacked agreed-upon qualifications and was thought to represent only the East and, particularly, New York City. To improve their national influence, in 1916 academic scholars joined with accountants from business in absorbing the old organization into the Institute of Accountants of the United States of America, whose major purpose was establishing higher and more uniform standards.

Although the 1,150 charter as well as later members joined the Institute as individuals, it was recognized that to reform local laws and their administration the new body must act largely through the state associations. In 1917 the Institute offered a model examination in accounting theory, auditing, and commercial law, but of the nine states that put it to use only four had large business centers. One weakness of the Institute was that it accepted members who were not CPAs; another was a lack of real vigor in working for reform. Consequently, in 1921 the younger and more progressive members of the profession formed the American Society of Certified Public Accountants. The two organizations had many members in common and did not openly conflict, but the dualism undoubtedly diminished the influence of either group.

As has so often been the case in the United States, business solved its problem independently of confused state laws. The spread of branch offices of the big accounting firms and the ideas of their members became the strongest influence both on the record-keeping of their clients and on outside local practice. The age was beginning when accounting would come to be recognized as one of the two or three most important operations of business administration.

FINANCIAL SERVICES: REAL ESTATE

With the consolidated mortgage, representing a fund of many individual claims divided into uniformly priced bonds of $500 or $1,000, a well-established form of investment by 1900, new vistas opened for the real estate developer. In the flush days preceding the panic of 1907 the greatest land boom of American history took place in Texas. Trains brought prospective buyers from the big cities of the Mississippi valley and fares were to be refunded in the event land was purchased. It is scarcely an exaggeration to say that California enjoyed a nearly continuous boom in land on urban fringe areas from 1890 to 1929. Land speculation in Florida reached a high point from 1923 to 1926, only to collapse from a combination of bad seasons and excessive prices.

The spread of urbanites to the suburbs, speeded after about 1910 by the automobile, led to a growing real estate business. Fortunes were made, and frequently lost, in planned suburban developments participated in by architects, building contractors, real estate agents, and promotional investors. Since, after 1913, real estate mortgages were acceptable investments for all banks, the suburban promoters often started such institutions chiefly for holding such securities. Another of the main features of the speculative years from 1923 to 1929 was the building of skyscraper office and hotel buildings financed by large consolidated mortgages. Often issued on the basis of gross overestimates of cost and value, these mortgages were sold both to financial institutions and, in the forms of bonds, to thousands of individual investors. The construction contractors were usually paid, but after 1929, the first mortgage holders found that they had claims on half-empty buildings then worth only a fraction of their cost.

FINANCIAL SERVICES: INSURANCE

Among the most important suppliers of capital for real estate development were the rapidly growing life insurance companies. In 1890 there were 60 such firms with about half of their reserve funds of $700 million invested in mortgages. While reserves had climbed by 1905 to $2.7

billion, investments in stocks and bonds were growing most rapidly.[9] But a state legislative investigation by the Armstrong committee held in New York City, the nation's life insurance center, revealed corrupt practices by both financial managers and agents. New York and other states promptly enacted regulatory laws prohibiting investment banking activities by the companies and limiting their portfolios to policy loans, real estate used for their own use, high grade bonds, and mortgages. The result was an upswing in mortgage investment to $7.6 billion in 1930 out of a total portfolio of $18.9 billion, not far from the ratio of 1890, but the total portfolio, twenty-five times as large, was now held by 438 companies. This upswing had made life insurance investment a major factor in the mortgage market, particularly for large urban certificates.

The Armstrong investigation also led to major changes in the managerial practices of life insurance companies. Previously, general agents had been granted large territories, sometimes whole states, and allowed commissions on all policies written by their salesmen. The agency emphasis was on maximizing initial sales and commissions without sufficient regard for the long-run welfare of either the policyholder or the company. Now the general agents were made salaried officers of the company and salesmen (agents) had to take training courses acquainting them with how best to serve the interests of their customers.

Meanwhile, the companies promoted research on classification of risks that reduced some premiums and led also to many new types of policies, such as endowments to cover inheritance taxes, future education of children, or retirement income. Government military, life, and endowment policies in World War I also made many more people familiar with insurance, as did the continued spread of small "industrial" policies with premiums collected weekly from wage earners. By 1930, there was $100 billion worth of personal insurance in force, exclusive of state compensation plans.

As might be expected, increasingly intricate actuarial calculation and employee education moved insurance in the direction of a profession. After teaching courses in insurance for some years, Professor Solomon S. Huebner of the University of Pennsylvania published a textbook in 1915. In the companies there was a movement to require certified life underwriters, similar to CPAs, and in 1927 this group established the American College of Life Underwriters to administer proper examinations. As in many other fields Americans were seeing more connection between commerce and scholarship than were the businessmen of other nations.

FINANCIAL SERVICES: A STUDY OF BANKING

Banker-politician Levi P. Morton said in 1895 that "the bank is the general agent of civilization in its advance."[10] But as in other types of marketing, the size of the United States continued to present difficulties in the activities of this important agency. The problems were not only in communication over great distances but in the reflection of isolation and localism in attitudes, and hence in resulting variations in state laws. Added to these difficulties were the jealousy of federal power by the states and the distrust of the power of money men in particular, producing a collection of problems in the field of commercial banking that the nation was unable to deal with satisfactorily.

Prior to the National Monetary Commission's studies of foreign systems from 1908 to 1912 it may well have been that many bankers even in major American centers of finance were unaware of the detailed operation of French, German, and Japanese banking, while that of Great Britain appeared by 1900 to operate under circumstances that were prevented by law in the United States. In addition, national characteristics subtly influenced the actual practice in each system in spite of any apparent similarities in structure. The differences between the United States and the other nations stemmed from the size of the country, the relative lack of fluidity in capital, and the degree of divided authority. But each of the other four nations differed from the rest, so that, as in the case of accounting, there was no accepted theory of banking structure and operation applicable to all nations.

Up to World War I, German practice varied the most widely from that of the United States. While the empire was composed of separate states, by 1890 the central government and the *Reichsbank* controlled German banking. About a score of business or all-purpose banks (*Kreditbanken*), of which eight were recognized leaders, performed all types of banking, including investment, and also held stock in certain industries. These banks continued to absorb the smaller private and chartered banks by merger. In response to government promptings the *Kreditbanken* continued to invest in mining, heavy industry, and military equipment, and to promote foreign trade. The investment process was often to loan money initially at low rates to a favored firm, then convert the loan into the company's securities and market some of them to the public, while retaining substantial amounts in the bank portfolio. By

1905 members of the big eight held 819 directorships in industrial firms. In 1913 loans on current account, which were equivalent to open lines of credit in American banks, and were freely used for capital purposes by the big borrowers, amounted to 73 percent of the portfolios of the leading banks.[11] For American commercial banks to become deeply involved in corporate stock or equity capital would have been both illegal and dangerous, but in Germany the *Reichsbank* stood behind the *Kreditbanken* and would rediscount to provide necessary cash in times of trouble.

The *Reichsbank*, with a monopoly of currency issue, had 100 main offices and 4,000 branches that discounted for private individuals in amounts as small as ten marks, but at rates slightly above those of the 140-odd incorporated banks doing local business.[12] In comparison to the Federal Reserve System, the *Reichsbank* was not only a banker's bank, but also a haven in time of trouble for all German borrowers.

The English system in banking practice was closer to that in the United States, but differed greatly in structure. Through continual mergers in the late nineteenth century the joint-stock banks had been absorbed into half a dozen nationwide corporations, some of them with 2,000 or more branches. While these systems stuck to commercial banking and short-term loans, they also bought preferred stock and bonds, both foreign and domestic, which would not have been acceptable to national, or most state, bank examiners in America.

Alongside those of the big banks were the branches of the bank of England which, like the *Reichsbank*, supplied the currency and served as an ultimate source of cash. Unlike those in Germany, however, the big English banks, such as Lloyd's or Barclay's, left investment marketing to the private bankers of London—an arrangement somewhat similar to that in the United States, except that before 1933, American commercial banks often joined security-selling syndicates or set up investment banking affiliates. Germans, however, called both American and British banks specialized in contrast to their all-purpose *Kreditbanken*.

The French system had more similarities to the British than the German. By 1900 a few big credit companies such as the Lyonaisse, the Societé General, and the Comptoir d'Escompte carried on commercial banking in over 500 branches around the nation; they also marketed, but seldom retained, securities of many types. With over 400 branches of the Bank of France and more than 2,000 local banking organizations of various types the competitive picture was too intricate to explore here. In general a local bank, run by a family, would lend to neighborhood people who could not borrow from one of the national credit companies—a situation that reminds one of the arguments advanced against branch banking in the United States.

Again, as in Germany and England, there was the Bank of France as a supplier of all currency and a lender of last resort. Perhaps reflecting the more agricultural character of the two continental nations, checks were seldom used, as was true before 1900 in the rural regions of the United States, whereas in England cash was seldom seen except for small purchases.

In the last years of the nineteenth century, Japan was emerging as an industrial state with a banking system that superficially, at least, resembled that of Germany. There was a central Bank of Japan and half a dozen large, all-purpose banks with branches as well as a large number of small commercial and savings banks. Each of the big banks was the financial center of a group of allied industries, a *zaibatsu*, often dominated by a single family. Recent scholars, however, have pointed out that the *zaibatsu* banks were not large holders of the securities of the allied firms and that they did much general banking business with outsiders. Only in times of financial trouble would the bank reduce its outside loans in order to maintain or increase those to the *zaibatsu* associates.[13]

FINANCIAL SERVICES: INVESTMENT BANKERS

The nearest American equivalents of the German *Kreditbanken* or the Japanese *zaibatsu* banks were the large investment banking houses with strong foreign connections. From 1890 to 1917 these international houses greatly expanded their influence in the investment and money markets. The old alignment of American partnerships around the Anglo-French sphere of J. P. Morgan or the German-continental European one of Kuhn Loeb continued, while they wielded an increasing managerial influence on the railroads and utilities that they financed. In the early 1900s Morgan led the way in financing some large industrial mergers as well, such as United States Steel and International Harvester.

The investment houses not only controlled trust companies by stock ownership, but also did commercial banking for large customers. In spite of offering this competition the syndicate leaders maintained good relations with the big commercial banks by giving them shares in the financing operations. In fact, a big security marketing syndicate of the early 1900s might include not only the metropolitan commercial banks as full-fledged participants, but even banks in smaller cities.[14]

It has been charged that the German *Kreditbanken* and Japanese *zaibatsu* held back the development of their nations by giving in to the government pressure for promoting mining, heavy industry, and military equipment at the expense of agriculture and consumer goods by charging higher rates for financing the latter.[15] While there was little or no government pressure in the United States, bankers, preserving their nineteenth-century views up to World War I, directed the principal flows of capital into excessive railroad construction and city and inter-urban electric traction development at a time when many such routes were about to become useless. The Chicago Milwaukee and St. Paul, for example, completed an extremely expensive connection to the Pacific coast the year the Panama Canal opened, and just before that Morgan had sponsored the purchase, at a fantastic price, of the New York Westchester and Boston electric line in the suburbs of New York City. Meanwhile, the automobile industry grew with practically no equity financing from the investment houses.

FINANCIAL SERVICES: OLD BANKING PROBLEMS

Big city bank managers on both sides of the Atlantic faced keen competition for good loans and deposit accounts. Bank advertising was an old practice in, at least, both England and the United States, but the arguments in the periodical advertisements ran in terms of service and securiy rather than lower discount rates. Interest on deposits was a different matter and directors usually gave cashiers, appropriate vice-presidents, or in Britain branch managers, discretion within limits. In the late nineteenth century, for example, Lloyd's managers were allowed to bargain from $2\frac{1}{2}$ to $3\frac{1}{2}$ percent for long-term balances.[16] In New York City the biggest banks were disinclined to pay interest on country bank balances, but the smaller banks bid up to 2 percent or more.

The time of the advent of the bank salesman is not established by the historical literature, which pays little attention to bank marketing, but by the 1920s he was a very important aid to the American big-city banks that were trying to outdo each other in size. Visiting important potential depositors or credit seekers, the banks salesman told them of the superior services of his bank. One reason that the first hiring of such specialized selling agents may be hard to date is that from early times similar visits had been made by officers or directors of banks. To elect a leading merchant as president was generally assumed to be followed by the transfer of the business of many of his friends or debtors to his bank. Fast-growing cities of the West might send a vice-president around the country to coax manufacturers to establish plants in his area with the help of his bank.

Dodging these difficult questions of bank marketing and comparative management practices, the most obvious distinctions between American and foreign banking continued to be lack of a central bank and widely differing federal and state regulatory laws. In the United States currency came only from such amounts as individual national banks choose to issue against the dwindling security of federal bonds, and from a limited amount of specie or certificates paid out by the Treasury Department for bond redemptions in gold, government services, and mandatory silver purchases. While the treasurers usually tried to get as much money into circulation as the laws and their resources would allow, the national bank currency tended continually to diminish.

In the big cities, where charge accounts and checking were the rule, the amount of paper money and specie made little difference, but in country areas, where most Americans still lived, checks were little used. In the absence of a system, supply and demand for money were negatively related geographically. The national banks were mainly in the cities of the Midwest and Northeast, and these regions normally had surplus currency. Before 1913 national banks could not lend with land as security, and thus rural banks were generally state-chartered and had no power to issue notes. This currency dilemma, plus the lack of a true national money market that could quickly and cheaply transfer cash to where it was needed, undoubtedly held back the business development of rural areas.

Seen another way, it has been estimated that for many years up to 1890 savings actually exceeded new capital formation, but partly because of the conservatism of Eastern banks and partly because of the deliberate discouragement of interbank discounting by the controller of the currency, savings accumulated in the money centers and failed to meet the needs of the rapidly growing areas. To make matters worse the biggest commercial banks of the East coast were reluctant to enter into any other new forms of investment. Through an organizational innovation that took the form of nationwide commercial paper houses with salesmen, plus some increase in insurance company investment in Western mortgages, credit was becoming more evenly distributed by 1913.[17] On the one hand these failures make bank management in the United States appear backward in comparison with that of Europe, but it must be remembered that no central bank stood ready to rescue Americans in case of trouble.

In spite of its rigidities and outward conservatism, American banking was exceptionally disjointed and insecure. Adding to the inevitable weakness of excessively small unit banks was a clause in the law prohibiting national banks from managing trusts, and a ruling of the controller of the currency in 1895 forbidding national banks from opening branches unless they were expressly provided for by state law. But the strongest threat to the stability of the central money markets was the rise of practically unregulated trust companies as competitors to the cautious and federally constrained big city national banks.

In New York City the number of trust companies nearly doubled between 1895 and 1904. Some were created chiefly as marketing outlets for the reserves of insurance companies and the securities of investment banking syndicates. For their banking business the trust companies cleared through banks that were members of the New York Clearing House, but when the latter imposed the requirement of a 10 percent reserve against deposits on the trusts that enjoyed this service, most of them went back to individual clearing by runners.[18]

By 1907 a situation existed in the New York money market—the recognized national center—that in many respects represented a decline in the efficiency of American finance over the previous three decades. The biggest commercial banks, National City and Chase, together with a handful of others, held the ultimate specie reserves of the banking system. They also controlled the board of the New York Clearing House. These banks were allied by friendship and mutual favors with the principal investment banking partnerships such as J. P. Morgan and with their controlled trust companies. The problem posed was that this unorganized and partly unregulated group that stood at the head of the nation's financial activities had no reason to feel any direct responsibility for the rest of the confused banking structure.

When a speculative panic occurred as in 1907, money moved out of threatened banks and trust companies into the security of National City or the other largest banks. Therefore, the big banks, as controllers of the Clearing House, saw no need for quickly coming to the aid of trust companies that had defied the 1903 effort at regulation. The house of Morgan gave some help in saving approved trust companies from the devastating effects of runs on organizations with minimal cash reserves, but a wise contemporary scholar, Professor O. M. W. Sprague, reported to a federal commission that the banking situation was handled "less skillfully and boldly than in 1893, and far less so than in 1873. . . ."[19]

Obviously some organizational innovation was needed to arrest the effects of nearly eighty years of inefficiency and confusion in the structure of American banking. Since in large part the confusion was the result of politically motivated laws and rulings, the reform would have to begin with the political and legal structure. To study what should be done by examining American and foreign banking systems, Congress in 1908 established the National Monetary Commission.

FINANCIAL SERVICES: NEW BANKING TROUBLES

The result of the commission's report, delivered in 1912, was the Federal Reserve Act of 1913, another law that ultimately reflected as much the obligations of congressmen to small city bankers and other constituents as any contemporary theories of central banking. The act applied only to the 7,500 national banks and not to the nearly 20,000 other banks and trust companies. These could join if they wanted to, but aside from some prestige useful in marketing there was little inducement. In place of a central bank there was merely a board in Washington whose power over the twelve regional reserve banks was largely advisory and negative. Members of the system owned the stock of their regional reserve banks and had the privilege of rediscounting prime business paper (short term loans) in return for a new type of currency, federal reserve notes. Since for small fees nonmembers could rediscount with members, state banks and trust companies lost little by staying out and avoided more stringent federal rules and examinations.

Over a long enough period perhaps any collection of private organizations left to themselves can work out tolerable ways of performing their necessary functions, and to a considerable degree this happened over the next sixty years, but the first two decades of the new system were the most disastrous in American financial history. In part, this was because the new system had been patched together, not to create an ideal banking system, but to cure the worst failings of the old order. Through rediscounting the currency had been made more elastic but not necessarily better adjusted to maintaining stable conditions for credit; this latter function might be aided by the right of the reserve banks to buy or sell government securities; and national banks could now make mortgage loans up to 50 percent of the assessed valuation of property. World War I, however, brought a host of new problems, some of them real dilemmas, and the politically restricted organizational innovation of 1913 proved inadequate.

Aside from inflationary war finance, which cannot be dealt with here, American investment and commercial bankers were suddenly faced with the responsibilities of being the market of last resort—the ultimate reserve of the world financial system. This was not only a task for which none but a few East coast bankers had any training, but also a responsibility that both they and the federal government were loath to assume.

Meanwhile conversion of privately held federal bonds into cash seeking new investment, prosperity from 1922 on, and a high proportion of untaxed income in the hands of investors in the upper brackets produced the easiest domestic money market in American history. Yet the old problem of regional differences remained. In the cotton growing South and wheat raising Plains states farm values and incomes were down, and each year many banks were failing. In the big cities banks were merging and new suburban banks were appearing largely to finance real estate development through the granting of mortgages on property assessed at unrealistic prices.[20]

Competition for all commercial banks was increased by trust company land banks deriving their funds from government Farm Loan Banks (1916–), savings banks, and the rapid growth of finance companies. The land mortgage trusts were largely confined to the Midwest and had unfortunate histories both before and after 1929, but finance companies that had originated just before World War I spread rapidly and permanently in the 1920s. They were able to take such advantage of the disabilities placed on national banks by law and the slowness of all bankers in financing installment sales and personal loans that the three or four big finance companies became strong competitors in the lending market.

However, even the managers of the normally most conservative metropolitan banks, while shunning new types of financing, were led into granting mortgages based on excessive property appraisals, investing in new types of bonds, and extending big loans against collateral in the form of common stock. All three trends were enhanced by the ability of many large companies to finance working capital and expansion more

economically through security issues or retained profits than by bank
loans, making for a rather steady decline in the relative amount of high-
grade commercial paper. Meanwhile, in high-pressure races for relative
size the big banks attracted deposits at record-breaking rates. The con-
tests were accentuated by a ruling in 1922 that national banks, unless
forbidden by local law, might establish branches within their own cities,
although the trend of state laws, particularly in the Northwest, was in
the opposite direction.

The situation of rising deposits and a scarcity of short-term investments, which the metropolitan banks had not faced since the early
nineteenth century, presented managements with investment difficulties
probably insoluble on the basis of maintaining safe liquidity for the
isolated individual bank. Forced ultimately to choose between mortgage
bonds or loans against stock market securities, the big city banks began
to favor the latter. Such loans were callable on demand and with a
generally rising market seemed highly liquid. And so they were in
amounts of a few thousand dollars, but a $5 million loan against some
hundreds of thousands of shares of one company's common stock was
prone in time of trouble to be completely nonliquid. Since there was no
way of selling such a block on a weakly supported market, by 1931 the
banks had defaulted call loans on their books and the securities, for
what they were then worth, in their portfolios, with the deficiency between the face value of the loan and the market value of the stock
taken from the capital of national banks and put in an unusable reserve
in accordance with federal law. This rigidity alone may have doomed
the success of much of the Americans' efforts to become world bankers
in competition with the far more flexible banks of the other financial
leaders.

Yet, because of its size and the ability to lend, the United States
was inevitably involved in European financial troubles. These complicated the efforts of the executives of the Federal Reserve or the leading
banks to control either the unwarranted stock market upswing or the
ultimately disastrous decline in liquidity. While the individual commercial
banks could probably have done relatively little, in any case, their efforts
were far from expert because of the lack of experience of their officers
with the problems.

The market for selling either foreign or domestic securities became
highly competitive and many of the marketers were quite irresponsible.
Chase National Bank, the descendant of the old National Park, National
City Bank, and some big banks elsewhere had already set up security
selling affiliates that in 1928 and 1929 marketed foreign bonds of very

inferior quality. The old controls, such as they were, once exercised by the dozen big investment banking houses became ineffective in competition with some 3,000 concerns initiating the marketing of security issues and the 6,000 houses selling and trading in them. While the house of Morgan had curtailed its activities and had a relatively good record, the fact that some of the issues it sponsored suffered heavily in the depression illustrates the general overoptimism and breakdown in standards.[21]

Some control of the credit inflation based on mortgages and securities might have been exercised by the Federal Reserve Board through selling government securities, to draw in cash from the banks (thereby reducing their reserves), and by raising the rediscount rate to further discourage bank lending, but there were difficulties that blocked either course. The first impediment was simple: by the late 1920s the Federal Reserve system did not own enough government securities to significantly affect the credit situation. The rate problem was more complex and involved the relation of the American money market to those of other nations.

The inflationary effects of overborrowing to finance World War I, and the international transfers of large sums in indemnity and debt payments had thrown the money markets of all the leading European nations into confusion. It took from 1923 to 1928 to again stabilize currencies in terms of gold. In 1925, Great Britain returned the pound to its prewar gold equivalent of $4.85—an overevaluation that adversely affected British trade and produced monetary problems in relations with the United States. To discourage the flow of pounds into more realistically valued dollars, Benjamin Strong, governor of the Federal Reserve Bank of New York, promised Montague Norman, head of the Bank of England in 1926, to keep the rediscount rate low; in other words, in order to perform his function as an international stabilizer, Strong had to risk credit inflation in the United States. But Strong also believed that domestic business could stand the further stimulation that might come from reasonably priced credit. The miscalculation was that low rates, unaccompanied by much increase in consumer demand, appear to have stimulated real estate and security speculation far more than the use of new capital by industry and trade.

By mid-1929 call market rates for stock exchange investments were far outstripping the relatively stable rediscount rate. The big metropolitan banks had by 1928 become cautious and generally stopped expanding call loans, despite their profitability, but big corporations were putting surplus cash on call, and money from European banks was crossing the ocean to take advantage of the extraordinarily high rates.

As a result, one of the most immediate strains of the October 1929 panics on American banking was that to preserve any semblance of an orderly stock market banks had to substitute domestic bank loans, by voluntarily concerted action, for the European money that had fled at the first signs of impending disaster.

While two of the chief monetary theorists in the United States give the Federal Reserve System low marks for its handling of both the security inflation and the ensuing domestic depression, it was operating under handicaps imposed by both its structure and its international position.[22] Or to put it simply, neither the Reserve System nor the American banking community were prepared to be, as London had been in nineteenth century crises, the stabilizer of last resort. The Federal Reserve Board had in general only negative controls over the twelve regional banks, and they in turn could exert only indirect pressures on member banks, and none at all on individual businesses. Meanwhile, the various Reserve Banks' monetary policies, while uncoordinated at best, seem to have reflected conflicting domestic and foreign pressures. By 1933, American banking was in need of fundamental organizational changes or innovations which, as will be discussed in Chapter Eleven, failed for the usual political reasons to take place.

9

Rationalizing the Big Firm

I N the Western world and Japan the turn-of-the-century was a
period of mergers that in the fields of processing and manufacturing produced new large business combinations. Some of these
ownership systems remained collections of separate firms, others came
from the growth of single companies that wholly absorbed their new
acquisitions. But the drive in most cases was for a stronger position in
an export or domestic market. In Europe and Japan the export market
was a major factor in growth of the firm; in the United States the
domestic market was large enough to reward potential economies of
scale in processing or selling power. Inevitably, bigness pursued for more
effective manufacture or a stronger marketing position threatened to
produce diseconomies in management.

AMERICAN LEGAL RESTRAINTS

In the United States small businessmen and farmers had always feared
monopolies. Partly to win the votes of such constituents for higher
tariff duties, Congress passed the Sherman Antitrust Act of 1890 declar-
ing "every contract, combination in the form of trust or otherwise, or
conspiracy, in restraint of trade or commerce among the several states"
illegal, and prohibiting agreements among competitors for the purpose

of dividing markets and controlling prices. But the act did not condemn monopoly of manufacture by a single company or make any statement as to what share of a market in the hands of one firm constituted "restraint of trade." In the following twenty-one years the United States Supreme Court finally concluded that it would have to use its judgment as to what share of the market or what actions constituted violations of the law. Meanwhile, near total monopolies not based on patents were broken up, but the marketing of 75 percent of a product by three or four firms was permitted.[1]

To facilitate mergers and bring in state revenue, New Jersey passed a general act for holding companies in 1889. From at least 1853 on, holding companies had been chartered by special act, but few other than big railroads had sought such acts, which were regarded with suspicion by both politicians and businessmen. The method of surrendering the stock of merging companies to trustees in return for certificates of trust had been, from its innovation by Standard Oil lawyer S. C. T. Dodd in 1879, a less conspicuous and equally effective way of creating central control. By the late 1880s, however, states were passing antitrust laws, and their courts were prohibiting the operation of such trusts within their jurisdiction. In contrast, the holding company had no fixed place as yet in state or federal judicial interpretation and ultimately met trouble only from the Sherman Act. Up to 1907, however, it was not clear that this national antitrust law would operate against centralized monopolies of manufacture that did not involve agreements in restraint of trade. Conversely, after the Addystone Pipe Association case of 1897, it was certain that intercompany marketing agreements would be prohibited. The relative legal safety of mergers into a single company or sale of stock to a holding company undoubtedly stimulated bigness in business, but because buying power was so dispersed, and price or production agreements were prohibited, the American market continued to be the most competitive.

Congressional antitrust forces, frustrated by the Supreme Court's "rule of reason" in judging market controls, passed the Clayton Act in 1914 containing a long list of specific things that were illegal if done "with a view to lessening competition." Among them were acquiring stock in other companies, entering into agreements with another company regarding the sale of its products (tying agreements), and certain types of interlocking directorships. A Federal Trade Commission was established to collect information on business practices and recommend prosecution for violations of the antitrust laws.

While none of the other countries prohibited pools, cartels, or some form of legally binding association, everywhere there was a tendency to bring companies under a single set of stockholders and a single board of directors in order to be able to close inefficient plants or agencies and to expand operations that promised higher profit. Consequently, big companies appeared in all the nations, and the American antitrust laws and common law rulings against cartel agreements did not make the nation as much the exclusive home of the big unified company as one might expect.

THE WORLDWIDE RISE OF BIG BUSINESS

An American student of the general movement toward consolidations and mergers came to the conclusion that in America and England, at least, the ease with which stock in a heavily capitalized new corporation could be marketed was the most important force in the timing of mergers.[2] At all events, it is clear that around the turn-of-the-century a number of forces leading to bigger companies—such as technology, market controls, easy money markets, and stock speculation—were operating all over the industrial world.

The German situation, for example, resulted in much the same rise of large firms in a quite different political and social environment. Here the public regarded bureaucratic forms and cartel organizations as normal and in the national interest. The *Reichsbank* encouraged the big *Kreditbanken* to build up firms like Krupp or Thyssen, and the government often provided capital and participated in cartels that might lead to new holding companies. The chief difference between Germany and the United States was the persistence and spread of cartels in the former, rising from 350 in 1905 to 3,000 in 1925 and embracing practically every type of business in which keen competition might disrupt the market.[3] In highly competitive situations the central government often took the initiative in bringing firms together and sometimes remained active in administering production quotas and price policies.[4] State intervention was welcomed by German business, in part, because of the fact that voluntary associations, even though legal, failed as in the United States to prevent their members from cheating by secret selling at special prices.

Japan's course was much like that of the *Reich*, with a similar emphasis on building the economic and military power of the nation.

Spurred by government advice and aid, mergers occurred rapidly between 1885 and 1905. Smaller firms that did not merge formed binding
associations, and many of the largest companies were members of a few
family-dominated *zaibatsus*. The latter generally radiated from a family-
owned bank and tended toward vertical as well as horizontal integrations.
Mines, metal processing, and machinery companies might be in the same
ownership group with textile, banking, insurance, and foreign trade
corporations.

As in Germany, Japanese arrangements, according to classic English
market theory, often seemed likely to limit efficiency. Scholars surveying
German and Japanese policy in this period do believe that state
pressures contributed to uneven growth by favoring enterprise that was
desired by the government at the expense of domestic agriculture and
consumer goods.[5] Yet, up to World War I both nations experienced very
rapid rates of economic growth.

Stimulated by the pressures of increasingly competitive world
markets and internal competition (under free trade) from big American
and German firms around the turn-of-the-century, Great Britain went
through a period of mergers and consolidations resembling that in the
United States. Domestic retailing in Britain also included a similar growth
of department stores and chains. Agreements between independent
competitors, however, were not condemned by the courts unless clearly
contrary to the public interest. As in America, promoters of mergers
often created the new firms with more attention to selling stock than to
improving business efficiency.[6] Below the fifty largest nontransportation
companies, the next level of British firms averaged slightly larger than
in the United States.

France forms somewhat of a contrast to the other four great industrial states. While there were a few large French firms in heavy industry,
on the whole business concerns remained smaller and more regionally
oriented. In part this was because of the luxury character of French
domestic sales and exports in textiles, wine, perfume, and automobiles.
Such high-priced goods sold in small special markets that demanded
much work that could only be done by hand. Since the effects on economic growth appear to have been favorable, France was fortunate in
having such products. From 1901 to 1929 French income per capita,
aided by near stability in population, grew twice as fast as that of Great
Britain, and among the three Western nations examined here, remained
up to 1960 the leader in the rate of such growth.[7] This record suggests
the possibility that partly because of types of production and marketing
France may have gained by avoiding between 1890 and the 1920s both

a rapid rate of population growth and much of the fumbling and adjusting period of big business management. The size of French enterprises only expanded rapidly in the period after World War II, when managerial problems were more clearly recognized.

The real impact of apparent international differences is difficult to assess. The poorly designed American antitrust laws and the rise of voluntary trade associations, for example, may have provided some of the same limitations on competition as in foreign nations. Furthermore, France, Germany, and Japan were at a stage of earlier development in heavy industry during which they would have, in any case, grown more rapidly than the relatively consumer-oriented United States. The need to adjust to a large inflow of non-English speaking immigrants imposed heavy burdens on American business in contrast to managing the more homogeneous and compact working populations of the faster-growing states.

THE MAJOR PERIOD OF
MERGERS IN AMERICA

From 1898 to 1902 the United States went through a period where more very large mergers took place than in any other nation. As discussed in Chapter Five, the trunkline railroads and the public utilities serving major cities had been large companies since the mid-nineteenth century, but by 1897 only eight industrial companies were capitalized for $50 million or more. By 1903, largely as the result of mergers, there were over forty, and a hundred other concerns were big enough to have some competitive advantage in marketing.[8] In part this rapid organization of big combinations was a "delayed response" by highly capitalized firms to the problem of competition in nationwide selling in the rich but spread-out American market. Such an explosive change in so few years was caused by a return to general prosperity after some years of depression and a much readier supply of capital available in the public money markets. As a result of the mergers Harold C. Livesay and P. Glenn Porter, using the *Census of Manufactures* twenty-one main categories of industry and classing those with half the product marketed by six firms or less, or three-quarters marketed by a dozen or less, as representing a degree of monopoly, found that in 1909, 31 percent of such industries would be included. The large companies marketed bigger, but un-recorded, percentages of the dollar value of products.[9] While economies from scale of operations and strategic location in manufacturing resulted, the stage of production open to the greatest saving from size was marketing.

THOUGHTS ABOUT BIG COMPANY MANAGEMENT

So far we have sketched the rise of bigger companies, but the chief concern of this chapter is with the managerial problems created. It is ironic that in the United States, where management probably gave the greatest weight to practical experience and the least to theoretical literature, the cultural value placed on financial success led to the earliest development of higher education for business. Following the Wharton School endowment at the University of Pennsylvania in 1883, a handful of other large universities, including Harvard in 1908, opened under-graduate or graduate schools of business. But before the second decade of the twentieth century there were few courses devoted to such business problems as marketing, administration, or high-level management. Since the publication of texts requires a market in the form of courses, there was little such academic writing on these subjects before 1920.

In the late 1880s, as technology became more complex, and real wages rose in the United States, practical or graduate engineers, such as Edward Atkinson, gave increasing attention in books and articles to more systematic organization of factory work.[10] Of these early technical men Frederic W. Taylor gained by far the widest reputation. Developing theories of time and motion study, incentive pay, and supervision of tasks by "functional" foremen, his papers received worldwide attention after 1900. Although foreigners as well as most American managers regarded much of Taylor's approach as impractical, different aspects of his "scientific management" were taken over by the new firms of "con-sulting" or "industrial" engineers and recommended to their clients.[11]

While Taylor advocated the application of functional divisions at all levels of management, the emphasis in his work and that of all but two or three other Americans was on rational plant organization. The next step forward in this type of administration was to recognize the importance of morale or good psychological motivation among workers. Lillian Gilbraith's *The Psychology of Management* (1914) and Mary Parker Follette's *Creative Experience* (1924) were important early publications, although Seabohm Rowntree's *The Human Factor in Business*, published in England in 1921, was probably more read abroad than the contemporary American writing.

The most influential conclusions of the worker-psychology school did not appear until just after 1930. In the late 1920s, Elton Mayo, a Scottish medical doctor employed as an anthropologist at Harvard, carried out experiments on the productivity of selected groups of workers at the Hawthorne plant of Western Electric Company. He concluded that the whole logic of technical efficiency failed to explain productivity "because it omitted the sentiments and non-logical components of the social system." He found better performance associated with emotions such as feelings of importance and responses to group attitudes. To arouse favorable feelings supervisors should communicate the reasons for assignments and listen attentively to complaints.[12] For the next two decades Mayo's ideas were to be a powerful force in shaping American and Western world thinking regarding the causes of efficient factory production.

Throughout the period before 1930 there were very few American books on administrative and structural problems within the ranks of management. There was no United States equivalent of J. Slater Lewis's *The Commercial Organization of Factories*, published in England in 1896, or the much more influential two-volume *Administration Industrielle et Générale*, by Henri Fayol in 1916. Fayol, a French engineer who had become a successful industrialist, gave specific rules for how to control an organization from the top and how to arrange for proper communication and delegation of authority. The principles that no manager could work effectively with more than six immediate subordinates, and that staff experts should take orders only from the top echelon were popularized by Fayol. But the spread was slow. Translated into English in Geneva in 1927, his ideas do not appear to have reached the United States before the 1930s.

Meanwhile one American business executive, Alexander H. Church, had written *The Science and Practice of Management* in 1914, but his ideas were less fully developed than those of Fayol. Also, as we shall see presently, these early books were devoted to perfecting controls in a unified structure of management, presently called the U-form, and did not give consideration to alternative systems of organization. Or put more broadly, all the Western writing accepted the general principles of unified governmental bureaucratic structures and tended to apply principles of public administration to business.

In Japan the culture patterns were so different and study by Westerners so lacking that their practices probably had a negligible effect on American managerial thought before 1930. Had more attention been paid to Japanese practice some of the understanding of the firm that came to the West only after World War II might have appeared earlier. This could have included: the recognition that along with a very strict observance of hierarchical status could go a loose definition of functions; much sharing of ideas up and down the hierarchy (the *ringi* system); and recognition of the useful role of cliques or informal groups.[13]

INHERENT PROBLEMS OF THE
LARGE ORGANIZATION

Such considerations lead to a sociological or psychological view of some of the inevitable problems of bureaucracy, and to troubles that take different forms in different cultures. A wise British scholar of the present day has written: "The fear of organization is the beginning of wisdom."[14] But what to be most fearful of varies, and because of trying to reconcile contradictory factors the best solutions may be far from perfect.

One basic cause of trouble is the contradiction that managerial employees, expected to cooperate with enthusiasm and efficiency for the welfare of the company, are in competition with each other for the more personally important goals of recognition and promotion. The larger the organization the more difficult recognition or visibility becomes, and, therefore, the more opportunistic the subordinate must be in order to secure it.

One way to speed recognition in the large, practically anonymous bureaucracy has been through cliques or informal social groups, the members of which look out for each other's welfare. The basis for such groupings may be regional background, as for example Boston area men on western American railroads, or the time and place of entering the company, as with men from merged outside firms, or school or university affiliations. All of these bases were common in the European nations and Japan. In the latter country such groups, called *Habatsus*, were recognized as a part of administrative life. An English writer has suggested that in all types of large organizations people with some common bond tend to form subgroups of eight to twelve, whose size stems by biological inheritance from the primitive hunting band.[15]

Another cause of nonfunctional behavior inherent in the bureaucratic situation is divided responsibility. From on top it is often impossible to tell what specific man or practice may be responsible for either good or poor performance, hence as long as a whole managerial group shares equally in a task, company time and money may seem unimportant to the immediate welfare of the individual member. These problems were recognized by Henry Poor in the 1850s and by railroad executives before 1880, but they were still being studied, with some desperation, in the 1960s and 1970s.

Finally, among these basic dilemmas is the fact that the characteristics that lead to advancement in the hierarchy are not necessarily those needed in the top administration. This has been well-satirized as the "Peter Principle"—that each man ultimately rises to a job for which he is not qualified. Even in the middle ranks it has proved difficult or impossible to write precise job qualifications or to set specific standards for promotion.

TRANSITION TO A RATIONAL STRUCTURE

Adding to these basic problems are other more specific and curable ones having to do with patterns of structure and control. A problem affecting business in all nations was loosely defined autocratic control by a single individual. In 1890 most big companies were scarcely a generation old in any country, and in the manufacturing companies the men who had put the complex together, or their sons who inherited absolute power, were usually still at the top. Even in Germany, where bureaucratic structure and rules were accepted as normal, leading companies such as Siemens and Halske remained poorly coordinated autocracies while under the control of their founders.

When Wilhelm von Siemens took over from his father in 1890 there was no systematic organization at the top, qualified "strangers" were seldom hired for important posts, and family connections were largely the basis for foreign branch or top domestic authority. Wilhelm introduced a relatively decentralized divisional system of management, ten to twenty years ahead of such developments in the United States, while at the same time retaining absolute personal authority—a power mix perhaps only possible with the German combination of highly developed ideas of structural order together with a value-laden belief in the right of hereditary control.[16]

Family control remained the core of managerial authority in France and Japan, whereas in Britain and the United States professional managers frequently took the reins of power in big companies from the surviving relatives of the founder. Some large companies were weakened by perpetuating the poorly rationalized structure that had functioned well enough in a period of strong leadership into a time when many professionals shared authority.

Around 1900, the dying-off of the pioneer generations and growth through the accumulation of many companies by merger created a pressing need for better management, particularly in large manufacturing firms. Railroad management could serve as a rough model for divisional and functional authority and staff work, but one that did not suit firms with many products, remote branches, and the associated marketing problems. Nowhere were governmental models of bureaucracy translated literally to business. With or without theorizing, entrepreneurs recognized that a government bureau does a limited job on a limited budget, whereas each department of a successful business is trying to expand its activities. The government situation lends itself to routinized interdepartmental relations, whereas the business firm is the scene of largely desirable internal competition.

Based on the published literature, the Du Pont Company appears to have been a leader in the transition to a centralized manufacturing and marketing structure described on a management diagram and largely operated by professional managers—an ironic twist, since this was one of the oldest family firms, headed during this time by two generations of able du Ponts. The basic organization plan, prepared in principle by Coleman du Pont, and in more detail by Arthur J. Moxham, president of a family affiliated steel company, was adopted in 1903. It provided for a president without specific duties and an executive committee made up of the president and the heads of six departments: one each from finance, sales, and development, and from the divisions producing the three different types of product. Coleman du Pont was president, three du Ponts were in charge of departments, and the remaining three department heads were unusually able professional managers, including Moxham in charge of development.[17] The latter became, in fact, the head of a staff department that planned not only product development, but sales strategy and corporate expansion, all of which led to further refinements in organization.

Under the wise guidance of Moxham and Hamilton C. Barksdale, with increasing help from Pierre S. du Pont, a unified structure of operation was brought about gradually. World War I, which catapulted the company into major national importance, both speeded and complicated the process. Du Pont only achieved a fully rationalized, central structure in 1919. Unfortunately a fully centralized plan was not well suited to a company as large as Du Pont—over $300 million in capital—or with the need to market products embracing dyes, plastics, and chemicals as well as explosives.[18] The development of the more decentralized divisional form that later emerged had, however, its most elaborate early exemplification at the Du Pont-influenced General Motors Corporation.

A PLAN FOR MULTIDIVISIONAL STRUCTURE

Between 1908 and 1920, William C. Durant acquired a collection of automobile parts, accessory, and assembly companies that he operated under the holding company title, General Motors. About the only unifying element was Durant, a highly dynamic, intuitive thinker rather than a systematic executive. In this industry size offered great advantages in marketing, and while many of Durant's purchases were extravagant, he had some of the best selling brands of automobiles. During the war the du Ponts had been encouraged by Durant, who had had financial troubles, to invest heavily in General Motors, and by 1920 the du Ponts had enough stock (27.6 percent of the common) and national financial influence to constitute the most important group on the board of directors. Consequently when uncoordinated expansion and inventory policies put GM into severe financial straits in the price decline of 1920 and 1921, the house of Morgan and Pierre S. du Pont, retired president of the Du Pont Company, decided that the one-man power of Durant would have to be superseded by a carefully designed and coordinated system of management.

At the urging of Pierre du Pont in 1920, Alfred P. Sloan, former president of a GM subsidiary, worked out a multidivisional plan of management that was to become one of the few classic documents of American business history. It is interesting that while the multidivisional structure, or M-form, was to become a standard recourse for companies such as Du Pont marketing diverse products in separate markets, in the case of GM it was chiefly a response to a breakdown because of size and complexity in the internal system of control. Since the company had not yet developed its household utility or agricultural equipment lines, its products all sold in the pleasure car or truck markets. Some of its parts-producing companies sold to both other car assemblers and to wholesalers, but there was no marketing outside the automotive industry. Thus the original M-form seems as much a result of the need for rules governing the delegation of authority in very large bureaucracies as of the demands of selling in diverse markets.

The Sloan Report of 1921 to the GM board strikes this note with an opening statement on delegation: "The responsibility attached to the chief executive of each operation shall in no way be limited. Each such organization . . . shall be complete in every necessary function. . . ." But, on the other hand, "Certain central organizational functions are absolutely essential to the logical development and proper control of the Corporation's activities."[19] These sentences also state the inevitable dilemma that harasses all large-scale organizations.

Turning to the overall corporate structure, Sloan distinguishes "major control," which is exercised by stockholders, directors, a finance committee, and an executive committee, or, in other words, control of grand strategy affecting external financial relations, from the necessary "executive control" that reaches down through the organization. The bulk of the report is, of course, devoted to problems in this latter category.

The basic principle was to determine which activities could be grouped under each top executive and to limit the latter to a number that could report personally to the president, who was "to have the entire responsibility of properly interpreting the policies formulated by major control and distributing them through the organization in such manner as he may elect."[20]

As in almost any very large corporation GM had inherent anomalies that prevented logical neatness and balance in any system. Eight car or truck divisions selling finished products provided the bulk of the company's income, and to exclude the vice-president in charge of any of these from direct access to the president seemed unwise. Thus, without proceeding further, the president had more men reporting to him than Henri Fayol or his later American disciples such as Chester Barnard would have regarded as efficient. General Motors also had a dozen accessory companies, such as Delco, each of which sold as much as 60 percent of its output to outside buyers. These companies, each under a separate manager, were collectively headed by a vice-president. There were fourteen other companies that produced solely for GM, and these were grouped geographically under four regional managers reporting to another vice-president.

What may broadly be thought of as staff activities were in charge of two vice-presidents, one for all advisory services and one for finance. In addition, there was a vice-president for export and installment finance and one for GM of Canada. There were thus a total of an even dozen vice-presidents reporting to the chief executive, who also had to serve on the committees for the major control of financial and executive matters.

Unquestionably the report was logically weakened by being drawn up with specific men in mind. W. C. Durant was still president, and it was foolish to think that he would stop issuing orders personally to all parts of the organization. In addition, some valuable and trusted executives trained at Du Pont required representation among the vice-presidents. But in spite of these imperfections, Sloan's was the first well-publicized organization chart for a divisional structure in a giant American corporation.

In application, the theory of the Sloan plan that each division "shall be complete in every necessary function" had to be more and more modified in the direction of centralized control. The corporation, after all, sold only one principal product—automobiles—and the real challenge was how the central organization could best contribute to economical purchasing and effective marketing. Central office control of inventories was soon established. Executives from the head office spent much time on the road "visiting plants, seeing suppliers, and most of all talking to dealers."[21] All capital expenditures of any size also went through the head office.

Consequently the Sloan plan appears more important as an historical manifesto than in its specific application to GM. In the succeeding years this great bureaucracy, ultimately to be the largest private one in the world, required more centralized control than comported with most models for a divisional system or M-form. By 1927, Donaldson Brown, next to Sloan, the most important executive at GM, explained to the American Management Association that policy had to be centralized and the division managers limited to administrative control. A decade later Chandler writes that general officers rather than division managers carried on the basic entrepreneurial activities in the company.[22]

As Du Pont, GM, and other large corporations further diversified their products in the 1930s and 1940s to lines that might require wholly unfamiliar methods of marketing, the multidivisional form ultimately came to seem almost mandatory. Sears Roebuck, for example, found in the late twenties that retail stores could not be effectively supplied and managed in a department formerly devoted exclusively to mail order.[23] In a Du Pont plan, adopted late in 1921, eight vice-presidents were separated from all specific duties, which were left to divisional managers, and became purely an advisory group on general corporate problems. But there is little evidence that executives in other companies such as those at Standard Oil studied these early M-form models, rather they learned the hard way from experience in their own organizations.[24]

CONTINUING PROBLEMS IN ORGANIZATION

Consequently while a few leading firms were moving toward more sophisticated and effective systems of professional management, the centralized structure with authority in the hands of one or two men remained the general pattern. Even if the chief executive was not a member of the principal owning family, he probably held power by virtue of family confidence in his abilities. Such managerial structures, built on experience rather than theory, the rule all over the world, continued strongly to reflect national characteristics.

In some respects France and the United States represented polar opposites. A French manager or worker demanded the illusion, at least, of individual discretion and did not readily enter into informal teams or groups. To shield French sensitivities from face-to-face confrontation, the source of authority was habitually placed one level above that of the manager giving the order, or, in other words, made bureaucratic or impersonal. In the United States, on the other hand, no good manager or worker was much bothered by face-to-face arguments with immediate superiors. Their authority was regarded as only a temporary situational matter and emotionally less important to the subordinate than good personal relations with some informal company group. Both patterns had their advantages. The French led to well-rationalized, logical structures and a degree of personal isolation that encouraged individual speculation about improvements.[25] The relatively loose American structure put people into unexpected situations and produced unanticipated problems that could lead to useful innovations. Yet, lest this seem to favor the American way unduly, it should be added that operations in the United States were harder to control, and men were more inclined to trust to the sense of a group meeting, rather than to work on a rigorously thought-out pattern.

In any hierarchical organization the making of decisions and their translation into action is a very imperfect process. To begin with the top-level decision is only a choice between those alternatives that are perceived, and perceptions suffer from many personal, cultural, and situational biases. Sampling studies have indicated that about 10 percent of the full content and explanation of a policy is lost each time it is verbally transmitted, so that six levels down from the top the policy line may not be understandable. If the lower executive thinks the decision is an error when applied at his level, his explanation of "why" suffers emasculation on the way back up. This loss from communication technically called "control loss," plus the desire of every manager to have as wide an area of discretion as possible, has led all large companies to delegate authority as far down the line as possible, and to try to avoid single-man stages in transmission of information by the use of multilevel committees. There seems little disagreement among scholars that all bureaucracy is dysfunctional, but since it results, inevitably, from economies in processing and marketing, the problem is one of minimizing the adverse effects.

Big Japanese companies undoubtedly led the world in building an internal company society that bound its members to each other and to the firm and compensated them for failures in promotion. American companies were also active in trying to create loyalty, particularly in the early years of the twentieth century. Company magazines devoted to a mixture of news of departmental achievements combined with social notes became increasingly popular, until by 1925 practically all big firms had them. Athletic teams, appealing mainly to the manual workers, and also clubs for various levels of employees spread, although before 1930, American companies seldom had the equivalent of the attractive vacation resorts or welfare benefits provided by the Japanese. Furthermore, intercompany mobility, almost certainly higher in the United States than elsewhere in the world, undermined the development of emotional loyalty to the firm. Before 1930 there was no theory and little practice of tenure or security, even at managerial levels in the American corporation.

CHANGES IN ASPECTS OF MAJOR CONTROL

In the easy money market of 1898 to 1904 hundreds of firms "went public" by marketing stock issues. But hundreds of others, afraid of letting stock get into the hands of outside interests, raised money only by mortgages, personal solicitation of investors, or the usual reinvestment of earnings. In general, the ones that took a chance and spread their securities widely were never troubled by effective challenges from stockholders opposed to existing management. Had turn-of-the-century executives studied the history of the railroads in this respect, they would have been reassured. While railroad managements were occasionally overthrown by the action of major banking and financial interests they had had nothing to fear from any number of small or independent stockholders.

The rise of public relations counselors at the end of World War I led to the doctrine that stockholders were a protection against adverse public opinion or political regulation and that their ranks should be enlarged as fast as possible. An added advantage was that the larger the number of stockholders the less likely it was that they could be marshaled against management. In tune with the public relations view, new stockholders were often welcomed to the company by a letter from the president; annual reports were made more complete and attractive; and in a few firms special magazines were sent regularly to the shareholding constituency.

As might be surmised, the real power of both stockholders and nonmanagerial directors was declining as companies grew bigger. On a few boards, such as American Tobacco, all members were also officers of the company; and on others, such as General Motors, the ones who were not officers were deeply committed to company affairs. While not yet repudiated altogether, the idea of directors as the elected representatives of the stockholders, confronting management in the interests of ownership, had become obsolete.

In fact, the relationship of stockholders to big companies had come to be an external one, in which they risked some of their capital in hopes the stock would go up and good dividends would be paid. If dissatisfied they would sell their stock, not try to reform the company. On the other side, the chief executives saw stockholders as one of several groups, including employees, suppliers, customers, and bankers who should be kept reasonably satisfied. Raising dividends to let stockholders share in higher earnings was valuable chiefly because it helped in new financing by issues of common stock and also made it harder for financial raiders to accumulate enough shares to overthrow management. A company with a large surplus and stock so cheap that it did not reflect the true value of the company was a target for outside takeovers. The soaring stock market of the 1920s, however, made this possibility only a small threat up to 1930.

In the period before World War I the bankers responsible for the public marketing of a company's securities were generally represented on the board of directors and might exercise ultimate control over financial policy. By the 1920s representatives of investment banks were still frequent on the boards of big companies, but in the easy money market of that decade their power was greatly diminished. Aside from Britain, foreign boards of directors were somewhat differently organized than in the United States and will be discussed in more detail in Chapter Twelve. Certainly in Germany and Japan the banking interests, often closely allied to the management of the firm, were continually a stronger force than in the United States. During the Weimar Republic legislation forced the representation of company labor on boards, with apparently negligible results. As with much minority representation, labor members enveloped by the atmosphere of the board and the demands of responsibility for the financial welfare of the company, followed the sense of the meeting.

THE PLACE OF BIG COMPANIES

While the organizational problems of big business are perhaps the most interesting and certainly the most complex and elusive aspects of American business, since 1900 they have never involved more than a few hundred firms out of a total of millions and, up to 1920, these few companies were largely confined to manufacturing, mining, utilities, and railroad transportation. Even in manufacturing the giant companies did not account for half the value added or employ a majority of workers. As Edith Penrose has written: "There are many businessmen, and very efficient ones too, who are not always trying to make more profits if to do so would involve them in increased effort, risk or investment."[26] Many manufacturers had specialties with limited markets, made relatively secure by lack of big company competition. The most telling advantage from size was in marketing and the resulting influence on price levels in various markets. Up to the 1920s in the rapidly expanding automotive, electrical, and chemical industries the solution of technological problems was of major importance to the economy as a whole, if not to the competitive position of the big companies. But as technological advance came to consist more of a series of engineering or scientific decisions made below the level of top management, the latter was able to devote its thought more exclusively to finance and marketing. In the period after 1930 the development of markets by advertising, design changes, and shrewd pressures on trends in public taste brought big American companies some decades of world leadership.

IV

The Age of
Demand,
1930-1976

10

New Relations Between
Business and Government

T HE AGE OF DEMAND has to be seen against a background of changing relations between business and government. While the social needs of an urban society forced state and local authorities continually to increase spending, the fundamental changes of the 1930s were on the federal level. Instead of acting as a relatively disinterested and remote arbiter of the distribution of private wealth and power, the national government became a major force redistributing income, altering demand, strengthening workers' organizations, and ultimately becoming and remaining the major customer of business.

THE HISTORIC BACKGROUND

Americans had a peculiarly mixed tradition of attitudes toward government. In the late eighteenth and early nineteenth century, in the days of Alexander Hamilton, Gouverneur Morris, or Thomas Willing, the state was probably more regarded as an economic utility controlled by men of property than has ever been the case in any other nation. But this optimistic, rather utopian view faded in the public bankruptcies of the late 1830s and the decline in the calibre of state, local, and federal civil servants. In the next half century Americans came to view their governments as corrupt and inefficient, and hence as bodies whose activities should be strictly limited.

In this later view of the negative character of government, Americans were probably coming closer to that of the common people of most nations. While important businessmen respected the efficiency and prestige of some European administrations, to the small man government was chiefly a tax-collecting power over which he had no control. Freedom for most of the people of the world was an inward state rather than a publicly respected right of action. Americans and a few other people such as the British still clung to the Lockean idea of external personal freedom, but they were increasingly forced to recognize that the right had to be circumscribed by the needs of an urban industrial society.

From the late 1890s on American states passed a goodly number of laws both helping business through franchises and urban improvements and imposing obligations on it for social welfare. Meanwhile, the federal government became a mediator between railroads and shippers, bankers and reserves of cash, big companies and their suppliers or competitors, and a regulator of a few business practices. The sum of such legislation, both state and federal, was considerably less than in the leading foreign nations.

In 1930, compared to our four nations used for reference, both businesses and people in the United States, particularly at the federal level, were comparatively unregulated. The Interstate Commerce, Federal Trade, and Federal Power Commissions, the Antitrust Division of the Justice Department, and the Federal Reserve System were the chief federal agencies affecting business. Tariff and tax policies were, of course, important, but involved no direct control of business practices. Furthermore, during the 1920s, the Antitrust Division and the regulating agencies were all quiescent, while tariffs were kept high and federal taxes low. The force that was to destroy the business-government harmony of the 1920s was unprecedentedly severe depression. World War I had temporarily increased the scope of federal policy, but wartime agencies and regulations were quickly ended. In contrast, the changes brought about by the depression of the thirties and reinforced by World War II became permanent.

DEPRESSION

That the business cycle results from business policies is a truism, but the initial causes may be political and international. The consequent business decisions form a collective movement that the individual firm, even the largest, can do little about. The decisions are made by thousands or even millions of entrepreneurs both at home and abroad, and their affect depends greatly on the structure and operation of government and international finance. From almost every standpoint except national wealth, business in the United States in 1930 was less prepared to cope with depression than was business in the leading foreign nations. Only in Germany, where the credit structure had been disorganized by reparation payments was the depression nearly as severe as in the United States.

In the light of history, the major elements in the disastrous American decline seem to be both occasional and systemic. Under the occasional or accidental heading may be put an income distribution that in the late 1920s encouraged saving at a higher rate than business required for labor-employing expansion. But this had its systemic side also in tax policies that increased saving while checking consumption, and the lack of federal administrative recognition of the need to provide economically useful public works such as highways and bridges, and to maintain more adequate employment. Thus from 1926 to 1929 the economy operated with excess plant capacity and a diminishing rate of investment in new productive facilities.[1]

It was during these same years that the investment policies of banks, discussed in Chapter Nine, and the resulting lack of liquidity grew rapidly worse. On the systemic side, a governmental structure composed of forty-eight separate state jurisdictions that collectively accounted for the largest amount of governmental spending, and a banking structure lacking uniformity, or any adequate central authority, made the United States in time of financial trouble an uncoordinated giant. In addition, lack of provisions for adequate unemployment relief, which were present in the other leading nations, allowed demand to fall more rapidly. In fact national income in Britain and France declined only mildly from 1929 to 1933.

If for the purpose of simplification one focuses on just three factors that by themselves brought ruinous consequences, they would be: the banking crisis from late 1931 to early 1933 caused by a lack of liquidity; the widespread belief, particularly among businessmen, that a capitalist economy must be self-regulating, which inhibited action by such leaders as President Hoover; and a belief among businessmen and politicians of both parties that recovery would arise from deflation of costs to levels that would again tempt investors. American businessmen were not unique in holding these last two beliefs. Except for ardent militarists in Germany and Japan, the worldwide economic cures were thought to be balanced national budgets and strict economy.[2]

The most active force in the downward spiral in both Germany and the United States was banking trouble. In Germany it was a matter of having come to rely on too much short-term credit from foreign nations that could be withdrawn in time of need. Thus the German problem was primarily lack of liquid capital, not a faulty system. In contrast, in the United States there was, if properly mobilized, ample credit but lack of a system that could force collective action. Apart from misguided federal laws and regulations, the particular liquidity problems arising from the investment policies of the 1920s afflicted banks of all sizes. By 1933 more than half of the banks in the United States had suspended payments, and many of the pillars of finance in New York, Chicago, Philadelphia, Detroit, and San Francisco were remaining legally open only because the federal Reconstruction Finance Corporation, hastily created early in 1932, had made them loans or added to their shrunken and sequestered capital by purchasing special issues of preferred stock. Of the banks that failed between 1920 and 1932 only about one in ten ever reopened.[3]

For bankers, both commercial and investment, the winter and spring of 1933 were made still more horrible by the revelations of Ferdinand Pecora, Counsel for the Senate Committee on Banking. Men in the highest financial positions were shown to have engaged in dangerous speculations, a few dishonestly, and many common practices favoring insiders, such as offering them new issues at less than the public selling price. While the banking structure was already collapsing from lack of liquid capital in the weaker banks, the troubles that culminated in the national bank holiday, proclaimed by President Roosevelt on March 5, 1933, were undoubtedly made more severe by a general loss of confidence in the men who only four years before had seemed to be the leaders of American business.

A FORCED MARRIAGE OF
BUSINESS AND GOVERNMENT

Whether the economy of the United States, along with those of the other industrial nations, would have recovered if left alone can never be told. Sir William H. Beveridge said in February 1932: "The way of escape from world crisis . . . is barred and doubly barred by disagreement among economists, and the lack of international will among governments."[4] Yet, regardless of profound economic disagreements, practical politicians in all the nations took some steps to aid "self-regulation," and the United States moved the greatest distance in new regulations of any nation save Germany. The New Deal of Franklin D. Roosevelt was a series of relatively unrelated and opportunistic measures attempting through legislation to provide greater security for workers, farmers, home owners, depositors, and investors. It also tried to move federal taxaion sharply away from tariffs and excises in the direction of progressive personal and corporate income taxes.

All of these measures had some effect on business, but an effort to control wages and prices by a National Industrial Recovery Act (NIRA) of June 1933 temporarily had the most widespread influence. In noting that the United States Chamber of Commerce and various important businessmen played major parts in shaping this legislation, it should be recalled (Chapter Eight) that America had continued to have the most highly competitive market and that as the market contracted to half its normal purchasing power, cut-throat competition became the rule in the majority of industries, those in which no small group of firms could influence prices. In return for granting code authorities, resembling trade associations elected by firms in the industry, the power to fix prices, the friends of labor in Congress and the administration gained Clause 7A, which provided for an eight-hour day, adjusted wage rates, and collective bargaining.

The promise of higher prices from code agreements gave the economy an inflationary boost in the summer of 1933, but from then until the NIRA was declared unconstitutional in May 1935 it is hard to estimate the act's economic effects. The reaction of businessmen, unaccustomed to so much regulation, however, became increasingly adverse. Codes were difficult to agree upon, and in the absence of industry action the law provided for a uniform set of regulations, offered by the president, that aided labor but gave code authorities no power over prices. For any long period such a completely regulated economy would appear to be a near impossibility in a capitalist system, but certainly such hastily improvised codes and regulations as those adopted by the National Recovery Administration (NRA) could not be made to work with reasonable satisfaction. Small business was overwhelmed by rigid rules and paperwork and, necessarily, poorly represented on the code authorities. Medium-sized, highly competitive businesses, such as the larger firms in cotton textiles, received the greatest benefits but feared the long-run effects on labor organization. Big business was not much interested, frequently refused to abide by 7A, and in general relied on their lawyer's well-founded assurances that NIRA was unconstitutional.

One would wish that some useful business lessons had emerged from nearly two years of experience with a far more regulated market than any before or since. But it seems that the experience was much too short and disorganized to produce satisfactory conclusions. The rather uniform effect was merely to increase resistance to government regulation.

At the same time that NIRA was being formulated a number of other emergency laws were hurriedly passed with the combined support of moderates of both political parties, including their adherents in business. While those on high income levels feared the transfer of such functions as relief payments from states and localities (whose taxing power was limited by interstate competition for business) to the federal government (which could not be escaped from by those who remained in the country), the majority reluctantly recognized that these were costs that had to be spread nationally. A city manufacturing heavy producer's goods, for example, with three-quarters of its population out of work, could not pay for its own cost of relief. Neither could one state reopen its banks and free deposits while those surrounding it worked only with money already in circulation and charge accounts.

Consequently "emergency" federal relief, reopening of solvent banks with deposit insurance, guarantees for packaged home and farm mortgages, and support of staple crop prices were all readily adopted. In fact the various laws aimed at achieving greater security in financial markets largely represented proposals advanced by banking or investment banking associations between 1920 and 1929.[5] Some effort was made to include a properly centralized national system in the banking bill, but it was defeated by state banking interests led by Senator Huey P. Long of Louisiana. The business separation of investment and commercial banking and the requirement of more public information regarding new securities were distinctly reformist and regulatory, but in the anxious spring of 1933 they aroused little opposition.

DIVORCE OF BUSINESS AND THE NEW DEAL

Since Roosevelt was a strong president with no special regard for businessmen, it seems inevitable that in so difficult and controversial a situation they should eventually quarrel, but business opposition to the administration mounted only gradually. Coinage of silver, written into the
farm bill, refusal to redeem government bonds in gold, rather than
currency, and the granting to the president of discretionary power to
devalue the dollar by more than 40 percent, all enacted between March
and July of 1933, led to growing criticism in the business press. By the
end of the year complaints against the NRA were also mounting, yet
many commentators place the beginning of strong concerted opposition
with the passage of the Securities Exchange Commission Act in the
spring of 1934, which coincided with the previously enacted date for
divorce of investment from commercial banking.[6]

The New York Stock Exchange and its bond department had always
been a private club administered by a board of directors and controlled
ultimately by the owners of seats that permitted trading on the floor.
The public was allowed to trade through the members by paying a set
fee, but strictly on a buyer beware basis. As late as 1927, of the corporations with securities listed on the exchange, 57 percent failed to
report either gross income or sales.[7] The new law forced every company
whose securities were traded to issue a considerable amount of annual
information in the form of balance sheets and lists of the compensation
of top executives and their holdings in company stock. A number of ways
of manipulating the market were also forbidden.

The new restrictions were somewhat similar to those enacted in
Germany between 1884 and 1897, and in the British Company Acts of
1908 and 1928.[8] Just as in the case of the SEC law the British made the
company responsible for the accuracy of information, but the older German laws provided more stringent regulations of corporate financial
policies.

Whether the SEC bill was picked upon merely as a focal point for
opposition to the general policies of the administration or because of
sympathy with the brokers, protest was substantial and the failure to
influence Congress was a significant indication of the waning political
power of business. The law was probably a slight deterrent to some of
the few companies contemplating new security issues, but it was a boon
to lawyers and public accountants.[9] Within a generation corporations
became reconciled to this scrutiny of their affairs, and the stock

market became more attractive to the average investor than ever before.

In the fall of 1934 the Democrats swept the congressional elections and their leaders viewed the result as a vote for more government underwriting of security. The following spring a large number of reform bills of this type were introduced in Congress and became laws by the summer of 1935. Of these the Social Security Act was merely a catching up with the practice of other industrial nations, one that had been delayed by the combination of the state system and a relatively high standard of living. As with strict national regulation of corporations, Germany had led the way in the 1880s, Britain had followed before World War I, and France had met the problem in the 1920s. In Japan a paternalistic company system and some government aid combined to minimize the need for legislative action. At the time of the passage of the American legislation the number of private pension plans in comparison with the number of medium-to-large firms was negligible, and only a handful of state plans offered any substantial help. Businessmen were more opposed to the unemployment insurance provisions of social security than to old-age pensions. Correctly they saw that workers would be less likely to work hard to avoid layoffs, but in addition business feared the prospect of increasing taxes to finance the system.

A law requiring the simplification of multilevel public utility holding companies, a particularly American phenomenon of the 1920s, aroused a great deal of opposition among business journalists. A more progressive income and inheritance tax bill, nicknamed "soak the rich," was also resented, as was a complicated law of the following year imposing a tax on undistributed profits.

In the long run the tax laws of the 1930s made little difference since they were largely superseded during World War II, but the Banking Act of 1935 made some lasting changes. The overall aim and effect was to vest more power in the Federal Reserve Board and to force more state banks to join the system. The presidentially appointed Board was revised to exclude the treasurer and the controller of the currency and to give the members fourteen-year terms at top government salary levels. The president of the United States could, subject to approval by the board, appoint its chairman, but he could not remove him. More important was the board's power to control the rediscount rate, open market operations, margins on the stock exchange, and, within limits, member bank reserve requirements. In short, instead of being merely a policeman with negative powers, the board became the effective administrative center of a coordinated system. The fact that the heads of the

Reserve banks were now called presidents instead of governors did not conceal their real loss of power in centers such as Chicago and New York.

Herman Krooss wrote that "bankers formed an almost solid phalanx of opposition" to this act.[10] The metropolitan banks objected to the transfer of power from their own district bank to Washington. Country banks affiliated with members objected to control of reserves and stricter regulations. On the other hand, the law created for the first time since 1836 a system with a single national center that could wield some positive power. While it may well be inferior to a strong central bank with branches, the system must be judged more effective than the power vacuum that existed during the preceding century.

The law of 1935 that aroused by far the most united opposition among businessmen and perhaps among the population as a whole was the National Labor Relations or Wagner Act.

GOVERNMENT AID TO UNIONS

While, as noted in the Introduction, this short book cannot explore the complex relations of business with labor, particularly in the absence of much general writing on the subject, the Wagner Act was too basic a change to neglect. Whether because the size of the country greatly increased the costs of organizing, or because of a relatively high standard of living, extreme geographical mobility, or active opposition by management, labor unions had been confined to the skilled crafts, or about 6 percent of the labor force. Following World War I the American Federation of Labor, representing a large majority of the craft unionists, failed to organize large-scale manufacturing and was unable to substantially penetrate service or trade.

Except for a few secret agreements among big corporations, or some regulations agreed to in employer's associations, each company had conducted its own labor relations. From 1900 on, and particularly during World War I, large companies introduced employee representation plans which soon came to be called company unions. Almost no company would voluntarily deal with a national union on a closed shop basis and with some exceptions there was no need to.

Even in the prosperous years of the twenties the AFL lost members, and by 1933 it seemed possible that employers could restrict national unions to just a few skilled crafts. The number of employees in company unions had by then reached a membership of about half the total of those in independent unions.[11] At this juncture Section 7A of NIRA, with its statement "That employees shall have the right to organize and bargain collectively. . . ." threatened to reverse the trend. Medium to large business concerns put on a strong battle through private detective agencies and company police to keep outside union organizers away from their plants. Partially to meet the provisions of the law, many more firms adopted company unions. As a result, while by 1935 there were more union members in relation to employment than in 1929, the major gain had been in controlled company unions, and the fight to prevent industrial unions from spreading into large plants or other branches of business had by no means been lost.

Passage of the Wagner Act in the summer of 1935 seems at first glance to violate the general principle that Congress only passes laws that have some substantial business support. It was a radical act protecting union organizers from either verbal or written interference in their operations on company premises. When the organizers judged they had the support of a majority of the workers they could request the National Labor Relations Board to call for an election by secret ballot. The employer had no right to set the date of an election or to campaign against the union. The organization winning a bare majority of the votes could force the remaining workers to become members, have the employer collect union dues from paychecks, and bargain for all of the workers.

To understand how the act passed Congress with only lukewarm support from the administration, one must take into account the situation in 1935. The United States Supreme Court had just declared unconstitutional half a dozen New Deal measures that interfered less drastically with property rights than did the Wagner bill. Labor lawyers were afraid and business lobbyists confident that passage of the bill would amount only to a meaningless gesture by legislators toward their labor constituents. Under these circumstances few congressmen or senators wanted needlessly to advertise themselves as opponents of national unions, and the bill swept through both houses.

Then to the consternation of a majority of businessmen and conservatives in general, Roosevelt won a landslide victory in 1936 and quickly had a bill introduced to add justices to the Supreme Court. Possibly the threat led to a reconsideration of the national situation by Justice Owen J. Roberts and Chief Justice Charles E. Hughes, but at all events, the Court upheld the Wagner Act in April, 1937, and subsequently the bill was modified so as to leave the supreme bench undisturbed. Not until 1948 would Congress modify, by the Taft Hartley Act, the most objectionable features of the law of 1935, and by this time executives of large manufacturing enterprises had been forced to set up administrative machinery to bargain with organized labor.

The confidence given to union leaders by the reelection of Roosevelt, and the power wielded by the National Labor Relations Board made the United States, which had been far behind Britain, France, and Germany in percentage of independent unionization of its labor force, one of the world leaders. From 1940 on the American figure was over 25 percent, largely confined before 1960 to construction, manufacturing, and transportation. In subsequent years government service became unionized and there was some spread in trade and service, but the total percentage of the labor force organized did not vary greatly.

From the standpoint of management control of shop procedures, and perhaps of productive efficiency, the two-to-three-year union contract, which became the rule, was a disadvantage. Seniority was substituted for the judgment of the supervisor in layoffs or promotions. When inflation was anticipated, which was the case most of the time from 1945 on, a multiyear contract built in a wage-push factor for subsequent years. On the other hand long-term contracts discouraged frequent work stoppages and may, in some instances, have given workers more of a feeling of being a part of the company. Operating on shorter term agreements, Britain was more bothered by strikes than was the United States. British, French, and German unionism had political overtones that made relations more complicated than in the "business unionism" of America. Japanese unions were organized on a company rather than industrywide basis, and hence, in spite of relative independence in decision-making, they could not bring the full resources of a national union into a company dispute. Lifetime employment remained an ideal in Japan, and there was undoubtedly more company loyalty than elsewhere, but the Japanese system was coming more and more to operate on a Western basis of competition in the distribution of earnings between labor, other claimants within the company, and probable consumer reactions to price increases.

BUSINESS ADJUSTS TO DEPRESSION

"'The danger in our situation," warned Dean Wallace R. Donham of Harvard Business School, "lies not in radical propaganda, but in lack of effective business leadership."[12] Failing to subscribe to the new theories of John Maynard Keynes and a few American economists to the effect that potential demand rather than saving was the stimulant for capital investment, businessmen had little positive advice to offer. Both in their own operations and in their pressures on government they preached economy and deflation. The same attitude was generally true of business thinking in France. In Britain, Keynesian ideas were securing recognition, and moderate government spending policies for public works and housing helped to create tolerably good times from 1933 on. The German and Japanese situations are not comparable because in both nations militarists overcame business objections to increasingly large-scale armament programs.

The impact of depression from 1930 to 1933 varied greatly between types of business. Seen in relation to numbers of enterprises, manufacturing, construction, and finance declined by a third or more while trade and service remained nearly at the same level. This did not mean that the latter firms were profitable, but rather that people could not do without food, drugs, doctors, or hospitals but could postpone new purchases of durable goods. Many retailers made no money but managed to feed and house their family that lived and worked in the store.

Within the larger American companies orders were given to curtail all unnecessary expense, which in general meant staff work such as personnel, advertising, public relations, and outside consultants on marketing or engineering. With an eye to the future, companies dropped lower-level employees more quickly than those on an upward course in the management hierarchy. Even in companies where production fell 60 percent or more, valuable skilled employees were retained by spreading work to a three-day a week basis and reducing pay accordingly. Building construction and heavy producers goods were hit so hard that even skeleton staffs could not be retained. In 1932, for example, the famous Baldwin works at Philadelphia turned out only four locomotives.

The sharp increase in demand from mid-1935 to mid-1937, which brought the volume of goods produced up to that of 1929, had only a moderate effect on unemployment. Several factors worked against rehiring. The increased demand was largely for consumer goods, including durables, assembled by the big companies that had plenty of excess capacity. As a result, the construction, producers' goods, financial, and real estate sectors of business were scarcely stimulated. A thousand large companies made profits, while the remaining corporations continued to average losses.[13] Business leaders correctly diagnosed that the upswing was based on government spending. Since they regarded this as wrong and dangerous in principle they thought the prosperity would not last. When, to win some conservative political support, Roosevelt suddenly balanced the budget for 1937–38, with disastrous consequences, the executive's fears proved justified.

From the standpoint of long-run effects on business structure and operation, the effects of the depression period are mixed. In order to employ unused resources and secure a broader base for income, big companies diversified their operations, often acquiring smaller companies that needed help. By 1940 the diversified activity pattern which has characterized big companies since that time had become the rule. During the depression some simplifications were made in the structure of management, but in the long run more elaborate structures returned. The economies during the depression were usually achieved by curtailing activities not absolutely essential at any one time although regarded as necessary costs over the long run.

The need for economy might have stimulated innovation, but, while the number of new ideas applied in business during the decade has not been studied, one suspects that lively demand and the pressures of expansion were stronger stimulants than frugality. Perhaps the greatest business innovation of the decade was the spread of the packaged mortgage repayable in even monthly amounts over a long period. This was the result of cooperation between the Federal Housing Administration and bankers. Without the federal guarantees bankers would have been prohibited by law from issuing mortgages for 90 percent or more of property values. The practice of payment in many equal installments extended a method long used in selling consumer durables to larger capital commitments, and one that was later applied through the withholding system to federal income taxes in 1944, when they reached high levels on a broad base of taxpayers.

NEW TYPES OF GOVERNMENT CONTRACTING

As was the case with losses from the depression, the financial benefits from World War II were very unevenly distributed. Inevitably manufacturers who could convert to or manage new plants for military supplies were bound to get the new business, while activities not connected with the war effort were bound to be curtailed and perhaps lose money. The need for speed of manufacture unquestionably distorted the distribution of profits between large and small companies more than would have been necessary with a more deliberate pace, and in doing so set a continuing business pattern for government contracting.

The big companies of the automotive industry and their subsidiaries producing aviation parts were obviously the group that could most rapidly assemble planes, tanks, and military vehicles. The president assured the primacy of these firms by placing William S. Knudsen of General Motors in charge of the manufacturing aspects of war supply. He told Roosevelt: "What I think we should do . . . is to bury the automobile manufacturers under defense orders—three times as much stuff as they can make with their present facilities."[14] While other big firms were not as neglected as would appear from this remark, orders were given by the Army and Navy Munitions Board to large companies that far exceeded the available materials or the capacity of the firms involved. The result was a national scramble for workers and supplies that left the small manufacturer who was not a subcontractor for any of the big primary firms out in the cold. The government under congressional goading tried to spread contracts to small business, but the whole situation worked against this. To best utilize and distribute scarce supplies the military found it increasingly necessary to make a few prime contractors responsible for coordinating both information and production.[15]

Some types of trade, such as the sale of new automobiles to the general public, disappeared altogether. With construction limited to the needs of the war, contractors in some areas were overwhelmed by demand, while others, especially the smaller ones, had little to do. Urban rents on household properties were frozen, but not those on business locations. Yet, all in all, there was less hardship for businessmen than in the preceding decade. Many proprietors shut down small operations during their military service and later secured government aid in reopening or going into some new activity. Civilian demand from full employment and overtime pay was extremely high, and anyone who could get or produce goods could sell them.

As a result of their wartime connections the military procurement agencies of the government continued in later decades to deal with about 150 prime contractors in the motor, aerospace, electronics, and chemical industries. In aerospace, particularly, government orders became the chief reliance, and such orders were continually subject to modification as technology progressed during the term of the contract.

This military-business relationship led to the creation of company departments staffed with some of the ablest executives solely for the purpose of government contracting. In a typical peacetime deal the military would tell what they wanted and the businessmen, after study, would outline either what the Pentagon could then expect, or what amount of research might be necessary to achieve the desired model. While by 1970 the government was advancing about $15 billion a year for military research, much of the remaining half of total national research expenditure was for work connected with government contracts. The total represented a new dimension in the business activity of defense-related firms, and their successes stimulated more research in other fields, but not always enough to keep ahead of foreign advances in the production of nonmilitary goods.

INCREASED GOVERNMENT REGULATION

Aside from taxes, the government regulation that affects the great majority of American businessmen has been at the state or local level. This has generally come from extensions of the police power in such forms as regulation of the size of trucks, motor vehicle inspection, prohibitions on Sunday business, licensing, zoning, and some antipollution ordinances. The smallest entrepreneurs lacking any staff for keeping track of or lobbying against legislation, operated politically, if at all, through membership in a trade association or some local business organization. In medium-sized firms (those with some fifty to 500 employees) affected by regulatory measures, someone usually has the responsibility of being active in trade or other associations and appearing at municipal or state hearings. But thousands of firms, perhaps the majority, have not been particularly affected by new regulations and have undertaken no activity in politics.

While the New Deal added a number of regulatory commissions and administrations important to the few thousand large corporations operating in the national market, these affected smaller firms only in lines such as broadcasting or air service. Except for civil rights, equal employment legislation, and environmental protection, the federal regulatory agencies changed little after the Taft-Hartley Act of 1948. Consequently large companies through appropriate staff departments have become familiar with the agencies affecting their businesses and have often hired federal administrators whose terms had ended.

The low prestige of government service in the United States in comparison to its high standing in other nations has worked in some opposite directions. The fact that most board or commission members were appointed for only five- or seven-year terms, often as a political reward, has made them susceptible to the lure of a future job in the regulated industry. Yet by failing to make commissionerships attractive to men with high ability, the government has made the federal agencies of limited use for advice, planning, or business leadership. The ninety-year history of the Interstate Commerce Commission illustrates these weaknesses.[16] What planning has been attempted, and neither side has done much, has usually come from company staff bringing pressure on the federal agencies. It should be noted, however, that in France and Japan, where general government planning and leadership have been carried on ably and been important, there has also been much business opposition.[17]

The agencies with which the biggest companies of all types have had to deal are the Federal Trade Commission, the Antitrust Division of the Justice Department and the Internal Revenue Service. The Federal Trade Commission generally tries to prevent practices that will lessen competition or mislead the public. Its docket has been swamped with many more small cases than its top staff can properly attend to, and under the continuous pressure for decisions the importance of any particular case may be overlooked unless strongly represented in some way. There has also been little cooperation between the FTC and the Justice Department regarding the definitions of unfair competitive practices.

The Clayton Act of 1914 was extended by the Cellar-Kefauver Act of 1950 to cover mergers that might, although well short of creating monopoly, be "against the public interest." In general, antitrust actions attacking specific practices or mergers have been far more frequent since 1940 than in the first fifty years of the antitrust laws. Experience had taught lawyers and economists both in and out of government that except for clear cases of dominance by one firm, the situation should be assessed realistically to see whether or not inefficient restraints were imposed on the entry of new competitors or on the marketing of products.[18]

Federal tax policy, monitored by the Internal Revenue Department has become extremely important for the large firm. During World War II an excess-profits tax was imposed that ultimately rose to 95 percent on earnings above those calculated as normal. The latter was a rate taken from earnings during a base period, and this vitally important figure had to be arrived at by agreement between company and government accountants. The World War II excess-profits tax was ended in 1946, but a new one of similar character with a 30 percent maximum was imposed during the Korean War. In tax laws after 1945 corporations were allowed to spread losses over a number of years as an offset to profits. This made companies that had for some correctable reason sustained a temporary loss, attractive purchases for corporations with large or particularly with "excess" profits. Since the general level of corporate income taxation was around 50 percent, taxes had become a major element in profits and accounting a major department of any large company.

SOCIAL ASPECTS OF DEMAND

As demand came to be widely recognized as the most important element in business forecasting and in plans for production, the government became further involved in controlling it. Social needs that could not be met by any business at a profit increased in volume and came to be put on a par with the needs that could attract enterprise. Inexpensive or free higher education, care of the aged, unemployment relief, lower-income housing, and passenger transportation by rail represented a very mixed group of services. They shared in common the fact that they could not be successfully carried on by business at a profit. The number of such activities has not only been growing, but their relative costs have increased. Community colleges, for example, represent a very large new expenditure for public education, and passenger rail service of all types gains steadily as a government expense. In major cities the costs of services are currently exceeding available sources of revenue.

In all the economically advanced nations industrialization was creating integrated societies with many pressing demands that could not be met through the mechanisms of the market. Hence private business has had to become reconciled to playing a relatively decreasing role, particularly in supplying services, although the total value of goods and services produced for profit was still advancing.

In adjusting to situations in the later twentieth century some of the problems of the nineteenth have continued. The United States, lacking the prestigious civil service of all four of our comparative nations, and fragmented by state jurisdictions, probably carries on government activities less efficiently. The government operation of telegraph, telephone, airline, and railroad systems, for example, has a century or more of experience behind it in Germany, France, and Japan. In America the first steps in the direction of wider spheres of government action were only being undertaken, with proper doubts and misgivings, in the 1970s.

11

Marketing Shapes Management

IMPROVED TECHNOLOGY in the nineteenth century had led businessmen and scholars all over the world to glorify production. In all the leading nations, and particularly in France, there still were journalists and politicians who regarded trade as parasitical. Somehow the products of factories should reach consumers free of costs for advertising and distribution, and if some small expenses were necessary they should be regarded as losses to society.

These ideas had their origins no doubt first in the fact that during the centuries of handicraft production, trade for the small customer had usually been simple and local; and second, in the paradoxically opposite fact that the importing and exporting merchants had trade well-organized and were prepared to both stimulate and distribute the early products of machinery. While new technology could be seen and marveled at, new trade devices were known only to experts.

CONTINUED WORSHIP OF PRODUCTION

Although marketing became clearly the major problem for most American businesses by the 1920s, the language of factory productivity continued to dominate business speeches and popular articles. One reason for this persistence is that production was a problem within the firm, where lines of communication and authority were clear, while marketing involved relations with the outside world in which the elements to be negotiated were uncertain and often uncontrollable. A chief executive could usually talk on how much his company had improved the current product over an earlier version, but he might not be so sure of the marketing network.

Another reason for the persistence of plant orientation was that by having mechanized large-scale production earlier than the other nations, the United States still had technological leadership in such operations as the handling of heavy materials, the use of very big or multiple machines, electrical generating, transmission and communication, and some specialties associated with the mass production of automotive equipment. The fact that the United States in 1940 lagged in the processes for many chemicals and pharmaceuticals, optics, electronics, and metallurgy was easy to forget.

THE SHIFT TOWARD MARKETING

The shift in business activity toward marketing, which was first noticeable in the 1920s and was still continuing in the 1970s, took many different forms. As American and world business adjusted to more normal routines in the middle fifties the trend became obvious statistically. Next to services, including those of government, wholesale trade grew most rapidly in percentage of national employment between 1955 and 1970, while manufacturing declined. The real shift was undoubtedly greater than indicated by the census, because "manufacturing" firms came to house more personnel in marketing and fewer in fabricating. Another indication was a doubling between 1954 and 1967 of the number of jobbers, agents, and so forth classed by the census as merchant wholesalers. Since about three quarters of producer's goods continued to move directly from one fabricator to another, most of the increase represented a response to increased consumer demand for more and more special types and brands of goods. In fact, wholesale agencies were tending to become relatively smaller but more varied in their specialties as big companies increased sales directly to retailers.

Within the large company selling directly to retailers, the qualitative shift in emphasis is clearer than what can be gleaned from statistics. The automotive industry was not only America's largest business by 1930, but its sales at retail were and have remained second only to food in the nonfinancial sectors. Here the emphasis in the first two decades of the century was on producing reliable cars. The great early success of the Ford Model T stemmed from its reliability and low maintenance cost rather than from initial price or fuel economy. On the same basis Buick, a medium-priced car, was the mainstay of General Motors. But during the mid-1920s the virgin market was pretty well exploited, and new purchases were increasingly made by those who already owned a car. Many customers were not buying to secure automobile transportation, but only because the new model was attractive enough to compensate them for the cost. Assemblers were no longer trying to sell the automobile, but their particular brand of automobile.[1]

The basic promotional device was an annual change in models that both made the new car more attractive and proved its newness to all interested observers. Since the automobile was more of a status symbol in these decades than in the society of the 1970s, obvious newness was an important factor in promoting sales. Minor improvements in technology were continuous but less obvious after 1925, and because basic changes in design were costly, most annual differentiations were in trimming and minor restyling. The marketing art came in estimating what investment in retooling would achieve the maximum net return from sales. It was not, of course, a simple matter of economic calculation. Comparative sales depended on public taste, which might be poorly estimated by the ablest designers and chief executives. Both Buick and Chrysler in the late twenties and mid-thirties, respectively, made costly misjudgements as to how much change in appearance the public would accept in a single year.

During these same years of increasingly competitive selling between a diminishing number of large assemblers, their relations with retail distributors became more tightly supervised. The manufacturer was in a strong position because the advertising that was actually important for sales was largely paid for by the maker, and only the latter could grant a franchise for an area. Consequently, starting with those of

General Motors in the mid-twenties, as described in Chapter Eight, dealers had to submit to many types of company scrutiny.

These earlier automobile marketing practices resembled the system of franchising that developed after World War II, particularly in motels and restaurants. In these latter cases the property-owning or leasing company could grant a franchise that required the holder to maintain certain physical facilities and sell foods that would be supplied to him. In return he received mandatory accounting and managerial help, and drew customers largely as a result of the national advertising and reputation of the chain.

As proprietors working on strictly controlled franchises became more numerous, the extent of medium-sized free enterprise in the United States came increasingly to depend on whether or not one classed these regulated entrepreneurs as independent businessmen. A strong argument may be made for the fact that such operators were only submitting to somewhat more of the same controls that money lenders had always sought to impose on their business debtors. Banks for example, had wanted to see balance sheets, equipment renters wanted to inspect, and companies advertising national brands wanted to advise on the display of their merchandise. The franchise holder was not limited as to his profits, he hired and fired his employees, and dealt exclusively with his customers. By supplying valuable property and equipment the franchiser enabled a man with small capital to enter what might turn out to be a highly profitable business, while the capital contributed by the local operator was an aid to expanding the business. Some successful automobile dealers, for example, became very rich men.

CONTINUITIES IN BUSINESS STRUCTURE

In all business activities, size conferred an advantage in marketing, but most so in manufacture or assembling of consumer goods. In such production the concentration of the dollar volume of output in the hands of one or two hundred firms gradually increased, although general indexes of concentration based on the number of industries with a dozen or less dominant firms have slightly decreased since 1929.[2] With ever-wider diversification into new types of production the whole question became confusing. A very large company such as Du Pont might have only a small share of the market in a particular industry, yet the division or subsidiary was backed by the marketing and development resources of the parent company.

In 1954 the 200 largest industrial companies, rated by dollar volume of sales, accounted for about 38 percent of the value added to goods by manufacture; by 1970 the figure was 42 percent. Yet in both years there were more than 200,000 other manufacturing firms, of which well under 1 percent had gross revenues of over $10 million a year. A large part of these enterprises with a dozen to 500 or more employees sold to other manufacturers. To cite an extreme example, in airplane production a big prime contractor might buy from over 13,000 small manufacturers. A more normal relationship in the assembling of complex products would be for the giant company to buy from a few hundred primary suppliers, who in turn might buy components from other firms.

PROBLEMS OF MANUFACTURERS

Since few small firms wanted to risk price warfare with much larger ones, the thousand or so companies that put their brand names on the final articles normally set prices. Among these big marketers pricing was an undefined process in which various factors such as costs, market trends, probable decisions by competitors, and special appeal of the company product had to be tentatively balanced. No final decision was ever more than an informed guess. Markets were stratified or segmented in odd and ever-changing ways. Large companies found on occasion that the same product sold better at a higher price than a lower price. Severe problems might attend the marketing of unfamiliar products. One of the very largest firms in the food industry was unsuccessful in entering the "fine food" market, for example, basically because the giant was "entering an area where these resources (of size) were of no great advantage and its limited experience was a clear deficit."[3]

Perhaps the most important determinant of business structure was the capital necessary for successful entry. This might vary all the way from a negligible sum for financing manufacture in one's home, to unknown billions in the case of motors or telecommunication. If the firm in control of marketing could buy more cheaply from many competitive suppliers it was not likely to extend ownership further down the line of production. The shop run by an efficient proprietor was likely to have lower costs than one bearing the overhead of a large corporation and run by a salaried supervisor. In fields with rapidly developing technology the looser structure and greater face to face contact of the medium-sized firm was widely regarded as an advantage.[4] General Motors, for example, had accounting methods for carefully checking whether particular components could be bought or produced more cheaply.

Ideally, the small manufacturer wanted to make some component or assembly that required careful workmanship and supervision and sold directly to other manufacturers, that is, to find a secure niche in the process of assembly. Not only could his personally known workers perform the operations more reliably than those on a large assembly line, but if he had half a dozen steady customers he avoided most of the expenses and uncertainties of marketing to a wide public. If he could make his product distinctly different from and superior to others, and was able to adopt improvements, so much the better, but if he was a wise businessman he might neither desire nor attempt to expand to other lines.[5]

Needless to say many such businessmen were engineers, but others with technical knowledge, such as skilled workers and men transferring capital from some other venture, might also succeed. A few years in the employ of a company buying the components might also serve as a training school. This emphasizes that business qualifications and connections were as important as knowledge. Knowing the right people, especially local bankers, attending association meetings, avoiding unnecessary investment, and most of all inspiring confidence in employees were almost essential to the initial success of the great number of manufacturing enterprises with under 50 workers.

An inevitable problem of small business of all types was the variety of talents required in the original entrepreneur. A man good at raising capital might be poor at routine operations; one with imagination in marketing might not understand technology. Aside from the manufacture of machine parts, the more important elements were usually the ability to raise capital, to apportion expense, and to secure customers, and in trade and service these were vital.

Thus the business abilities and decisions essential to permanence or expansion in most manufacturing firms were much the same as they had been ever since the Business Revolution: careful husbanding of capital, accounting that produced the proper information, and a wise choice of products, markets, and customers requiring credit. If a local or special market was to be exceeded, selling agents and relations with wholesalers were necessary but introduced new problems. This might be necessitated by a change in the local market or demand for a new type of product. When a firm was big enough to have several executives, personal compatibility was nearly essential.[6] Since most firms, even in the mid-twentieth century, started as family enterprises, it took a wise majority stockholder to exclude his sons or brothers from top management in favor of abler outsiders.

TRENDS IN DISTRIBUTION

In wholesale trade there were few essentially new types of business change. The process of increasing specialization, which had been going on from the 1790s, continued, stimulated by the literally explosive increase in the varieties of goods. In 1967 there were a few more firms in wholesale trade than in manufacturing, with sales of $206 billion through such middlemen, as compared to $157 billion for sales to retailers through manufacturers' branches, and $61 billion through agents or jobbers who did not store goods. Wholesale trade was the second most rapidly growing major category, and employment in this sector increased by 36 percent in the fifteen years preceding 1970.

Wholesaling divides in its type of activities rather sharply between the following: those who deal with undifferentiated basic commodities such as grains, fibers, or metals sold on exchanges; those dealing in perishable products such as food or drugs; and those handling manufactures that deteriorate only from style changes. The first group had to have skill in buying and hedging in goods for future sale, and usually delivered to processors. The wholesale office handling perishables was more like that of the old-style merchant dealing with jobbers, agents, or retailers and having continually to assess credit risks. The third group handling nonperishables had much the same problems, but with less necessity for continuous movement of inventory, they could act as stabilizers of their markets. All wholesales continued to perform the important function of assessing local credit seekers and shouldering the risks. In spite of 2,000 credit rating agencies operating in the nation by the 1960s, plus the older mercantile credit firms such as Dun & Bradstreet, a perceptive area wholesaler could judge the immediate financial conditions of his local customers better than a factory salesman armed only with reports.[7]

It cannot be emphasized too often that while the internalization of marketing in the big firm allowed for stronger and more varied sales campaigns, the cost for most products ran higher than if the items had proceeded through conventional multilayer distributors. Each of the latter would be specialists at operation in certain markets and would have to quote competitive rates that ran lower than for the cost of the same operation conducted by less knowledgeable or hard-driving employees of a large bureaucracy.

Retailing and service have continued to include most of the smallest businesses. In the former, supermarkets increased during the depression, and became central to the shopping centers that multiplied rapidly in the suburbs after World War II. The associations of retailers on various bases with single large wholesalers, which had checked chain store expansion in the 1920s, proved less effective against chains of super-markets. The sales of multiunit chains accounted for 42 percent of retail sales in 1954 and 47 percent by 1967.

Yet there may be a hard core of small retail and service enterprise that can permanently compete with large companies. *Time* magazine, in its issue of July 28, 1975, noted the number of supermarkets made vacant by depression, together with the "mini-markets" that had sprung up nearby. As discussed in Chapter Eight, the labor costs of shops staffed by proprietors and family members are less than those hiring on the market. In addition, hours of work are more flexible, some living expenses may be combined with the business, and personal relations are estab-lished with customers. For the "mom and pop" enterprises, assets in relation to debts appear to have been more important than profits. While the average life of such small retail or service enterprises has been around five years or less, failure often meant taking a paid job for a while and then trying again. In background and education these small proprietors are a fair cross section of the population, but they are over the average age.[8] In an exhaustive government study made in 1938, the authors found savings from wages the most important source of initial retail store capital, and the amount saved was usually inadequate for a proper start. The authors concluded that there had been little change in eighty years in the average life span of small business.[9]

FINANCING SMALL BUSINESS

The Reconstruction Finance Corporation (RFC), established in 1932 for emergency financing of business that could not raise sufficient money in the private market, remained as an institution making loans to businesses that seemed desirable for the national welfare. Such loans were very hard for small enterprises to secure and by 1953 seemed unnecessary for large corporations. The RFC ended in that year and was succeeded by the Small Business Administration (SBA). This agency could make or guarantee 90 percent of private loans up to $150,000 (otherwise hard to place) for enterprises of not more than 100 to 1,000 employees, depending on the type of business. Thirteen regional offices were opened, and since the loans could apply to more than 90 percent of all business firms, one would have expected important results. But like the RFC before it, the agency was inclined to apply conventional financial tests to applicants and the difference between those of the SBA and of a commercial bank or credit company covered relatively few firms.[10] Encouraged by SBA loans equal to half their capital, some 360 finance companies had been formed by the early sixties and had lent about $300 million to small business. Both the SBA and some of the finance companies professed to favor ethnic, particularly black enterprises, but the flow of funds in this direction was disappointing. For all purposes, the SBA had only guaranteed a little over $2 billion in loans by 1971.

From 1958 on Congress gave special tax advantages to small business and the companies financing it. Firms with less than ten shareholders and a million dollars in assets were exempt from part of the regular corporation tax, the stockholders could deduct their share of business losses up to $25,000 from personal income taxes, and the firm could take accelerated depreciation on new equipment costing less than $10,000. In 1960 these advantages were estimated to save these "small" companies $250 million a year, which seems large, but dwindles in proportion to the tens of thousands of firms in this central segment of American business.[11]

How much these mild measures of support accounted for the continuing vigor of small- to medium-sized business in the United States is hard to estimate. Everywhere in the world small enterprise was the prevailing form. The Japanese descendants of the *zaibatsus* subcontracted much of their production, while trade and service remained largely in the hands of moderate-sized single units. The same was even more the rule in Britain, France, and Germany. The continuities in size relationships often in the face of big company competition seemed to indicate a state of perhaps precarious equilibrium between the many internal managerial economies of the small company and the processing and marketing advantages of size.

THE GENERAL BUSINESS STRUCTURE

While in the United States a few thousand big companies accounted for about half the dollar volume of final payments, the other half, greater up to 1970 than the total money volume in any other nation, was done by some 12 million proprietorships, partnerships, and corporations. Of these, 9.4 million proprietorships accounted for about 15 percent of business receipts. Partnerships numbered a little under a million and accounted for only about 6 percent, while the 1.7 million "small" corporations accounted for the remaining 79 percent.[12]

By far the most rapidly growing sector of business in both size of income and number of enterprises was service. Motels, auto and other repairs, and amusements or recreational facilities were all rapidly increasing in both categories. But their rates of increase were completely overshadowed by the total of various business associations and consulting services. From 1950 to 1970 this minor census category grew over 300 percent in number of participants, with "medical and health" services as its only close rival. In comparison with the growth in the total labor force of about 30 percent, the service group as a whole expanded employment some 50 percent.

Employment of over 1.6 million people in services to business in 1970 calls attention to how many small to medium-sized organizations are trade or professional associations, or agencies for various types of business advice. For example, in the field of advertising there were: the American Association of Advertising Agencies, the American Communications Association, the American Marketing Association, the Association of National Advertisers, the Advertising Research Foundation, the Association of Radio News Analysts, the Research Society of America, the American Society of Composers, Authors and Publishers, the Institute of Radio Engineers, the National Association of Broadcast Engineers and Technicians, the Radio Directors' Guild, the Radio Executives Club, the Radio Research Council and doubtless a half dozen more that might fit their services to the advertising category.

As a result of the multiplication of associations and agencies, with their various publications, it was no longer possible for a busy executive to keep up with this vast output of published material. Intake of such information had to be delegated to staff men who would decide on the few items worth passing on to line officers. In the small firm that lacked staff employees the enormous literature might never be read. In the hundreds of thousands of really small businesses marketing only locally, the proprietors generally did not even belong to a trade or professional organization.

LARGER COMPANIES

A basic dilemma of modern business is that there are undoubtedly economies of scale in purchasing and marketing, but beyond a certain size there occur diseconomies of scale in the complicated management needed to carry on big operations. As of the 1970s this was still an unsolved dilemma of world business. The problem affected big business in all the leading nations, but since the United States had the largest companies, it was forced to be a leader in seeking solutions, and hence its domestic experience up to almost 1970 may be surveyed independently from that of Europe. The thesis that in the long run it is better to be a follower than a leader when it comes to adjusting to problems of size may have been borne out.[13] France, in particular, was able to continue regional selling by medium-sized companies until the 1950s and 1960s, by which time the basic American adjustments to large-scale marketing were well known.

Yet, even in 1976, the process of adjustment was still proceeding in all nations, and it was by no means certain that the paths being pursued anywhere were the correct ones. In marketing, for example, a desire to win customers by unusual food packaging had produced 2,500 different package sizes, whereas the European Common Market nations had agreed upon a small number with a great saving in handling and shelving. American marketing may well give too much attention to elaborate management structure and expert advice on catching the eye of the fast shopper and not enough to basic matters of quality and efficiency.[14] That the Europeans may be doing better than they realize is suggested by the drop in the United States income per capita to about sixth place in the world.

Undoubtedly either experience or more knowledge of social science can in the course of future decades contribute to the evolution of processes and an organizational structure in all leading nations that will conduct large-scale operations without the usual losses of bureaucracy. But such progress has been so slow and uncertain that experienced executives wrote of the "management jungle" of the 1970s, while students of organizational innovation saw their work as just beginning.

The basic problems were the same as when the railroads first expanded into long lines in the 1850s (Chapter Five). No executive could absorb and utilize more than so much information, called by organizational theorists "bounded rationality"; each level of management produced a certain degree of "control loss," or a loss of clarity in orders transmitted from above; and each manager was engaging in "subgoal pursuits," or trying to satisfy his own egoistical aims as far as his discretion in decision-making would permit. The ideal organization, therefore, would have only essential information fed to the top executives, have a minimum of hierarchical levels, and design each managerial job so that the normal goals of its occupant and the welfare of the company would be the same.

The inability of any single company to patent or keep secret an innovation in organization was a deterrent to investing large sums of company money in supporting research.[15] Consequently, as long as they all suffered from about the same degree of inefficiency in the use of human resources, big companies competed on equal terms. Therefore while a very few giants such as Du Pont and General Motors in the 1920s (Chapter 10), Westinghouse in the 1930s, and General Electric in the 1940s and 1950s devoted special study by chief executives to these problems, in general, companies readjusted their structure only under severe external pressures from the market.

The depression of the thirties was such an external stimulant to organizational restructuring. Big companies that had grown haphazardly generally had such activities as production, purchasing, finance, or marketing headed by a vice-president, and these men joined with the president in running the company. These U-form companies in the 1930s found that they had both surplus capacity and surplus officers. Since recovery was anticipated, the best solution seemed to use the idle resources in men and space to make products for new markets. When this was attempted, the demands of new types of marketing operations led, as it had at Du Pont after World War I, to the setting up of special divisions. Thus diversification and the adoption of the multidivisional or M-form went hand in hand. World War II had the same effect but for opposite reasons: new divisions were created to process and distribute the new products demanded by the government.

As explained in connection with the Sloan plan at General Motors in 1921, the aim of the M-form was to create a central office staffed by men whose sole responsibility was for the welfare of the company as a whole, and to supply them with the staff necessary for collecting and processing what appeared to be the requisite information. In theory each division operated as a separate company whose management was judged by financial results. The central office staff might offer suggestions to managers within the divisions, but mandatory intervention from above was to be kept to a minimum so that the division alone could be held responsible for its profits or losses.

The later history of General Motors, however, illustrates two abiding weaknesses of the theory as put into practice. One was present from the start. The divisions were so numerous and so big that several needed a sub-M-form for their own complex management. Hence there still remained a loss of control brought about by transmission of information and instructions through many levels of bureaucracy.[16] Sheer size also brought problems to the central office. The input of information was so great that the "office" became in fact a large hierarchical organization of special assistants, vice-presidents, committees, and such top officers as treasurer, president, vice-chairman, and chairman.

The second weakness at GM was either the unwillingness or inability of the central office to give true autonomy to the divisions. They had to have their annual budgets accepted, to have investments of more than a relatively small amount approved, and had to justify their purchasing policies. Meanwhile, as we have seen (Chapter Ten), central office representatives such as Sloan traveled around acquiring information from men down the line and checking on divisional marketing policies with their dealers. By 1950, the divisions had become mainly convenient structures for the conduct of routine operations, and Sloan himself thought that General Motors had perhaps become too large.

This remark by the aged chairman before a congressional committee illustrates another aspect of organizations. If given a chance they grow readily, but there is no practice or theory of splitting-off the ownership of profitable subdivisions, save by prosecution under the antitrust law, and such action is not normally instituted to promote internal business efficiency.

A more advanced stage in the development of the central office as the distributor of financial and managerial resources between semi-autonomous divisions came, by the late 1950s, to be called the con-glomerate. As distinct from the M-form, in which diversification took the form of new divisions to market somewhat allied products, the conglomerate bought control of companies on a purely financial basis. In one sense this was a logical extension of the theory of the central office as a specialized money market whose resources were more re-stricted than those of the outside world of finance, but whose officers had far better access to information. The efficiency of the M-form stemmed from the possibilities of reallocating resources from a branch of the industry that was contracting to one that was expanding, but the range of choice for a big conglomerate that owned companies in many different types of business was much greater. Furthermore, the existence of both M-form corporations and conglomerates (there is no precise distinction) prowling through the corporate forest looking for firms that might want to sell out, or ones that could be made more profitable by stronger management or acquired for less than their real worth, has undoubtedly given a competitive vitality to the market for corporate securities.

On the other hand, if in fact this central office of the conglomerate does not know enough about a business to improve its efficiency and has merely purchased it for a temporary security manipulation or a tax write-off, the purchased firm and the economy in general may be poorly served. Furthermore, this appears as of the 1970s to be organizational innovation in the wrong direction. More expert central office handling of a limited amount of information, kept down by restrictions on the scope of activities, seems more desirable than unlimited expansion that must eventually pile office on office and result in decreased effectiveness in both processing information and in exercising essential controls. It should be remembered that "in an information-rich world, most of the cost of information is the cost incurred by the recipient."[17] The fifty-cent business review may consume a hundred-dollar's worth of the reader's time.

By concentrating on new corporate developments in the last two generations the discussion has inevitably exaggerated their aggregate importance in the world of business. Since all big companies are still only a minority sector of either enterprise or employment, and companies in an M- or conglomerate form are not always the rule even among the very large, they are far from representative of American or, for that matter, foreign business. Companies producing relatively undifferentiated products in metals, rubber or petroleum have either preserved a U-form or have adopted ad hoc mixtures of centralized and divisional structures. This is also true of companies producing a variety of products but selling only to other manufacturers. In such companies product development and quality may be the most important duties of management. Both groups of companies, however, underline how important the problems of diverse types of marketing were in creating the M-form.

There has always been a widely shared opinion among executives that the problems of their company are unique. Therefore, little company time has been spent in studying purely organizational changes in unrelated corporations. Also, in practical management theoretical neatness plays a minor role. Some companies have a U-form for domestic operations and an M-form for foreign branches. Others have an M-form based on domestic regions rather than type of product. Supermarket chains tend to have regional divisions but central purchasing, whereas Woolworth and J. C. Penney have scarcely altered their U-form organizations. In the late 1930s, Shell Oil set up two central offices coordinated only through committees of the board of directors. Some companies like United States Steel tried a modified M-form from the 1930s to 1950 and then returned toward more centralized control.[18] Usually organizational change occurred not as the result of continuous research and planning, but rather when a strong new chief executive came to power. One generalization, however, can apply to all large companies: there has been a steady growth during the twentieth century in the relative number of middle managers, and the United States has probably been the leader. It should also be remembered, however, that productivity per worker, of all types, has increased greatly.

MANAGEMENT THEORISTS

The idea that each company's problems can only be understood by insiders goes far to explain the lack of impact on chief executives of the theories emanating from business schools or professional associations. The men in the big companies who read the theoretical literature had, in general, no power beyond offering advice. They also soon came to understand that their reputations were not helped by their becoming known as advanced theorists. When advising line officers who wielded the power, it was best to wrap theory in a cover of anecdotal experience and to offer such advice very tentatively.

Since both business schools and professional associations multiplied rapidly in the 1920s and have continued to increase since then, the American literature on management is voluminous, and since one of the ablest thinkers in the field wrote in 1972, "We do not understand enough . . . to have developed comprehensive theories," one can scarcely blame busy practical men for skirting this theoretical mountain. Yet for the business historian the chance that some of the theories of the future may have had their origins in this formative period makes a brief summary seem valuable.

The academic excitement caused by Taylor, Follette, and Mayo in the period before 1930 had, as we have seen (Chapter Ten), largely to do with plant supervision. Only in the thirties did books begin to appear on the structural relations of big company management. Of these, Chester I. Barnard's *The Functions of the Executive* (1938) had the most lasting influence. To the theories of administration advanced by Henri Fayol in France, Bernard added a more developed understanding of social psychology. Like Fayol, he had been a business executive, and also like contemporary French theorists, he emphasized the relatively small number of subordinates with whom an executive could have proper interchange of information.[19] While in a general way books on the structure of management can be separated from those on its psychological problems, Barnard's book temporarily brought the two schools together.

Herbert A. Simon and his disciples carried on a primarily social science approach, which because of its application to all bureaucracies has come to be called organizational theory. Chester Barnard wrote an introduction to Simon's *Administrative Behavior*, published in 1947. As expanded in numerous later works, Simon's writing has called attention to the almost infinite complexity of human relations in any large organization, and the tendency of the company environment to limit the executive's perception of reality. Simon's greatest contribution may turn out to be the undermining of simplistic structural theories.

More influential in the world of business has been the work of Peter F. Drucker, which first attracted attention in *The Practice of Management* in 1954. Taking a broad, nondogmatic view of the problems of business companies, both internal and external, he restored an emphasis on economic goals that the extreme exponents of the human relations approach were neglecting. His insistence on the profit objective in management made him a favorite among the few businessmen who read theoretical discussions. Justifiable pragmatism in a discipline where accepted theory is scant is expressed in his admonition: "To substitute typical functions for an analysis of the activities actually needed is dangerous mental laziness."[20] His avoidance of elaborate hypotheses regarding organizational behavior attests the intelligent man's judgment of the earliness of the stage of thought about such complex mixtures of art, science, and human emotion. Or, put another way, perhaps when men have solved the problems of the large organization they will simultaneously have solved the same problems in society as a whole.

Efforts to bring more analytical thinking into the performance of middle management have led from 1939 on to the advocacy of various systems designed to make sure that important factors were not overlooked. Generally designated by letters that stand for parts of the problem (such as PERT for program evaluation and review technique), these systems essentially urge the middle manager to do careful thinking. "Operations Research" has involved more collection of data, particularly on elements external to the firm such as the market, and more use of computers to put the data in forms useful for management.[21] A major difficulty in this kind of approach is the cost in time. A complete simulation model may take three years of staff time to prepare and in the end not prove particularly useful. As a result the use of systems and mathematical approaches declined at some large companies in the hard times of the late 1960s and early 1970s.

But none of the systems proposed by the scholars in business schools could relieve top management of the necessity of making decisions based on inadequate knowledge, of acting more as artists than scientists. As with generals in the confusion of battle, they had to rely for success as much on the errors of their competitors as on the accuracy of their own guesses.

INTERNALIZING EDUCATION

Vocational training programs in business companies go back to the mid-nineteenth century, but intensive training in management only spread widely after World War II. As one executive put it, emphasis changed from getting more out of workers to getting the most out of management. By 1953, *Fortune* noted that some companies were spending as much as $10,000 per trainee and that the average was about $2,500—then substantially more than the highest business school tuition. General Electric, one of the leading advocates of advanced training, was stocking its management pool with a thousand graduates a year who spent some fifteen months in what was in effect a company college.[22] At Standard Oil (New Jersey) emphasis on training programs was said to be the most important postwar development in management.[23]

In a few big companies, such as General Electric, training courses and seminars were held for executives up to the highest levels of middle management, while men on the rise were also encouraged to enroll for graduate work and secure doctorates from major universities. Thus after graduating from college and joining the company, a successful manager might be a student for some twenty years. At the same time the promising younger men were shifted from plant to plant and division to division, so that if ultimately they reached central office level, they would have had experience in production, finance, and sales.

But the system produced many problems that had not been satisfactorily solved by the 1970s. Shifting the locale and duties of managers every two to four years upset their family life and prevented the development of intimate work teams in which the members knew each other's eccentricities and capacities. It also made it difficult for men two or more levels below to know their ever-shifting superiors. To be sure, not everyone went through the whole process. When a man seemed to have reached a level well suited to his abilities, he might be kept at that post or given the option to remain.

In major German industrial firms, mainly in the Ruhr section, a policy of training and movement was also pursued, but in France, particularly, there was much less shifting. Regional executives were generally kept in their provinces and central office men were often educated in Paris and stayed there. British and Japanese firms tended toward the American system of managerial transfers without the added feature of higher business education, and with the mitigating factor that plants and offices were far more geographically concentrated. Aside from science and engineering, higher education for business was not highly regarded in any of the four foreign nations, and there was such a lack of prestigious local curricula that many of their promising young managers came to the United States for courses or an MBA. Whether in fact higher education for business was making a valuable contribution, the language, structural forms, and marketing practices taught in the leading American schools were winning acceptance around the world.

ACCOUNTING PROBLEMS BECOME MORE VITAL

It would be logical to suppose that as business education became more widely accepted and specialized, and financial analysts became more familiar with every type of situation, accounting would solve its problems of recording and disclosure and become internationally a rather standardized procedure. But, unfortunately, the problems of the nineteenth century never disappeared: accounting could answer a wide range of questions but not all questions with a single method. Or, in the language of the profession, "The Problem is . . . associating particular accounting goals with specific means of attainment." And the variety of goal-oriented questions that management, government, and investors asked of accountants increased over time.[24]

Up to 1933, American accounting practice had been much more a voluntary matter than in the other leading nations, which were divided between those countries having specific clauses written into company acts and those issuing uniform charts to be followed in preparing audits. In the United States the Securities Act of 1933 and the more thoroughgoing Securities and Exchange Commission Act of the next year, while applicable only to the small number of corporations with publicly held stock, tended to standardize accounting practice. Increased corporation and personal income taxes from 1935 on made the Internal Revenue Bureau an important general arbiter of what constituted income. But in all, American theory and practice probably remained less formulated than in nations such as Germany or Japan.

Up until the low point of the depression in 1932, the old British traditions of detailed analysis of records still prevailed, but the depression stimulated management to think more of accounting as a means of suggesting policies that would save costs, and also to be content with sampling procedures that would save auditing expenses. In fact, there may be a built-in or inevitable contradiction between the theorists' or stockholders' desire for complete disclosure (probably an impossibility) without too much regard to cost, and management's desire for only those figures that will facilitate decision-making and policy.

The decade of the thirties was one of such great change in price movements, laws, and earnings that it remains the most fertile period of accounting thought. Added to other upsetting changes, the bankruptcy of the wholesale drug company of McKesson and Robbins in 1939 showed that one of the most prestigious accounting firms had been completely unaware for a number of years that very large reported inventories of materials did not, in fact, exist. The shock led the professional associations to advocate the sampling of inventories.

The entire period from 1931 on was one in which the professional associations, particularly in the United States, were the most active in trying to relate principles to practice. In order to accomplish this, the Institute of Accountants' committee on accounting procedures issued fifty-one *Accounting Research Bulletins* between 1939 and 1959, but, befitting a body that was essentially a trade association, divisive questions were avoided; in addition, the bulletins dealt with current problems rather than with the construction of a coherent theory. Meanwhile, the more academically oriented American Association of Accountants issued statements of principles, concepts, and standards, together with supplementary papers. This activity led to a book entitled *The Statement of Basic Accounting Theory* in 1966. Yet, so many alternative methods had to be recognized in such vital areas as depreciation and inventory valuation that reading or assimilation by management was discouraged.[25]

It seems probable that in the big companies management relied more and more on summaries from their own accounting departments. This meant, in turn, the rise of controllers to key positions in top management. In 1950 the Controller's Institute had no member, who was a corporate vice-president. Eleven years later, 235 members were vice-presidents. The increasing need for financial controls and the ability to justify methods used to government agencies were reflected in the increase in the number of CPAs from 38,000 in 1950 to 90,000 in 1965. In 1973 the Institute of Accountants set up a financial accounting standards board with nine trustees selected by the leading firms of the profession. The trustees, in turn, appoint a salaried board of seven members, only four of whom may be practicing CPAs. It would appear that decisions of this group should have great weight with both government and business.

Meanwhile business and social changes put new demands on the techniques of accounting, and computers made it easier to meet them. Internal Revenue and the various government and state commissions frequently wanted data in forms differing from those most desirable for company use. Labor contracts and fringe benefits also required special calculations, so that big companies with many plants frequently had to run several parallel systems of accounting. In addition, each type of business had its own variation in accounting practice, which obviously complicated the compilation of overall figures for widely diversified companies.

Introduction of the computer eventually made these multiple operations, and account-keeping in general, cheaper and more exact, but during the period before about 1970, it posed serious and costly problems in programming and correcting errors. After almost fifteen years, and the use of some 60,000 computers, only half of 2,500 large companies polled by *Fortune* in 1969 thought they had received their money's worth. The same type of poll in 1979 would doubtless produce a sharply different consensus.[26]

In the decades after World War II, large companies also adopted new accounting practices to assist management. In 1947, Pittsburgh Plate Glass, for example, introduced a system of "direct standard costs," which, combined with studies of reasons for variance, proved popular with other manufacturers. Since corporate accountants preferred to deal with rising prices by special reserves for replacement or rapid depreciation, rather than by cost of living adjustments, years of lobbying for accelerated depreciation for new investment was finally rewarded in the tax law of 1954. Capital budgeting for future years also became popular in the 1950s, and the collective plans of business could now become a statistic in national forecasting. Accountants continued to advocate the following: realization of income through transactions; consistency in methods from year to year; conservative valuations of assets; and disclosure of all relevant information. But in the absence of more precise fundamental theory, each of the four aims could be variously interpreted.

While these and other refinements had become accepted in principle by the 1970s, century-old problems remained. The best systematic data still had their limitations for the purpose of management planning and much of the mounting statistics supplied could not be uniformly digested and interpreted for policy-making decisions. As Herbert Simon observed in 1971: "Today's computers are moronic robots. . . . They do not and cannot exercise due respect for the scarce attention of the recipients of this information. . . . Computers must be taught to behave at higher levels of intelligence."[27] Philosopher William Barrett says: "Perhaps our agencies of information accumulate enough data to complicate matters but have not yet advanced to a point where they can resolve the complications they introduce."[28]

RESIDUAL PROBLEMS

Basic to all the difficulties in transmitting information was the limited span of perception and concentrated attention that could be expected from any individual; no system that necessitated passing of information and orders from one set of men to another could avoid losses in content and control; and while it was best to give the maximum discretion to lower managers, or men on the spot, this also allowed them to serve their own ends rather than those of the company.

This last problem has several aspects: a lower echelon manager might, through laziness or lack of the proper abilities, serve the company honestly but poorly; he might be responsible through neglect or personal avarice for stealing by himself or other employees; and in the upper echelons there were essentially unethical personal goals that management justified as necessary. At the lower levels minor theft by the employees in chain store operations, for example, was regarded as a job perquisite whose elimination would cost more in detection and wages than it was worth. Kickbacks on orders or construction contracts might be secret from the public but regarded as necessary by normally ethical officers of the firm; or, as in several large companies in the postwar period, most officers might be involved in widespread internal corruption.[29]

There were still historic differences between legal codes and acceptable business ethics. Secret bargains for pricing purposes, for example, were against the law, but quite often regarded as normal procedure by businesses of the highest public standing. Top executives of large electrical equipment firms were sentenced to jail for such practices in the early 1960s. Bribery of foreign or even domestic political officials was often regarded in all the leading nations as a necessary cost of doing business. Whether business ethics or practices either at home or abroad were improving or declining is, because of the nature of the evidence, impossible to estimate.[30] While the inquiring traveler gains the impression that standards of honesty and devotion to company goals are highest in Germany and Japan, such cross-cultural views can be deceptive.

The other problems inherent in bureaucracy may be alleviated by more sharply focused studies of business organization, or a long-run solution may come from less hierarchical structures. As automation proceeds, the number of employees in very large operations should decline dramatically, and the small semi-independent enterprises successful in trade and service may multiply so that fewer people will be parts of long, impersonal chains of command, and more will be either franchised proprietors or employees working face-to-face with their bosses.

Thus while the advantages of size and resources in marketing will probably not disappear—capitalism is, after all, chiefly distinguished by open markets—the number of employees in the manufacturing departments of the large assembling firms that are the chief factors in selling to the consumer should diminish. Or, put another way, making goods, including branded items, should take up less of the labor force in relation to their distribution, repair, and use. Technological improvements in all goods-oriented processes will undoubtedly release many more people for service activities.

12

Finance Expands Its Markets

U P TO 1933, the owning and mortgaging of one's own home, investing in any type of security, or maintaining a checking account at a bank had been confined very largely to the upper fifth of income receivers, who in the relatively good year of 1935 had incomes of more than $2,200 or $2,300. From 1934 on government guarantee of mortgages, and after World War II, Veteran's Administration loans, the shortage of labor, and consequent higher real wages made home ownership available to nearly all people who had steady jobs. Bank advertising beamed at small depositors attracted checking and savings accounts, while reliable investment trusts led a much larger part of the population to become stockholders. In other words, financial institutions joined in the mass marketing of loans, mortgages, and accounts and came to think in terms of a wide public.

On the other side of the coin, World War II ended a long period in which, except for 1915 to 1920, saving, practically all by business and the well-to-do, had tended to exceed the demand for new physical capital. In the years after 1945, commercially marketable needs for new funds normally exceeded the real savings available for investment. To some extent this was a result of both higher real wages after 1941 and progressive taxation that redistributed income downward and curtailed saving in the upper brackets. At the same time, in addition to repairing war damage, large increases in government military and other investment, and an incredibly costly rehousing of people and business to fit the opportunities opened up by guaranteed mortgages, automobiles and trucks led to unprecedented needs for capital.

The increase in demand for durable goods relative to the supply involved a major economic sector that was still highly competitive and that conformed well to classic theory: the money market. Since money was a completely undifferentiated product available from many sources, even the largest banks or insurance companies lacked the control over rates for credit that the big industrial or marketing companies had over the prices of their goods. Furthermore, financial corporations were competing in rates not with a few similar dealers, but with hundreds of bidders of many types for profitable business. Therefore in discussing finance we come, almost by definition, to the heart of the free capitalist system, and to the most complex aspects of business.

Next to government services and wholesaling, real estate and finance, which are inextricably bound together, were in the years after World War II the most rapidly growing area of employment. Such "primary and secondary" activities as farming, manufacturing, mining, and utilities actually suffered declines in their percentages of the total labor force; but real estate and finance grew about 25 percent. Furthermore, except for a moderate number of clerical workers, most of the people involved could be classed as businessmen.

REAL ESTATE

In financial flows real estate remained, as always, the most important single type of business other than manufacturing, and the assets of the firms involved were several times larger than those of all industrial companies. In previous chapters (4, 7, and 9) real estate has been discussed chiefly as a factor in business specialization and geographical expansion. In the United States after 1930, when government and the automobile were literally revolutionizing home ownership, and the location of both homes and offices, real estate finance becomes the most important aspect of business change.

The Federal Housing Act of 1934, providing for government guarantees of mortgages for 80 percent of appraisal up to a value of $15,000, revolutionized both home ownership and the mortgage business. Heretofore mortgages had generally been on a one-year renewable basis, with a reappraisal every five to ten years. They also tended by state or federal law, and also by lending practice, to run only about 60 percent of value. This meant a need for equity or "front money" too large for the lower-middle income receiver to meet. Recourse to a second mortgage at a discount of its face value and quick amortization that made actual interest run 15 to 18 percent was usually not within a worker's ability to pay.

Not only did the Federal Housing Administration (FHA) guarantee approved mortgages, but the agreement provided for automatic amortization through small monthly payments over a 20-year period, a practice introduced by saving and loan associations only in the late 1920s. Ultimately the time was extended to 30 years and the maximum amount raised to $20,000. With these guarantees, mortgage grantors were anxious to make the loans.

Although such arrangements, plus the desire of families to move to the suburbs, would inevitably have increased home ownership, it was given greater impetus after World War II by higher real incomes and guarantees to ex-servicemen of 95 percent of value of the mortgage by the Veterans Administration. The millions of veterans were of an age to form or expand households, and given this backing, they were largely responsible for an almost continual real estate boom that lasted until the end of the 1960s.

The automobile and truck were principal forces in this great relocation of population from central cities to suburbs, from apartments or tenements to single or double homes, and from farms to nearby towns. As more people came to live in the suburbs or fringes of metropolitan areas, companies moved operations that employed middle-income workers from expensive urban sites to locations in the surrounding country. This, in turn, attracted more families, and as the semirural population grew it was followed by trade and service in new shopping centers. Other factors such as racial problems, schools, and the deterioration of central cities also contributed to this population shift, but without the FHA, VA, and the automobile, the great relocation could not have occurred. By 1970 more people were living in the outlying parts of metropolitan areas than in the central cities, and since World War II about $500 billion has been invested in residential construction.

FINANCING THE BUILDING BOOM

The business basis of the new society had many aspects. Because of its seasonal character, building construction had always been a high-wage business, and in the postwar boom only upper income families could afford to buy country acreage, install the necessary improvements, and have an architect design and supervise the erection of a house. There were great economies in doing all of these operations for from ten to a hundred houses at one time. Large acreages were relatively cheaper to buy than small, facilities could be shared, and designing and supervising costs spread. In addition, the subcontractors for plumbing, electricity, and other fittings saved all the time that would have been consumed in meeting an equal number of individual orders in different locations. By these means, plus the development of prefabrication for panels, bathrooms, windows, and kitchens, a three- or four-bedroom house on a half-acre lot or less could be sold within the range of price permitted by the FHA or VA. Some developers, such as the Levitt Brothers, or insurance or industrial companies built entire satellite cities with business and public buildings as well as homes.

Providing money for the great building boom was, except for war, by far the biggest financial operation in American history. The government guaranteed mortgages, but supplied no money except in cases of default, and meanwhile collected premiums on the insurance. Equity capital was needed for purchasing the land and improving it to the point where houses could be erected and sold. To secure such money developers usually formed either a corporation or a syndicate. The latter was a legal arrangement, fairly uniform among the states, whereby one or more general partners who controlled the management recruited a number of limited partners who had liability only for the money invested, plus any operating losses. Since the general partner bore all the excess liability, "he" was normally a corporation. Once the land had been prepared, short-term construction loans sufficient to cover payments to contractors could be secured from commercial banks, particularly if government guaranteed mortgages were to be available for the completed houses.[1]

Savings and loan associations, called by different names in some states, were major suppliers of the long-term mortgage money. These mutual organizations date back to the Philadelphia area in 1831, but they only multiplied in the twentieth century, reaching an all-time high of nearly 6,000 in 1950. As their title indicates, they collected deposits, usually by selling saving certificates, and invested the money in mortgages on improved property. To overcome differences in state regulations, efforts were made by the United States Saving and Loan League to secure federal charters for the associations. Blocked for some years by state banking interests, the League finally won in the desperate depression year of 1933. Federal savings and loan associations could secure charters and have their deposits insured. They were soon placed under the control of the Home Loan Bank Board, which will be discussed presently. By 1970, the 2,000 that were federally chartered held 54 percent of the assets of the 5,700 associations.[2]

Mutual savings banks, another old financial institution going back to the Philadelphia Savings Fund Society chartered in 1818, became increasingly active in mortgage lending after World War II. These banks had never spread substantially beyond the East coast. As of 1970 they existed in only eighteen states, and more than three-fourths of the total were in New York and New England. While dividends were paid to depositors, the banks were run by self-perpetuating boards of trustees. In early days state laws generally restricted the mutuals to short-term loans, and hence their mortgages were on a one-year renewable basis. With the coming of mortgages guaranteed by the FHA and VA, the state regulations were relaxed and the mutuals became major holders of such certificates.

State commercial banks had started savings departments in the late nineteenth century, and national banks were encouraged to do the same by a ruling of the controller of currency in 1903. When permitted to invest in mortgages by the Federal Reserve in 1914, member banks moved cautiously in this direction. Even one-year mortgages are not very liquid and until government action in the 1930s, there were no central banks in the United States prepared to buy large quantities of mortgages, or in other words, no stable secondary mortgage market such as existed in France and Germany through government institutions. Even with the coming of such facilities, however, commercial banks in the United States have preferred bonds to mortgages. In 1970, even though the assets of the savings departments of commercial banks were far larger than those of mutuals or of the few separate stockholder-owned savings banks, they had only a small percentage of their investments in mortgages.

The chief business problem involved in the buying of mortgages by both mutual and commercial banks was liquidity. Since, in fact, withdrawals from savings deposits were normally made on demand, while mortgages could only be sold quickly at a discount, they were not regarded as liquid. In contrast, federal, state, and local bonds had daily quotations on security markets, and when taken together totaled by 1970 more than all mortgages ($530 billion as against $498 billion). In general, therefore, mortgages were only attractive because of federal guarantees and higher rates of return.

The other major type of mortgage buyer was the life insurance companies. Since state laws confined the mortgage investment of most savings institutions to within 50 to 100 miles of their office, the insurance companies constituted the only national primary recourse for long-distance movements of mortgage money. Every decade from 1890 on, life insurance reserves doubled, until by 1970 they stood at $208 billion, with $25 billion potential new mortgage money from premiums each year. Less troubled than banks by problems of liquidity or by state regulations, and under continued pressure to invest large sums, the insurance companies became the major source for big mortgages, which for these companies were preferable to small.

Private pension funds, with $141 billion in assets in 1970, and similar government funds, with $117 billion, have not been major factors in the real estate market, nor has the individual investor. Pension funds have invested more often in tax-exempt bonds, which proliferated as the need grew for state and local improvements in housing and education. An advantage of listed bonds was that they did not require the continuing attention or servicing needed by mortgages.

Finally, a special type of mortgage investor has appeared in recent years. Partly to promote home building and to stimulate business, the federal Real Estate Investment Trust Act of 1961 provided for associations of shareholders managed by trustees who would have to invest at least three-fourths of their assets in mortgages, and make 90 percent of their gross income from real estate. The trustees also had to distribute 90 percent of net income annually to the shareholders. In return, the association paid no taxes on either the income paid out or on capital gains that were received. The existence of other attractive investments and the amount of specialized real estate knowledge needed for the operation of such trusts prevented much use of the law until 1969. Then, partly as a response to investors searching for hedges against inflation, about a score of such trusts were formed and promoted by major investment houses. Usually the trustees hired the services of the real estate departments of a bank to advise them on risks, and were involved with one or more banks for a line of credit.[3]

In the upswing caused by massive federal deficits and easy monetary policy in 1971 and 1972, the so-called REITS seemed to be doing well, but in fact they were advancing money on many types of mortgages, such as motel properties, that banks and insurance companies generally avoided. In the depression of 1974 and 1975, many of the REITS had to default on both bank loans and interest to their own debenture bond-holders, illustrating historic business experience that real estate is an excellent asset in times of prosperity and a burden in depressions. Britain also experienced a sharp break in the real estate market in late 1973 and 1974. There many real estate corporations had listed their stock and a number of unregulated "secondary" banks had lent on such real estate. The result was a more severe collapse than in the United States, but the bank depositors were protected by the Bank of England.[4]

THE MORTGAGE MARKET

So far the discussion has focused on general sources of money rather than on how the particular customer wanting a mortgage would find a lender. This process involved a type of marketing partly conducted by individuals and partly by branches of corporations; in fact, it operated much like the various trades in commodities. Some big insurance companies have had branch offices to which a "retail" customer such as a builder or home buyer could apply. Big banks also have opened real estate departments that bypass brokers. But a large part of the trade, particularly in residential mortgages, has gone through the hands of middlemen.

The intermediaries usually call themselves mortgage bankers, whether they are single operators working from their homes, or corporations with branches in a number of cities. Their principal services have been bringing potential borrowers to the attention of institutional lenders and servicing mortgages for the latter. Finding mortgages required a salesman or the banker himself to talk continually with men developing or selling property. Real estate brokers have been a prime source of information, but records of local property transfers were examined, and builders were often interviewed at their work. The success of a mortgage banker depended on the soundness of the applications he could offer to buyers, reasonable fee arrangements for finding and servicing, and rapid negotiations that satisfied borrowers.

Again, as in general trade, it might be considerably cheaper for a big company to keep track of payments, taxes, and maintenance on far-flung buildings by paying fees to outside mortgage bankers than to set up an inside department. In 1945, when the Mortgage Bankers of America was organized, there were only about 500 representatives of such activities, although agents of banks and insurance companies were allowed to join the associations. By 1970 there were 2,000 mortgage bankers servicing nearly $80 billion in mortgages.[5]

For the majority of residential mortgages, FHA and VA guarantees had provided ultimate security and allowed for their sale to absentee purchasers. Business properties, on the other hand, presented much more difficult problems in appraisal and proper servicing. Whereas the government agencies have carried out reliable appraisals on their residential applications, borrowers on business properties need to offer the reports of specialized private appraisers. From the nineteenth century on each big city has had a number of firms and individuals providing such service, and since 1932 there have been national organizations aimed at increasing confidence in the ability and reliability of their members appraisals. Banks train their own staff for appraising business loans and these specialists could also be called on to evaluate mortgages. Some very large mortgages on business properties, that have run into many millions, have been bought by one or a number of insurance companies on the basis of both staff and outside appraisals. A primary difficulty, brought out in periods of depression, has been that business structures that were built for special purposes might not be readily convertible to some other use. While homes have always been a standard commodity with a wide market, the same has not always been true of business establishments, beyond the value of the cleared land.

Unlike France, Germany, and Japan, the United States government prior to 1932 had never created a central authority to provide a secondary market, that is one for the sale of partially amortized loans on property. The Home Loan Bank Act of that year provided for a Mortgage Corporation to maintain such a market for residential certificates. Lending institutions were allowed to become members with trading privileges. In 1938 the Federal National Mortgage Association with a $10 million capital was set up as a subsidiary of the Reconstruction Finance Corporation (RFC). It could buy insured mortgages, finance large rental projects, and borrow money on its notes. Not very active until after World War II, it provided a needed secondary market for VA mortgages. Since it was successful as a business institution, "Fanny May" was made a private corporation by the Housing Act of 1968, and in 1970 its shares were listed on the New York Stock Exchange.

In all, some twenty-eight special agencies were established in the 1930s to finance or refinance homes, farms, businesses, electrification, or transportation. Some like the RFC have been closed, but most of them remain in some form.[6] Collectively they have made government-business financial relations closer than in Britain and more like those in France, Germany, and Japan.

INSURANCE: A GROWING BUSINESS

The powerful financial position of insurance companies since World War II calls attention to the two distinct aspects of the business: marketing profitable policies; and investing the enormous amounts received annually in premiums. From the standpoint of top insurance executives, the first problem has usually been more complex and time consuming, while in its effects on other business the second has been much more important.[7]

Guidance of marketing activities promises to be a never-ending problem. New policies are required to meet new social risks and these continually change. To meet the challenges, the big companies have internalized underwriting, actuarial training, and research, while business schools have set up major programs in insurance. As early as 1932 university teachers formed a national association. In fact, there was practically no part of business education not needed by insurance executives.

Unlike the purchase of any tangible commodity, buying insurance requires an immediate expenditure and offers nothing but a promise of some future security in return. As the Pennsylvania Company for Insuring Lives and Granting Annuities found from 1812 on, opening an office and doing some advertising has never been sufficient to attract business. Customers generally needed to be seen by a salesman who could explain what they might ultimately gain by a small current sacrifice. The managerial problem has been to select and hold an energetic, educated sales force, and the amount of education needed has steadily increased. After World War II a large number of untrained, part-time agents retired or died and were not replaced. Companies have since tended more and more to make selling chiefly a salaried occupation.

Since 1930, the automobile has given casualty and property insurance a new importance. This type of business has risen 66 percent faster than the GNP, making it one of the leading growth industries. Yet harrassed by inflation, difficult assessment of risks, and ballooning verdicts by juries, the business has had as many bad years as good.[8] Some diversified companies have dropped casualty, and specialized companies like the pioneer Insurance Company of North America (1794) have added life and industrial insurance. To diversify outside the field of insurance, state laws have made it necessary to set up a holding company that can own the stock of the original insurance firm as well as that of other types of business.

Because of the wide differences in knowledge and skills needed in different aspects of insurance, effective coordination by top management has been unusually difficult. By the 1940s leading companies were working out a system allowing for departmental (functional) autonomy coupled with a large amount of staff work emanating from the president's office. Whether or not the departments such as life, industrial, casualty, or property should be set up as separate corporations was a matter of state regulatory laws or convenience, but, in any case, they would be visited and "advised" by head office staff. Too much separation might either produce too many sales agencies or agents with too many interests to serve.

In the 1960s companies in other fields, such as Sears Roebuck, entered into insurance with direct selling by mail. By 1970 about a fifth of the volume of casualty was being sold in this manner, but most people preferred to deal with local agents who could advise them. These agents were frequently independent firms that handled the policies of several companies. In addition, the increase in group life or health insurance was cutting down on the relative amount of contact with customers, which had been the reason for having agents in the first place.

The depression of the 1930s created new problems for the investment side of the insurance business. Mortgages had to be foreclosed and insurance companies involuntarily became the largest owners of farm property with the largest federal benefits under the Agricultural Adjustment Act of 1938.[9] The burden of farm management, for which the companies were quite unprepared, became enormous, but fortunately World War II permitted a rapid liquidation of these equity holdings. Meanwhile, portfolios had been shifted from weakening railroad bonds into government bonds, but only at a sacrifice in interest of some 20 percent. How to secure higher yields became the major problem of insurance investment departments.

In the long period of general prosperity from 1945 to 1973, the insurance companies shifted back to mortgages, were permitted by law to make some long-term commercial loans, and took advantage of laws by New York and other states allowing equity investments in low- to moderate-cost housing. A number of planned metropolitan area developments across the country were directly financed by insurance companies, despite the reluctance of some conservative top executives. By the 1970s diversification was making it relatively unimportant to try to distinguish between life and other types of insurance companies. Together they held over 21 percent of the assets of all financial institutions, exceeded only by commercial banks with 46 percent. Compared to 1950, this was not a gain in percentage since savings and loan and pension funds had cut into the shares of both banking and insurance, but the total sums in real dollars had more than doubled. Since a larger part of the holdings of commercial banks had to be in liquid assets, the insurance companies played practically an equal role in long-term institutional investment.

BANKING EXPANDS ITS MARKET

The demands of liquidity made the early thirties worse for commercial banks than for other financial intermediaries. Between 1929 and 1933 about half the commercial banks in the nation failed, and few ever reopened. While defaulted mortgages and loans against large blocks of common stock caused serious losses, the general decline in the value of bonds hit most banks even harder. As noted in Chapter Eleven, had the Reconstruction Finance Corporation not made large loans to the big banks and bought their specially issued preferred stock, the financial disaster would have been so severe that the entire system of American banking would have had to be reorganized. For those that survived the lack of new private bond issues or commercial loans, and the flood of government bonds forced more and more investment in the latter at rates of return held down by federal policy.

This turned attention to a source of profitable business not exploited earlier, namely small personal loans. Lending in small sums to people with no security beyond their job had been growing rather rapidly from before World War I in the hands of the Morris Plan or "industrial banks," credit unions, and finance companies. In spite of state laws allowing high interest rates on these small loans, all but a few commercial banks, meaning those that dealt in demand deposits, had continued to regard this business as too risky and expensive in overhead per loan to be worthwhile. They preferred to lend "wholesale" to the finance companies and let them conduct the retail business. The record of the 1920s had shown the business to be safer than real estate mortgages, however, and the interest to be high enough to more than support the overhead. Since the charge was collected in advance, as a discount on the entire amount borrowed, and the loan had to be repaid in equal installments, a nominal rate of 6 percent actually returned around 12 percent, far in excess of any other paper in which a bank might legally invest. Risk was so subdivided that any sudden large loss was inconceivable, and continual maturities and new loans made a considerable part of the total liquid at any given time. As a consequence enterprising banks decided to bypass the middlemen and enter the retail market.

Nevertheless, because of increases in staff space and knowledge required, banks proceeded cautiously, some not at all for a decade or more, and they never advertised such services vigorously until after World War II. From one standpoint the small personal loan business was like insurance in that the lender had to rely on increasingly refined risk tables based on experience that might be made unreliable by everchanging social conditions. In 1950 personal loans standing at $10 billion made up only about 6 percent of bank assets. By 1972, after two decades of prosperity and heavy installment buying of high-priced consumer durables, personal loans reached double the former share of total bank assets (which had themselves grown three and a half times larger) and brought in a disproportionate 18 percent of disposable bank income.[10]

Along with the spread of bank and finance company loans, checking accounts, credit cards, and installment payments both by mail or at retail dealers, went an enormous expansion of the business of consumer credit rating and account collections. Over 2,000 such firms were operating by 1970 from 6,000 offices, and probably every American with a steady income and some accounts had a credit rating.

Affluence and bank advertising also spread checking accounts to types of consumers who had never thought to use them before. A disadvantage that banks had to overcome in order to attract both personal borrowers and depositors was their austere moralistic atmosphere. It took much radio and television advertising about friendly banks to teach much of the public that the business of banking was lending and servicing, not holding money. Perhaps most depositors were probably not overawed, but before 1945, low interest returns on bank investments and the high cost of manual sorting and disposing of checks made it necessary for banks to place relatively high service charges on small checking accounts.

Starting with routing numbers and electronic ink in the late forties, reinforced by computers a decade later, banks were able to handle checks inexpensively, and meanwhile inflation and capital scarcity had started the secular rise in the earning rate of money. Now checking accounts were solicited by the banks and in the 1970s service charges were removed. As a result more than two-thirds of American families paid by check in the 1970s, whereas one-third had done so in 1945.[11]

Electronic data processing (EDP) made many new types of bank services such as credit cards, overdraft checking, running payroll accounts, or renting computer time sources of profit. In fact, all types of accounts and payments seemed, in 1976, to be on the verge of revolutionary change in the direction of national computerized recording and transfer systems.

THE ENDURING STRUCTURE OF BANKING

In spite of the experiences derived from the disastrous collapse and subsequent revival of American business to a new position of importance, the same forces that had historically kept the banking structure weak and uncontrollable continued. Public distrust and fear of banks, the aim of the small-town banker to protect his business from metropolitan competition, and the resulting politically cautious approach to the use of national power were continuing forces, just as they had been in 1836, 1863, and 1913.

While the Banking Act of 1935 provided a less politically influenced central board, and gave it some positive power over open market policies, area rediscount rates, reserve levels, and some types of loans, it did not create any central financial institution or even compel banks to join the regional system. In contrast, after World War II, Britain, France, Germany, and Japan all had nationally owned central banks with almost unlimited power to act in financial emergencies. The result of the voluntary systems in the United States was a gradual decline in the number of national banks and the rise of both member and nonmember state-chartered banks, which by 1972 had 41 percent of all deposits. In 1936 there had been 6,400 members of the Federal Reserve and 7,685 non-member banks, but in 1970 there were only 5,768 members compared to 7,919 nonmembers, with the latter class continuing to grow. Many of these banks had inadequate capital to cover any substantial loss. Of the banks that failed prior to 1956, over half had capitals of $25,000 or less.[12]

State laws regarding branch banking continued to vary and prevent systems of nationwide branches such as existed in the other leading industrial nations. As of 1972 only twenty states, three more than in 1935, permitted statewide branch banking and only two, California and North Carolina, imposed no restrictions; nineteen states allowed branches within the bank's home city; and twelve prohibited branch banking. Under these restraints new unit banks, numbering 7,440 in 1970, appeared faster than those with branches, although the branch-operating minority, with over 20,000 offices, still controlled the largest share of the banking business.[13]

Space does not permit any detailed comparison with present-day foreign branch banking systems, which, in general, have offices of all the big banks in each city. Britain and Canada show the general nature of the contrast. In 1960 the government-owned Bank of England cleared for eleven joint stock banks with nearly 10,000 branches. In addition there were "secondary" banks, chiefly in London, which worked with one or more of the clearing banks and often specialized in certain types of business. When, as we have seen, some of those specializing in real estate ventures became insolvent in the collapse of 1974, the Bank of England intervened to protect the depositors. Canada has the same system, with a small number of banks with branches throughout the dominion and a central Bank of Canada.[14]

Effective central banking is an intricate and controversial subject, but some weaknesses in the possibilities of Federal Reserve action have been historically obvious. Open market operations, buying or selling government securities, are the most flexible way of adding to or subtracting from the cash used for bank reserves. Because bank lending is restricted to a maximum based on reserves, open market policy can make a tighter or easier money market. But two problems stood in the way of free exercise of the policy. First selling when the United States government was also selling securities (a majority of the time) depressed the bond market and forced the government to offer higher rates. In fact, until a confrontation and resulting accord with the Treasury in 1951, the Federal Reserve under government pressure avoided the use of open market selling. Since then the government has allowed its rates to rise when necessary to maintain the price of its bonds and notes. In a few earlier instances the Federal Reserve had been short of a sufficient quantity of bonds to greatly affect the market, but this seems unlikely in the future.

A second practical limitation on its effective power was in regulation of member bank reserves, because only when banks were close to their maximum lending capacity did an increase in reserves have much effect. Even then, the banks often increase their reserves by borrowing from another member with extra resources, or from a nonmember or foreign bank out of reach of federal regulation. Use of the remaining major control mechanism of the central board, raising the rediscount rate, has (as seen in Chapter Nine) contradictory effects. Increases to prevent speculation or inflation have hindered home building and small business as well as attracted foreign money to the country, and the latter has fed inflation.

Continuing problems in federal jurisdiction have been bothersome but less serious than the lack of centralized power. The Controller of the Currency, the Federal Reserve Board, and since 1933, the Federal Deposit Insurance Corporation, have overlapping authority. The states also have sovereign rights over banks in their areas that cannot be violated by the federal agencies. In addition to preserving local autonomy, a large part of the maze of national and state regulations that continued to hinder progressive developments originated in the public distrust of banking practices generated in the years from 1920 to 1933. Liberalization of state laws was a slow and uneven process, but significant relaxation in national regulations came during the regime of James Saxon as Controller of the Currency from 1961 to 1966. National banks were permitted to buy accounts receivable, own equipment for leasing purposes, serve as underwriters, run credit and travel bureaus, and engage in other types of business such as those mentioned earlier in connection with computers.[15] One might say that by the middle 1960s the distrust but not the localism of the 1930s was being overcome.

In these same years plans to circumvent laws forbidding statewide branch systems spread. Chain banking, where the same stockholders controlled a number of unit banks, was old, but group banking achieving the same result through a holding company was relatively new. In the middle fifties about 10 percent of bank assets were so controlled, mainly in the Middle West.[16] By the Bank Holding Company Act of 1956, member banks were permitted to set up such companies, but the Federal

Reserve Board had to pass on new corporate acquisitions, and the firms bought had to be in activities related to finance. Spreading systems by merger was strictly supervised by the Antitrust Division of the Justice Department and some large banks were prevented from uniting because, even though they would still not have been the biggest in their regional market, it was assumed that competition would have been lessened. It does not appear that any further major improvement in the structure of United States banking will come easily.

BANKING AS BUSINESS

In 1975, American banking, like practically all other major activities, was still run, in part, by thousands of small independent firms. Concentration of resources was slowly increasing in the medium-sized banks, through some relaxation of state laws against branch banking, more holding companies, and the rapid growth of metropolitan centers. At the top, however, concentration was diminishing. In 1940 the hundred largest banks had 58 percent of all commercial bank deposits, while in 1950 their share had diminished to only 47 percent, and in 1970 to 44 percent.[17] With the number of banks remaining roughly constant from 1935 to 1975, the increased ability of each bank to lend to business is indicated by a rise in the median of deposits per bank, from about $500,000 to more than $8 million. Lending ability was only slightly diminished by the fact that bank capital did not quite keep pace with the rise in deposits. Even where two banks with branches dominated the banking of a state (as in North Carolina), the business still seemed highly competitive.

Bank lending, which had in the twenties been chiefly to small- and medium-sized business, became increasingly involved with mortgage household, home improvement, automobile, and personal loans. Big business tended to be a short-term lender as much as a borrower. In the 1960s the surplus funds of large companies were used to buy negotiable certificates of deposit in $100,000 units, on which the banks could pay a higher rate than that allowed on regular savings accounts. In 1972 the banks had $26 billion in corporate time deposits, mainly covered by certificates that had become a major way of transferring funds in the money market. In addition very large companies met seasonal needs for cash by selling their own short-term notes in $5,000 denominations through the half dozen remaining commercial paper dealers.

The following trends occurred in total bank investments from 1950 to 1970: a drop in the percentage of United States government securities from over a third to about a tenth; an extremely rapid gain in state and local obligations from 5 or 6 percent to 11 or 12 percent; a rise to nearly 5 percent in the obligations of government agencies; a gain in personal loans and real estate loans; and a drop in cash from about 23 to 15 percent. In short, the banks were gradually getting out from under the wartime flood of United States securities and moving in the direction of financing the rehousing of population and the rehabilitation of cities through mortgages and local government bonds. Large holdings of municipal bonds caused concern to the banks after the New York City troubles of 1975.

Individual loans by national banks were still limited to 10 percent of their capital, and larger loans by state-chartered member banks would not be accepted by the Federal Reserve for rediscount. This restriction became more irksome as bank capital suffered severely in the thirties from mortgage and security losses and stood at only 10 percent of assets in 1940. During the war assets rose much faster than capital and further reduced its percentage of the total to five and one-half. In the postwar upswing in the value of assets the percentage in capital accounts gradually rose to a relatively stable level of about seven. This still meant that even a large metropolitan bank with a billion in assets and an average percentage of capital would not be permitted to make a $10 million loan. The solution has been loan syndicates or, in everyday language, participation by several banks. When a national bank in a small city had the opportunity to make a large and locally useful loan it usually had to ask one or more metropolitan banks to participate. Thus the country had long been divided into financial areas dependent on metropolitan centers, although such centers are not always defined by clear lines, as in the case of competing and nearly adjacent centers such as Chicago and Milwaukee.

In order to attract medium-sized business financing from the 1830s on, banks, in competition with insurance companies, developed term loans of five to ten years or even longer, sometimes on a self-amortizing basis and sometimes with adjustable or "floating" rates. The trend in banking theory in the forty years after 1935 was toward open recognition of propriety of longer terms, rather than the assumption of the earlier days that all bank loans should be short-term, although often with the informal assurance of continuous renewal. By 1957 a third of all commercial loans had maturities of over a year, and federal examiners were inclined to evaluate loans on the basis of their soundness rather than their duration.[18]

While since 1930 loans have made up less than half of most bank portfolios, their higher rates of interest made them the chief money-making assets, bringing in around 60 percent of bank income. Salaries, wages, and current expense have made up about half of bank costs. Other items of expense, each around 8 to 12 percent, have been charge-offs for bad debts, taxes, dividends to stockholders, and a steadily increasing amount for interest on time deposits. By 1970 both private and business depositors had learned to keep only a minimum in demand deposits and to transfer the rest of their money to a time account. With time deposits larger than demand, banks were paying more for their money than in the old days, when New York City banks, for example, paid nothing on business deposits.

All financial institutions have high salary costs because their business is primarily selecting risks on the basis of human judgment and experience. Each special type of risk, for example loans to local wholesalers, requires an expert evaluator, and for this reason banks often specialize in certain varieties of credit. In the 1920s the banks led all of business in using titles as a substitute for high salaries and, although copied by other businesses, banks probably remained proportionally in the lead in numbers of officers in relation to volume of income or total employees. Some critics think salaries too low to attract able managers.

SECURITY DEALERS EXPAND THEIR MARKET

The distribution and exchange of stocks, bonds, and other certificates was, in 1930, chiefly in the hands of a large number of specialized brokerage houses, most of which were no more than medium-sized partnerships. Only about 400 had partners with seats on the New York Stock Exchange, some of these and hundreds of others dealt on local stock exchanges in the major financial centers, some on the commodity exchanges that were usually centered in Chicago or New York, and still others specialized in certain types of over-the-counter sales.

The buying public for bulk commodities and over-the-counter

securities, except for bank stocks, was chiefly composed of businessmen, often buying or selling as a hedge against changes in price during the life of a contract for manufacture or delivery. Buying of common stock over-the-counter, which generally meant the shares of young, medium-sized companies, offered both greater rewards and risks than dealing in listed stocks or bonds, and was engaged in by passive investors only as a gamble.

In spite of continuing inflation and periods of prosperity between 1933 and 1946, common stock prices rose only moderately and the volume of trading remained small. High excess profits taxes, reaching 95 percent of earnings above a not very prosperous base period, prevented the acquiring of the kinds of business fortunes that had been earned in World War I, and judging by the published opinion of "experts," many investors feared a postwar depression similar to that of the early twenties. Not until the recovery in the fall of 1949 were these fears put to rest and the way paved for a decade of upswing in the price of stocks reminiscent of the 1920s.

There were distinct differences from the earlier period, however, that made for a more stable market. The Securities Exchange Commission monitored both margins and dealer practices in listed securities, and thus largely prevented killings by insiders, collusive trading, and thin margins. Consequently a sharp drop in the market no longer sent thousands off in a panicky search for funds to support their margin accounts. The other major factor was dominance of the market by institutional rather than individual investors. Not only did rapidly growing investment trusts spread stockholding to millions of small investors, but pension funds and insurance companies grew, as we have seen, into enormous financial powers with tens of billions of dollars to invest each year.

In minor market movements institutional buying proved a stabilizing force, as their analysts sold on rises and withheld funds to buy on declines. When the decline was too severe, however, as from 1973 to December 1974, the funds failed to purchase strongly until the New York Stock Exchange had dropped some 40 percent, nearly as much as from October to December 1929.

Higher real incomes, and a chance to get indirect diversification of their holdings through shares in government-regulated investment trusts, increased the number of owners of common stock to, at least, double the per capita figures of 1929. Few estimates of the earlier period place the total above six million, whereas sampling studies of 1970 led to a surmise of twenty-five million. In a nation with sixty-three million households (1970), this meant that the average middle to upper income family owned some common stock.

Meanwhile, the fact that shares in the funds were usually marketed to consumers by advertising, and institutional buying was in large blocks through a few big brokerage houses, had permitted economies of scale in security trading that the small brokerage partnership could not meet. A mounting withdrawal of individual investors in the late 1960s and early 1970s plunged many of the small and some of the larger firms into financial difficulties. Hasty mergers usually prevented complete insolvency, but the New York Stock Exchange set up a fund to insure the customers of brokerage firms in liquidation. As in the case of banking, the computer promised to bring about new means of trading and settlement that might radically alter the structure of the business.

A major factor in the growing power of the institutional owners of stocks has been the rise of employee pension funds controlled by trustees responsible to the potential beneficiaries. Typically a publicly-owned company's pension fund gets thirty cents of every dollar of earnings before taxes. By 1976 these sums had given the funds a majority control of the voting stock of the biggest American companies. What this portends for the future relations of unions, funds, independent stockholders, directors, and managers seems almost impossible to forecast. Peter Drucker calls the situation "pension fund socialism" and sees it as perhaps the "central problem" of our society.[19]

Running through all the discussion of recent finance is the problem of state regulation. While in some cases model statutes drawn up by national associations have been widely adopted, the resulting laws almost invariably involve small modifications from state to state. The jurisdictional system, never designed for an industrial society, is a lawyer's paradise and often a businessman's hell, and, unfortunately, the confusions can only be cured by legislatures, a majority of whose members are normally lawyers. The United States, with the most wasteful systems for use of the tax dollar of any of the leading nations, has throughout its history traded administrative efficiency for local autonomy.

13

The Changing Environment

MUCH OF THIS BOOK has demonstrated the greater power of business to shape its own environment in the young, expanding, and democratic United States than in nations that shared various feudal and monarchical traditions. While Americans were often highly critical of business, no political party standing for severe interference by the state ever gained more than a small percentage of the national vote. Until the startling revelation of inner weakness in the depression of the 1930s, and the resulting New Deal, almost no important national legislation had ever been enacted without substantial business support.

The New Deal moved the government-business relationships of the United States closer to those of the other four industrial leaders, and faced business thereafter with a national, governmental-military bureaucracy to which it had to adjust—usually with profit, sometimes at a loss, but always with some annoyance. In the same period the external environment of American business, which had been changed by World War I, was more fundamentally altered by World War II. In the twenties and thirties the United States should have been the world's financial market of last resort, but both its government and banking system were unwilling to accept the responsibility. From 1945 to 1970 the United States sought no escape from world dominance in finance and military power. These relations, in turn, involved American business in a return to its pre-1929 interest in direct investment in overseas enterprises.

EARLY GROWTH OF AN
INTERNATIONAL ENVIRONMENT

From the mid-nineteenth century the effect of the demands of the big American domestic market had created an environment for business that differed fundamentally between Europe and the United States. From about 1850 on the American market for middle-class consumer goods and labor-saving machinery was larger than that of any European nation. As relatively high wages encouraged more mechanization in America, a circular process developed. The machines ultimately turned out products more cheaply than hand labor, and these machine-made products, such as firearms or machine tools, could win some foreign markets even in the nations where labor was relatively cheap. To achieve this low cost it was necessary, of course, for the American company first to secure a position in the domestic market that allowed large-scale production.

A related cycle was the development of the knowledge of possible new processes in Europe, because of its much larger number of men with advanced technological training, but with the first commercial development of the process occurring in the more rewarding American market. Sewing machines, reapers, and electrical processes were originated in theory abroad, commercialized in the United States, and the products later exported to the nation responsible for the basic knowledge. Europe tended to innovate in basic processes and inventions, America in marketable products.[1]

A typical cycle for an American mass-producer developing foreign interests would be the following: first, the securing of a strong position in the domestic market with efforts to expand exports through normal mercantile channels, with foreign patenting if advantageous; next, the establishment of direct overseas sales agencies; then the licensing of foreign firms to make the product; and finally either buying control of such licensees or starting branch plants abroad.[2]

The supremacy of the United States in what by 1900 was becoming "high pressure" marketing, was illustrated by John H. Patterson in cash registers and the Eastmans in cameras. Patterson came to be regarded as a world leader in teaching personal salesmanship to his representatives, and Eastman Kodak company had the temerity to start chain retail outlets in London and Lyons in 1902.[3] On the whole, as would be expected, the early twentieth century foreign successes were in products needing a medium-high level of technology that lent itself to machine processes.

In spite of continuing tariff protection, the great buying power of the American market attracted foreign as well as domestic sellers. The value of merchandise imports into the United States, chiefly manufactured or processed goods, rose from $164 million in 1850 to $4.3 billion in 1929, and the two-way movement of products required many international trade and service agencies. In fact foreign trade partnerships between British and American firms go back to the early days of the Colonies, and cooperation by private banking houses in capital issues stems from the early nineteenth century. In these areas of business the environment had always been international. Exemplifying such ties were the innovation of the travelers check by American Express in 1891 and the formation of the American Chamber of Commerce in Paris in 1894.[4]

The tendency for foreign firms to manufacture in the United States was limited by high labor costs to a few luxury items. As we have seen, foreign investment in this nation before 1930 was generally in bonds, either private or government, that paid higher yields than in the most developed nations of Europe.

In 1929 the book value (well below the existing market value) of United States direct investments in Europe was $637 million in manufacturing, $135 million in sales, $239 million in all aspects of the petroleum business, $57 million in mining, and $138 million in utilities. Thus manufacturing accounted for about half of the American-owned foreign facilities. About one-third of this industrial investment was in Britain, a sixth in Germany, and an eighth in France.[5] The amount in Japan was negligible. Accurate figures were difficult to compile by nation since United States firms frequently operated throughout the Commonwealth from Canadian subsidiaries or covered Europe through firms owned in Britain. Consequently, while the $1.7 billion in direct investment in Canada was larger by about a quarter than that in both Britain and continental Europe combined, it is impossible to estimate what share served the Canadian market. In any case, compared with domestic figures these quantities were all small. The great majority of businessmen in 1929 thought complacently in terms of operations confined to the United States.

THE CHANGING ENVIRONMENT
FOR DIRECT INVESTMENT

Both the depression of the thirties and the later concentration of industrial effort on war production checked the growth of American business activities in Europe and Japan. In the latter nation local business policies and governmental regulations had always discouraged direct investment, and in the thirties the Japanese bought control of a number of the existing American subsidiaries.[6]

As a percentage of GNP, American direct investment abroad was much smaller by 1946 than in 1929, and by the later year the 181 foreign branches of banks existing in 1921 had fallen to 72. Furthermore, prior to about 1954, European conditions appeared uncertain both economically and politically. Consequently in the early postwar years investment came largely from earnings retained in existing foreign subsidiaries.[7] Aside from some bothersome antitrust prosecutions, however, the United States government favored direct investment, which it had not done in the 1920s.

By the middle of the 1950s the markets of the leading industrial nations of Europe were growing faster in per capita buying power than that of the United States, and demand was increasing rapidly for many types of mass-produced consumer goods. In addition in late 1958 most of the West European currencies were made freely convertible, and while foreign licenses were necessary for capital withdrawals in dollars, American profits could be repatriated with only a 7½ percent domestic tax. The United States Mutual Security Act of 1959 guaranteed direct investments in "underdeveloped" countries. Spurred by this incentive, $7.3 billion had been invested in seventy-eight such countries by 1970, and the government had paid out some substantial indemnities.

In the new environment of world interests and highly valued dollars, direct foreign investment rose rapidly. While from 1950 to 1970 the GNP grew 250 percent in current dollars, the book value of direct investments increased by 550 percent. In Europe, including Britain, American direct investment in 1950 was still lower in terms of real dollars than in 1929, but its postwar growth was the most spectacular of the major areas. The total rose between 1950 and 1970 from $1.7 billion to $24.5 billion, with somewhat over half the total at both dates represented by manufacturing other than petroleum.

This rapid, and to Europeans alarming, growth was mainly confined to the larger American corporations, and it conformed to the historic pattern of major investment by companies that had successfully mechanized processes dependent on medium to high technology. The chief exceptions were products like Coca Cola, where massive advertising campaigns could build markets. In fact, much of the European feeling of inability to resist the American invasion of the 1960s rested on their smaller companies' lacking both resources and experience to rival the invaders' costly marketing techniques.

Some of the inability had an inescapable factual base. An American corporation with a billion or more a year in sales could afford a crash advertising campaign costing many millions of dollars and then cut back when a secure position had been won. This was the usual practice in the United States for either new products or expansion into new sales areas. To some extent in Germany and even more so in France the idea of building a new market from scratch had seldom been considered. European businessmen tended to look only at American successes and American marketing achievements, often attributing these to superior management techniques rather than to smart advertising agencies and high cash outlays. A more careful analysis would have revealed some spectacular failures in marketing both at home and abroad by the biggest American corporations.[8] In the late 1960s, however, American marketing was being better understood, and its practices applied by Western European firms in both their home and foreign markets. Perhaps one could say that up to the 1960s the market for processed consumer goods had never been large enough in any single European country other than Britain to make a massive selling campaign pay.

American direct investment proceeded in the Middle East and Latin America, but more in developing sources of supply than in the creating of new local markets. Japan still restricted ownership by foreign corporations and successfully bought both technical and managerial advice from American and other firms, usually improving on the Western models in the course of adaptation. Yet the values and customs of Japanese, as well as other Asian cultures, still remained so far from those of the West that comparative business analogies are difficult.

A PROCESS OF MUTUAL LEARNING

While the book value of direct investments of 3,500 American firms in 15,000 foreign enterprises in 1970 was only a fraction of a percent higher in relation to the GNP than in 1929, the influence of these investments was much greater on the business environment. The world-wide governmental problems of the United States made even the strictly local businessman aware of the adverse balance of payments, comparative rates of inflation, and other problems of multinational business. Furthermore, the 3,500 firms involved were leaders in finance, trade, construction, oil, mining, and manufacturing. They were the corporations looked to for innovations in management and marketing, as well as for price leadership. Except for aircraft companies, which only exported, the multinational firms included nearly all those that carried on extensive product research, in some cases heavily subsidized by the federal government. The world setting had thus become the backdrop for American business action to a far greater extent than ever before.

Following World War II, serious attention in both corporations and universities was directed to the characteristics of various foreign business environments. Language made England the easiest to visit and study and the business environment was in many respects most like that of the United States. In the 1950s and 1960s large British companies were creating autonomous divisions for either special products or regional markets. Their boards of directors probably had a higher percentage of the corporations' executives than in America, but otherwise had a similar relation to the enterprise. While the managerial hierarchy appeared much the same in both nations, British firms were more production-oriented and made less effort to find and develop new markets.

A very basic cultural difference was the British belief that high-level management was a talent or art not susceptible to scholarly analysis or much improvement in business schools. Britain placed less importance on the role of business education in the undergraduate curricula of its major universities than did the United States; by the 1970s there were only three top-level graduate schools of business in Britain, and most professional management advice was chiefly at the plant level, as it had been in the United States during the days of Frederick W. Taylor. This tradition led to the paradox of the talented amateur in management who, as part of his general reading, had seen some of the literature of business administration, but doubted the value of experimenting with more systematic procedures. Although the civil service or professions were still more attractive than business to the well-born and best educated, there was also an element of aristocracy in the concept of natural competence to manage.[9] In all, however, it was not difficult for American managers to adjust to the British environment.

Externally Germany also seemed much like the United States except for its two-level system of corporate directors. There was a topmost board composed of outsiders that generally represented banking interests but in the coal and steel industries also included representatives of the trade unions. Beneath this board was a smaller one, the *Vorstand*, composed entirely of officers, that really ran the corporation the way an executive committee would in the United States. Big companies played a dominant role in manufacturing and also in banking, and although they had excellent technologists, German executives had much of the American respect for the importance of marketing.

Beneath the surface, however, there were differences in managerial power and attitudes. The half dozen big German banks exercised more internal influence on large companies than any financial institutions did in the United States. There was more respect for authority based on ownership, and an abiding suspicion of professional managers. Consequently less authority was delegated to the middle management level. Traditions and moral codes circumscribed the means used to pursue economic goals to a noticeably greater extent than in the United States. Furthermore, as in France, the professionals reaching the top were likely to be technical men. Except for the heavy industry of the Ruhr, managerial movement between firms or branches was more limited than in the United States. Men liked to stay in their ancestral state. Yet American chief executives found it relatively easy to adjust to German practices, and the central government was even more favorable to direct investment than in Britain.[10]

Of the three nations of Europe used for comparison, France offered American firms both the greatest challenges and some of the best opportunities. The French government, particularly after the election of De Gaulle, was opposed in principle to the American takeover of French firms. This was aggravated in the early 1960s by the United States government's prohibition of a computer sale to the French nuclear power authority, a political action so bizarre that its political antecedents can not be explored here. Partly as a result of continuing French hostility to the "American invasion," fed by extremist books and articles, direct investment was only $2.6 billion in 1970, compared to $4.3 billion in West Germany. But it must also be remembered that the West German market was growing at a more rapid rate than the French and hence offered more opportunities. In both finance and manufacturing all but a few of the American-owned enterprises in France had been there before 1950.

The friction between American ideas of management and those of the French was not a post-World War II phenomenon, nor had the views of the two national groups been more than moderately reconciled by 1976. As in Britain, American philosophies and studies of management were not held in high esteem. Chief executives in France were generally selected from among Parisians specially trained in engineering, law, or governmental finance. The civil service was still highly prestigious and many graduates of the Parisian écoles spent some years in government before being bought away by private or state-owned business enterprise. American managers lacked experience in dealing with the competition, either for personnel or markets, of government-owned business. But studies and interviews do not indicate any difference in the type of managers in the government-owned motor, utility, or financial companies from those in the private sector. Similar observations would apply to both Britain and Germany, but with considerably less consistency than in France.

Within the firm, lines of authority and its delegation departed radically from the customs of the United States. The board of directors was generally controlled by banking interests, the big credit companies, that voted the proxies of stockholders who deposited in their branches. Since only the *directeur generale* plus, at the most, one other officer sat on the board, its deliberations were much more concerned with overall finance than with internal affairs. The *directeur generale*, being often the only link with the board, exercised autocratic authority, in contrast to the discussion and voting of the German *Vorstands* or British or American executive committees.

The French appeared to prefer arbitrary decisions passed down bureaucratically to the comparatively free and easy discussions and modifications of policy that went on in the interlevel committees of the United States. Yet, while the system might seem more arbitrary, the policy directives were also fewer and more generalized, leaving a good deal of discretion to the individual manager. Seen from the French point of view, men are called upon to think creatively for themselves (within limits) rather than waste endless hours in the Anglo-American type of committee and group discussions.

Some of the French combination of high-level policy formation and wide managerial discretion in its application may be at the base of a new stage of management thought, but in the area of marketing their managers in most businesses appeared to have failed, perhaps temporarily, to match American practice. This is not surprising, since in the prewar French company the men in charge of sales and marketing were not generally part of the top level of management, and ideas for spending any substantial sums on sales promotion met cold responses from the heads of manufacturing firms who usually thought in terms of better technology, or finer products. The unexpected winning of a bigger share of markets by a few American companies and the development of television were moving the French in the direction of more respect for sales and less acquiescence to inter-company regional marketing agreements.

The fact that some American companies as important as General Electric, Ford, and Westinghouse have not, over many decades, been able to expand their French manufacturing operations indicates that American methods of marketing are not necessarily superior under all circumstances. Even in the 1970s, French middle-income purchasing power was small compared to that in the United States, and French buyers had different schedules of preference in spending any extra income. While France is currently in a stage of rapid growth and new markets are evolving, so are worldwide ideas regarding management, and it may turn out that the French have been able to skip those extremes of the last quarter century that had poor local applicability.[11]

More than in France, Japan presented governmental, managerial, and market impediments to American expansion, with the result that the direct American investment there is small and was far surpassed from 1970 on by Japanese direct investment in the United States (more than $2 billion by 1975). Consequently, Japanese management in these companies can be studied as well as that of the relatively few American managers who have had experience with local companies in Japan. In *Fortune* for May 1975, Louis Kraar wrote an article entitled "The Japanese Are Coming With Their Own Style of Management." His conclusions, together with writing by many Japanese and American scholars on the business history of Japan, emphasize the contrast already alluded to in earlier chapters. The Japanese traditional order was so hierarchical and status-conscious that means were developed for bypassing the normal rigidities. More communication and emphasis on common aims were basic to the Japanese compromise. The welfare of workers has been constantly emphasized as a goal of the firm. From the lowest supervisory levels there is free upward communication with the chief executives through the *ringi* system of written suggestions and each *ringishi* is discussed first among the organizational peers of the proposer and then sent higher up. Such procedures tend to enhance the feeling for the company as a group enterprise, but they also slow down decision-making. While the American branches of Japanese firms may have good nonunion employee relations and democratic managerial attitudes, they seem to have been slower to adjust to market changes.[12]

Of those of the five nations discussed, French companies probably have had the weakest informal structure. Michael Crozier, a leading student of French management, said in 1964 that stable informal groups were rare and that there was a low level of free group activities.[13] This may make it easier for a foreign manager to institute new systems of control, providing that they appear to respect the dignity and rights of the individual. In contrast the Japanese *habatsu*, or cliques, are the strongest and most enduring.[14]

A century of experience abroad has unquestionably had effects on American management that have sometimes been attributed to domestic ideas. American Radiator Company, for example, with newly established plants in England, France, and Germany in 1900 made the three local managers a European Advisory Board, or in later-day language, created a semiautonomous foreign division. Certainly much of the recognition of social and psychological problems among supervisors and workers, generally ascribed to Elton Mayo and his followers, must have come back to the central offices of companies with branches in half a dozen foreign countries, of which there were some two score by 1930. Perhaps the most persistent message was the value of delegating decision-making to the lowest possible level and thus giving managers of the foreign nationality a sense of discretion and importance.

On the other hand, computers, telex, and jet travel have allowed head offices to keep much closer track of what is happening in the field, both at home and abroad. Monthly figures of any available type are now easy to prepare and transmit. As a result central management is wrestling with two contradictory concepts: the value of divisional and even departmental autonomy; and the profits available from longer range central office planning and more frequent and exacting checkups. As a result of such conflicts in imponderables, Robert Stobaugh and Sidney Robbins, in *Money in Multinational Enterprise*, accused big companies of sacrificing as much as 25 percent of their possible overseas profit by not planning and dictating capital borrowing policies to their foreign subsidiaries, which would lead to tax advantages on money transferred back to the United States.[15] In fact, the computer alone is forcing upon all management more drastically than ever before in history the dilemma of centralization versus delegation of controls.

SOCIAL PRESSURES ON BUSINESS

The social responsibilities of business have been subject to highly different interpretations in the different nations. One might conclude that the greater the degree of business freedom, the more public relations departments would emphasize their recognition of social responsibility, and vice versa. In support of such a thesis it could be noted that in France there has never been a doctrine of social responsibility by business, but a wide area of public ownership and government planning. In Germany the state, from an early date, assumed a large part of the social responsibilities that were borne, if at all, by American business before the New Deal. In Britain the same was true at slightly later dates, but except for two brief periods of rising nationalization, the state interfered relatively less with British business than it did across the channel, and there was more support for the doctrine of private responsibilities. As has been so often the case in these comparisons, Japanese attitudes differed substantially from any of those in the West. Social responsibility in business meant primarily responsibility to the employees of the firm, and, as we have seen, included much lifetime employment, medical care, recreation, and pensions. This made the state slow in adequately assuming such functions, and in this way fits our thesis, but it is also true that government never hesitated to regulate business in the national interest.

Pursuing the inverse relation of regulation and the doctrine of private responsibility, in the late 1920s government in the United States still did less for the economic security of the private citizen than in other leading industrial states, and national business associations and company public relations departments talked continually about social responsibilities. Dean Wallace Donham of Harvard Business School, surveying this outpouring from professional spokesmen of business, said that it dealt with serious subjects in "platitudes about morality and service." Equally annoyed by the national deluge of cant regarding social responsibility, the progressive business leader Edward Filene remarked: "Nine tenths of a businessman's best public service can be rendered by virtue of the way he conducts his business . . . ," and the equally liberal Herbert Swope of General Electric said: "Society in testing the efficiency of any organization, is going to measure not only its services, but also its continual and progressive reduction of prices of its products to the public." The *Nation's Business* denounced "the rhetoric of service as little more than a sales device."[16]

After government assumed more and more of the social burden during the New Deal and imposed numerous regulations, there was never another such outburst of talk about social responsibilities. One of the contributing factors was the mandatory fringe benefits agreed to in union contracts from 1946 on. There was still, however, a more continuous American interest in business responsibility for social welfare and more writing on the subject than in the foreign nations.

Contributions for purely philanthropic purposes was a type of responsibility that business companies assumed to a small degree. In the late 1920s the Community Chest movement had gained rapidly, and the issue of whether corporate funds could be donated for purposes only indirectly connected with the welfare of the stockholders became increasingly important. In the "soak the rich" tax bill of 1935, companies were allowed to contribute 5 percent of income for gifts, but it was 1953 before the courts began to legalize moderate gifts for such purposes as education on the basis of their indirect benefit to the stockholders. Since corporate giving from 1935 on declined slightly as a percentage of all philanthropy and averaged about 1 percent of income, with no large company known to have approached the 5 percent mark, a major lawsuit was never brought to prevent such practices.[17] Hence the precise limit of what represented social responsibility of indirect value to stockholders has never been determined.

Many beneficiaries of corporate success, however, from Carnegie and Rockefeller to the Fords and Mellons, personally set up tax-exempt foundations that gave gifts to a wide range of social causes, but seldom to poor relief, which came increasingly to be regarded as a sphere for government action. For gifts to education, research, the arts, and civic betterment, companies as well as individuals established foundations, which were tax exempt until a number of legal restrictions were imposed by congressional action from 1969 on. Such organizations had two distinct purposes. The first was to maintain family control of corporations by placing much of its stock in the hands of the foundation, thus avoiding heavy inheritance taxes whose payment might force the sale of too many shares to outsiders. To this end large individual holdings of the voting stock of a company were placed in the hands of relatives serving as trustees of a foundation or, for more security, were converted into a new nonvoting category, a practice followed by the Fords. The second, more socially useful purpose was to separate yearly contributions to the foundation from its annual spending. In good years the company or family could make large payments to the foundation, which could accumulate the money and grant it in less prosperous times.

The congressional act of 1969 was a hastily designed bill aimed at curbing the use of foundations as tax shelters. In providing for both taxes and limited life spans, it handicapped the work of many useful organizations that had long since ceased to have family or company connections. As time goes on the law will no doubt be amended so as properly to distinguish between foundations created solely for private tax purposes and those performing valuable social functions.

FEDERAL REGULATION OF RESPONSIBILITY

In the 1960s and 1970s the federal government passed laws and established regulatory agencies to monitor business practices regarding hiring employees and those necessary to protect the health and welfare of the public. Both were problems of long standing which, except for food, drugs, and some safety devices, had generally been left to the discretion of business and the states.

The Civil Rights Act of 1964, prohibiting discrimination in hiring on the basis of race, sex, or color, interfered with the habitual practice of many if not most firms. Insofar as these practices had grown without sufficient analysis and with the qualifications demanded for many jobs having little to do with the needs of the position, a fresh examination was probably advantageous to a company. But the new law and the Civil Rights Commission established to enforce it did not demand a more rational hiring system, but rather one that gave a considerable place to women and blacks, whether or not such categories presented sufficient, reasonably eligible candidates. During the decade following its passage, federal enforcement at first became stricter and then more relaxed, concentrating only on certain aspects of the act.

Although few businessmen have thought it part of their role to take the lead in discovering new social responsibilities, they have usually tried to conform to government policies. Often this has not been easy. While a chief executive may order new policies for hiring, for example, he cannot know whether or not personnel officers put them into effect.

Of the new antidiscrimination regulations, the one requiring more hiring of women was relatively easy to comply with at the lower levels and probably beneficial for business efficiency. Promotion of women to executive positions, however, involved problems in the informal structure of company relationships. In many companies the higher echelon formed a group that belonged to the same clubs, played golf together, and joked about common male experiences. When a woman was added to one board of directors, the group had to stop lunching at the best downtown club because women were not allowed. It was easy, however, to exaggerate these problems. Many if not most medium to large companies had no informal structure that necessarily excluded women, and by 1976 they were rather rapidly infiltrating senior officer groups and boards of directors.

Blacks presented a more difficult problem. Victims of poor education in segregated schools, they often lacked the minimum requirements for corporate jobs. If the company was to meet the demands of the government for fair employment the only solution might be to set up special training courses. Of a sample of 247 companies studied by Jules Cohn from 1967 to 1970, special programs to recruit and train blacks were set up by 110, and most of the rest tried to increase black employment. Only 9 percent, however, did anything about equalizing opportunities for other ethnic minorities.[18]

Legislation by the states to check pollution had a hundred year history of rather minor local regulations and, on the federal level, from 1953 on, with the Public Health service reports on air pollution from a large number of stations. That same year President Eisenhower created the Department of Health, Education, and Welfare. Since it administers Social Security, which is run as a contributory pension fund, its outlays by the 1970s were about equal to those of the Department of Defense. The rise of public concern for health brought regulations to bear on business; but these regulations were more the result of mounting public concern in the 1960s about air and water pollution and the hazards to workers and consumers from chemicals than they were of government planning. Concern over air pollution was triggered by the fantastic increase in the total horsepower of internal combustion engines in use between 1950 and 1965; while health hazards were augmented by the increasing use of new synthetic chemicals and drugs.

The same problems were afflicting all the densely populated industrial nations, but prior to 1970 the effects were probably more marked in the United States, and since only one national government was involved, effective action was easier. In general, Europe suffered more from water pollution and, since there were fewer and smaller automobiles, less from unhealthy air. Smoke abatement had long been an aim of legislation in the European nations as well as in the American states.

A young lawyer, Ralph Nader, aroused the people of the United States with his book, *Unsafe at Any Speed* (1965), which attacked the design in automobiles. That same year the state of California adopted an automobile emissions control act, and two years later Congress passed a law for motor vehicle safety standards. While federal laws sought in the course of a decade to force manufacturers to reduce noxious chemicals in automobile exhausts, an important step in the same direction came from the Arab oil embargo of 1973–74 and the resulting rise in the price of gasoline. To bring the size of American cars and engines down to the average of the rest of the world would in itself eliminate a large part of the problem.

Nader's privately financed organization in Washington became one of a number of organizations (such as the Sierra Club) working for conservation and the protection of health. Disposal of sewage and industrial wastes came increasingly to be regulated by federal as well as state laws and in 1971 an executive decree created the independent Environmental Protection Agency, with broad powers to investigate and issue orders. The result of these various pressures was far from a war between corporate polluters and government agencies. As the president of Du Pont said: "Some urban problems are clearly the business of business, and demand our direct involvement. Pollution control is a case in point."[19] But as in any such campaign, there were disagreements as to what was adequate and possible.

The increase in chemical production from a national total of $3.2 billion in 1929 to $27 billion in 1969 was bound to produce health problems in both manufacture and use. No consumer could pass on the safety of the goods purchased, nor could any company immediately detect long-run ill effects from handling or consuming some new compound. The chemical industry created the Institute of Toxicology to study work hazards not already covered by state labor laws and to protect consumers. In 1970 the Occupational Safety and Health Act created an administration of the same name in the Department of Labor. In fiscal 1974 alone it inspected 75,000 plants and inspired the tightening of state laws. In 1973 the Consumer Product Safety Commission was added to the array of new federal agencies.

In fact, because of environmental change, essentially conservative presidential administrations signed bills or issued executive orders creating more new regulatory agencies than in any period since the New Deal. But while business could protest the earlier regulations as interfering with business as such, the new type had the patriotic appeal of saving the national environment and protecting the people. Extreme conservatives in business stood in principle for the removal of all regulatory commissions, but if the public demanded legislation it was easier for management to have it administered by commissioners than interpreted by costly legal action, as in the nineteenth century. The danger to both business and the public was that autonomous agencies might act irresponsibly.

Perhaps a more serious threat by government to efficient business operation came from the drain of so many of the best technologists into a few defense-related industries and government administrations. While there were by-products from government-sponsored research that were useful for the improvement of processes in production for civilian use in many lines, they did not compensate sufficiently to keep the United States competitive with the foreign leaders. Except where the big American market allowed for more development expense, or where there were high-technology spillovers from defense, American exports of manufactures, in spite of devaluation of the dollar, were having a hard time maintaining their place in the world markets.

THE BUSINESS FACTOR

Of more fundamental importance to the business system, however, was the continuing shift toward consumer goods and service, in which the United States had led the world. Even by 1970 this was necessitating business adjustment to new economic relationships. From 1960 to 1973, for example, capital investment in relation to national output was the lowest in the United States of any of the leading capitalist industrial nations.[20] Perhaps this was a passing situation, but possibly it forecast a new relationship of the high wage, service economy.

Adjustment to relatively lower employment in capital goods production, and compensating aspects of the shift such as the upswing of recreation were suddenly complicated, in 1973, by an unforeseen short-age of energy, a shortage that fed a high worldwide rate of inflation. Because of great distances and consequent large costs for communication and transportation, and real wage levels initially above those of its chief competitors, these changes posed unusual difficulties for the United States. Furthermore, since even in 1976 the nation was probably furthest along the road toward employment in service and away from employment in fabrication, it faced the greatest challenges in redeployment of its labor force in new directions. At the extreme one can imagine a future economy of automated factories supplying ample goods for a population devoted to marketing, recreation, and an increasing variety of personal services.

In addition, the economic problems arising from shortage of energy and inflation were aggravated by the weaknesses of a governmental system designed for an earlier agricultural society. Moreover, the adversary attitude between businessmen and government built up in the nineteenth century tended to persist so strongly that cooperation was difficult. But even on the best possible basis, the cost of maintaining three levels of government with poorly defined jurisdictions was unusually high; or put another way, quite aside from corruption, the American received a poor return for his dollar in taxes.

Cures for the ills of the environment, diminishing resources, economic change, and governmental inefficiency would not be produced by a single inspired leader in New York or Washington or by Adam Smith's unseen hand. In America they would have to come through business as a system. In our type of society business is the inevitable intervening factor between physical and technological change and social adjustment. It is in reality a network which, as we have seen, is greatly more complex and interconnected than is generally assumed by economists or politicians. The effects of altering the fabric of interrelationships at any point cannot be foreseen. Change has to proceed on a trial and error basis. Hence history or statistical series cannot supply the knowledge needed for predicting short-run change, but they can point to factors likely to be important in the long run.

One such element that probably makes for flexibility is that the normal decisions in American business are still those of the small- to medium-sized firm, the organization with well under a thousand employees. In this area the changing environment is having subtle effects. All over the industrial world average levels of formal education have risen dramatically since 1945, and the most so in the United States. The small businessman who might have had only a grade school education in the 1920s was now being replaced by his sons who had, at the least, graduated from high school. Yet in many cases well-educated sons preferred some other career to any type of business. In 1970 only about one-fifth of college graduates chose to be businessmen. The effects of this disinterest in commerce in an age of increasing knowledge were hard to foresee. Small business had never relied much upon recruiting leaders with academic proficiency and in the drift toward service enterprise it might do just as well surrounded by a "world of knowledge" as one of ignorance. Furthermore, it was hard to educate for unknowable future jobs. Big business was able to buy the specialists that were made essential by change, but chief executives of all companies were still necessarily more artists than scientists.

In the larger corporations American management was confronting other changes in values and social customs that affected all the industrial nations, but perhaps this nation most because of its equalitarian traditions. The United States had led the way in preaching democracy, in pioneering more permissive childrearing, and in an equalitarian attitude in office and plant. Perhaps all the other big industrial nations were being forced to move in the same direction, but as of 1976 they still seemed to carry with them more values or restraints from their aristocratic past. A team of management students from the United States sampling European "managerial thinking" in the middle 1960s concluded that "taking all countries together, 'to direct' has better connotations than to 'persuade,' and that to persuade . . . is closer to making a mistake." They found that managers "seem consistently to endorse authoritarian principles, *vis-a-vis* organizational structure. . . . Across all countries . . . two needs stand out as unsatisfied—autonomy and self-actualization."[21]

If these are the most important needs or motivations of businessmen the United States may well take a lead in fulfilling them. In the seventies both business schools and corporate managements were proposing flexible combinations of managers for projects in which each participant would have more of a personal interest. While informal authoritarian systems still existed around strong chief executives in the United States, as elsewhere, a more equalitarian climate was deliberately being cultivated. But bureaucracy still imposed restraints on rapid adjustment. The giant company did not operate with an easygoing flexibility. In 1975 a 48-year-old, top-level vice-president resigned from a $550,000-a-year position because, he complained, "one simply couldn't be an innovator or planner; . . . you were too harassed and oppressed by committee meetings and paperwork. . . . [The company] has gotten to be a total insulation from the realities of the world."[22] Obviously, in big business, at least, some inspired changes were needed if "self-actualization" was to be achieved, and it would surprise few managers anywhere in the world if the next organizational innovations occurred in the United States.

NOTES

Footnotes are used more to indicate useful sources than to document statements. Had the latter been attempted in a work of this scope, the footnotes would have overwhelmed the text. When, because of absence of historical literature, information has had to come from outmoded textbooks, I have tried to note the most useful one. With few exceptions, statistics come from *Historical Statistics of the United States* and the annual *Statistical Abstract of the United States*.

Introduction

1. Robert Lekachman, *The Age of Keynes* (New York: Random House, 1966), p. 89.
2. Daniel A. Wren, *The Evolution of Management Thought* (New York: Ronald Press, 1972), p. 505.

1: The Social Bases of Enterprise

1. See John U. Nef, *Cultural Foundations of Industrial Civilization* (Cambridge, England: Cambridge University Press, 1958).
2. For more detailed discussion see Thomas C. Cochran, *Social Change in Industrial Society: Twentieth Century America* (London: George Allen & Unwin, 1972), pp. 11–29.
3. Thomas Hamilton, *Men and Manners in America* (London, 1853), p. 74.
4. Benjamin Rush, *Plan for the Establishment of Schools and the Diffusion of Knowledge in Pennsylvania* (Philadelphia, 1786), pp. 5–6; James G. Carter, *Essays on Popular Education*, quoted in Newton Edwards and Herman G. Richey, *The School in the American Social Order* (Boston: Houghton Mifflin, 1947), p. 273.
5. David A. Barnes, *A Discourse on Education* (Boston, 1803), pp. 8–9. For general discussion see Thomas C. Cochran, *Business in American Life: A History* (New York: McGraw-Hill, 1972), pp. 91–102.
6. See Carl Bridenbaugh, *Myths and Realities: Societies of the Colonial*

South (Baton Rouge: Louisiana State University Press, 1952); and Aubrey C. Land, "Economic Base and Social Structure," *Journal of Economic History* 25 (Dec. 1965).

7. See Ralph H. Gabriel, *The Course of American Democratic Thought* (New York: Ronald Press, rev. ed. 1956); and Seymour Lipsett, *The First New Nation* (New York: Basic Books, 1963), p. 79 ff.

8. Thomas C. Cochran, "The Business Revolution," *American Historical Review* 79 (Dec. 1974): 1449–67.

9. James Willard Hurst, *Law and Economic Growth: The Legal History of the Lumber Industry in Wisconsin, 1836–1915* (Cambridge: Harvard University Press, 1964), p. 121.

10. Cochran, *Business in American Life*, pp. 114–16.

11. Murray G. Murphey, "An Approach to the Study of National Character," in Milford Spero, ed., *Meaning and Content in Cultural Anthropology* (New York: Free Press, 1965), p. 144 ff.

12. See, for example, John S. Abott, "Parental Neglect," *Parents Magazine* 2 (Mar. 1842); Anne Kuhn, "The Mother's Role in Childhood Education," *New England Concepts, 1830–1860* (New Haven: Yale University Press, 1947); John Hersey, *Advice to Christian Parents* (Baltimore, 1839); and Margaret Mead and W. Wolfenstein, eds., *Childhood in Contemporary Culture* (Chicago: University of Chicago Press, 1955).

13. See Herbert G. Gutman, "Work, Culture, and Society in Industrialized America, 1815–1919," *American Historical Review* 78 (June 1973): 525–89.

14. Perry Miller, *American Character: A Conversion* (Santa Barbara: University of California Press, 1962), p. 23.

15. For a discussion of early values, see Edward Pessen, *Jacksonian America: Society, Personality and Politics* (Homewood, Ill.: Dorsey Press, 1969), pp. 12–30. For the enduring quality of most of these values, see F. X. Sutton, S. E. Harris, C. Kaysen, and J. Tobin, *The American Business Creed* (Cambridge: Harvard University Press, 1956).

16. Charles E. Friedman, "Joint Stock Organization in France, 1807–1867," *Business History Review* 39 (Summer 1965): 190.

17. Some years of graduate seminar work on an American definition for individualism achieved no consensus beyond the control of personal property. For a discussion of the Latin interpretation, see Thomas C. Cochran, *The Puerto Rican Businessman: A Study in Cultural Change* (Philadelphia: University of Pennsylvania Press, 1959), pp. 117–32.

18. David S. Landes, "French Business and Businessmen: A Social Cultural Analysis," in Hugh G. J. Aitken, ed., *Explorations in Enterprise* (Cambridge: Harvard University Press, 1965), pp. 185–86.

19. I cannot agree with the methods used in measuring achievement motivation and believe it still has to be treated as a nominal or, at most, an ordinal variable.

20. See, for example, Richard R. Wohl, "Henry Noble Day," in William Miller, ed., *Men in Business* (Cambridge: Harvard University Press, 1952), pp. 153–92.

2: *Innovations in Structure and Processes*

1. *The Unbound Prometheus: Technological Change and Industrial Development in Western Europe from 1750 to the Present* (Cambridge, England: Cambridge University Press, 1970), p. 1.

2. See Peter Mathias, *The First Industrial Nation: An Economic History of Britain, 1700–1914* (New York: Charles Scribner's Sons, 1969), p. 10 ff; Phyllis Deane, *The First Industrial Revolution* (Cambridge, England: Cambridge University Press, 1965), pp. 54–68; Landes, *Prometheus*, 545–47; and Kazushi Ohkawa and Henry Rosovsky, *Japanese Economic Growth: Trend Acceleration in the Twentieth Century* (Stanford: Stanford University Press, 1973), p. 12.

3. For entrepreneurship, see Hugh G. J. Aitken, ed., *Explorations in Enterprise* (Cambridge: Harvard University Press, 1965).

4. Charles Wilson, "Transport as a Factor in the History of Economic Development," *Journal of European Economic History* 2 (Fall 1973): 327–30.

5. See Thomas C. Cochran, *Business in American Life: A History* (New York: McGraw-Hill, 1972), pp. 61–87. In the opening paragraph, written some half-dozen years ago, I am still repeating the classic emphasis on technology.

6. Business organization is not what most economists define as "human capital." The latter is usually meant to represent expenditures for education and training.

7. "Gross National Product 1834–1909," in National Bureau of Economic Research, *Output, Employment and Productivity in the United States after 1800*, Studies in Income and Wealth, vol. 30, (New York, 1969), pp. 5–7.

8. "New Light on a Statistical Dark Age: U.S. Real Product Growth Before 1840," *American Economic Review* 57 (1967): 294–306. The article is reprinted in *New Economic History*, ed. by Peter Temin (Baltimore: Penguin Books, 1973), pp. 44–60; see table, pp. 50–51. Robert Gallman has told me that he thinks these figures slightly high but would only reduce them about 10 percent.

9. *Urban Growth and the Circulation of Information: The United States System of Cities, 1790–1840* (Cambridge: Harvard University Press, 1973).

10. A. Dunsire, *Administration: the Word and the Science* (New York: John Wiley & Sons, 1973), p. 40.

11. Roy J. Sampson, "American Accounting Education, Textbooks and Public Practice Prior to 1900," *Business History Review* 34 (Winter 1960): 460–61.

12. Stuart Bruchey, "Success and Failure Factors: American Merchants in Foreign Trade in the Eighteenth and Early Nineteenth Centuries," *Business History Review* 34 (Autumn 1958): 278–79.

13. Curtis P. Nettels, *The Emergence of a National Economy, 1775–1815* (New York: Holt, Rinehart & Winston, 1962), p. 290. For a more specialized account of American business at this time see Elisha P. Douglass, *The Coming of Age of American Business* (Chapel Hill: University of North Carolina Press, 1971).

14. See Judah Adelson, "The Early Evolution of Business Organization

in France," *Business History Review* 31 (Summer 1957); Charles E. Friedman, "Joint Stock Business Organization in France, 1807–1867," *Business History Review* 39 (Summer 1965): 187–91; Mathias, *Industrial Nation*, pp. 33–38; and Joseph S. Davis, *Essays in the Earlier History of American Corporations*, 2 vols. (Cambridge: Harvard University Press, 1917).

15. State and federal aid to economic growth are well summarized in Stuart Bruchey, *The Roots of American Economic Growth, 1607–1861: An Essay on Social Causation* (London: Hutchinson University Library, 1965), pp. 95–138. For more detailed studies of Northeastern states see John W. Cadman, Jr., *The Corporation in New Jersey: Business and Politics, 1791–1875* (Cambridge: Harvard University Press, 1949), pp. 33–37; Nathan Miller, *The Enterprise of a Free People: Aspects of Economic Development in New York State During the Canal Period, 1792–1838* (Ithaca: Cornell University Press, 1962), pp. 14, 25–26; Oscar and Mary Handlin, *Commonwealth, A Study of the Role of Government in the American Economy: Massachusetts, 1774–1861* (New York: New York University Press, 1947), pp. 113–43; and Louis Hartz, *Economic Policy and Democratic Thought: Pennsylvania, 1776–1860* (Cambridge: Harvard University Press, 1948), pp. 37–103. The Handlins' and Hartz's volumes were planned by the Committee on Research in Economic History as parts of a systematic survey of business and government in sample states. The Cadman volume, begun independently, was later incorporated into the series. The Miller volume, also conceived independently on the particular subject of canals, was published by the Beveridge Fund of the American Historical Association.

16. Davis, *Corporations*, pp. 2, 20 ff.

17. See Eric Monkkonen, "Bank of Augusta v. Earle: Corporate Growth v. States' Rights," *The Alabama Quarterly* 34 (Summer 1972): 113–30.

18. For details of this complicated history see F. Cyril James, "The Bank of North America and the Financial History of Philadelphia," *Pennsylvania Magazine of History and Biography* 64 (Jan. 1940): 56–96.

19. Peter Mathias, "Capital, Credit and Enterprise in the Industrial Revolution," *Journal of European Economic History* 2 (Spring 1973): 129.

20. Bruchey, "Success and Failure Factors," p. 28.

21. See Glenn Porter and Robert Livesay, *Merchants and Manufacturers: Studies in the Changing Structure of Nineteenth Century Marketing* (Baltimore: Johns Hopkins University Press, 1971), for a general discussion of the wholesaler. As Mathias notes, most capital investment was (and continued to be) in buildings not in production goods in the form of machines ("Capital, Credit and Enterprise," p. 123).

22. Pred, *Urban Growth*, pp. 37, 44, 45.

23. Mathias, "Capital Credit and Enterprise," p. 127.

24. *Statistical Annals* (Philadelphia, 1818), p. 374.

25. Pred, *Urban Growth*, p. 86.

26. Ibid., p. 85.

27. Ronald W. Filante, "A Note on the Economic Viability of the Erie Canal, 1825–1869," *Business History Review* 48 (Spring 1974): 96.

28. See Robert G. Albion, *The Rise of New York Port, 1815–1860* (New York: Charles Scribner's Sons, 1939).

29. Pred, *Urban Growth*, p. 268.

30. See Gene Cesari, "Technology in the American Arms Industry, 1790–1860" (Ph.D. diss., University of Pennsylvania, 1970), for the unprofitability of Eli Whitney's and other early attempts at mass production.

31. Douglass, *American Business*, p. 88.

32. Ohkawa and Rosovsky, *Japanese Economic Growth*, pp. 217–32.

3: The Competence of Early Management

1. David S. Landes, "French Business and Businessmen: A Social Cultural Analysis," in Hugh G. J. Aitken, ed., *Explorations in Enterprise* (Cambridge: Harvard University Press, 1965), p. 186.

2. Thomas C. Cochran, *Business in American Life: A History* (New York: McGraw-Hill, 1972), pp. 88–89.

3. Robert G. Albion, *The Rise of New York Port, 1815–1860* (New York: Charles Scribner's Sons, 1939), pp. 285–86.

4. Robert G. Albion, *Square Riggers on Schedule: The New York Sailing Packets to England* (Princeton: Princeton University Press, 1938), pp. 106–11.

5. Albion, *New York Port*, pp. 272–83.

6. Albion, *Square Riggers*, p. 106.

7. R. S. Sayers, *Lloyds Bank in the History of English Banking* (Oxford, England: Clarendon Press, 1957), p. 63.

8. Andre Liessé, *Evolution of Credit and Banks in France: From the Founding of the Bank of France to the Present Time* (Washington, D.C.: Government Printing Office, 1909), pp. 8–10.

9. Ibid., p. 10.

10. Elmer Wood, *English Theories of Central Banking Control 1819–1858: With Some Account of Contemporary Procedures* (Cambridge: Harvard University Press, 1939), pp. 13–16; Sayers, *Lloyds Bank*, passim.

11. N. S. B. Gras, *The Massachusetts First National Bank of Boston, 1784–1934* (Cambridge: Harvard University Press, 1937), pp. 11–12; and Fritz Redlich, *The Molding of American Banking: Men and Ideas*, 2 vols. (New York: Hafner, 1951), 1: 5. For early banking history see also J. Van Fenstermaker, *The Development of American Commercial Banking, 1782–1937* (Kent, Ohio: Kent State University Bureau of Economic and Business Research, 1965); and Benjamin J. Klebaner, *Commercial Banking in the United States: A History* (Hinsdale, Ill.: Dryden Press, 1974).

12. Bray Hammond, *Banks and Politics in America: From the Revolution to the Civil War* (Princeton: Princeton University Press, 1957), p. 81.

13. Walter Bagehot, *Lombard Street: A Description of the Money Market* (London, 1873; rev. ed. 1904) p. 331. In 1829, New York State required an annual deposit of one-half of one percent of a bank's capital in the state Safety Fund for note redemption.

14. Albert O. Greef, *The Commercial Paper House in the United States* (Cambridge: Harvard University Press, 1938), pp. 7–8; and Bagehot, *Lombard Street*, p. 286.

15. Sayers, *Lloyds Bank*, pp. 64–68.

16. Greef, *Commercial Paper*, p. 71.

17. Marquis James, *Biography of a Business* (New York: Bobbs-Merrill, 1942), pp. 17–21.

18. Daniel Hodas, "Report of Research Possibilities at Eleutherian Mills," 1974 (Mss., Eleutherian Mills-Hagley Library, Greenville, Delaware), pp. 13–18.

19. Elisha P. Douglass, *The Coming of Age of American Business: Three Centuries of Enterprise, 1600–1900* (Chapel Hill: University of North Carolina Press, 1971), p. 77. Douglass puts the average rate of profit at 2 or 3 percent.

20. Douglass, *American Business*, p. 110.

21. For Japan, see David S. Landes, "Japan and Europe: Contrasts in Industrialization," in William W. Lockwood, ed., *The State and Economic Enterprise in Japan* (Princeton: Princeton University Press, 1965), p. 110; for the United States, see H. J. Habakkuk, *American and British Technology in the Nineteenth Century* (Cambridge, England: Cambridge University Press, 1962), p. 5 ff.

22. See George S. Gibb, *The Whitesmiths of Taunton* (Cambridge: Harvard University Press, 1943). For a discussion of early English management see Sidney Pollard, *The Genesis of Modern Management: A Study of the Industrial Revolution in Great Britain* (Cambridge: Harvard University Press, 1965).

4: *The Challenges of Space and People*

1. Allan Nevins, *Abram S. Hewitt, with Some Accounts of Peter Cooper* (New York: Harper, 1935), p. 95.

2. Simon Kuznets, "Notes on the Pattern of U.S. Economic Growth," in Robert W. Fogel and Stanley L. Engerman, eds., *The Reinterpretation of American Economic History* (New York: Harper & Row, 1971), pp. 18–20.

3. See Thomas C. Cochran, *The Puerto Rican Businessman: A Study in Cultural Change* (Philadelphia: University of Pennsylvania Press, 1959).

4. Everett E. Hagan, "British Personality and the Industrial Revolution: the Historical Evidence," in Tom Brown and S. B. Saul, eds., *Social Theory and Economic Change* (London: Tavistock, 1967), p. 37.

5. Charles Francis Adams, *Railroads: Their Origins and Problems* (New York: Harper & Row, rev. ed. 1969), p. 115.

6. See John A. Armstrong, *The European Administrative Elite* (Princeton: Princeton University Press, 1973).

7. Charles Babbage, *On the Economy of Machinery and Manufactures* (London, 1832), and Charles Dupin, *Discourse sur le Sort des Ouvriers* (Paris, 1831), cited in Daniel A. Wren, *The Evolution of Management Thought* (New York: Ronald Press, 1972), pp. 71, 78.

8. A. Dunsire, *Administration: the Word and the Science* (New York: John Wiley & Sons, 1973), pp. 72–79.

9. For example, see Thomas Willing's letter in N. S. B. Gras, *The First Massachusetts Bank of Boston, 1784–1934* (Cambridge: Harvard University Press, 1937), pp. 208–12.

10. French and Prussian technical schools were started in the eighteenth

century. In the United States, West Point started in 1803, Rensselaer Polytechnic Institute, in 1827, and major university schools from 1848 to 1870.

11. Thomas C. Cochran, *Business in American Life: A History* (New York: McGraw-Hill, 1972), pp. 139–40. Women, children, and blacks were treated in more authoritarian ways.

12. Herbert G. Gutman, "Work, Culture and Society in Industrialized America, 1815–1919," *American Historical Review* 78 (June 1973): 525–89.

13. William B. Gates, Jr., *Michigan Copper and Boston Dollars* (Cambridge: Harvard University Press, 1951), p. 33.

14. Thomas C. Cochran, *Railroad Leaders, 1845–1890: the Business Mind in Action* (Cambridge: Harvard University Press, 1953), p. 82.

15. Alfred D. Chandler, Jr., "The Railroads: Pioneers in Modern Corporate Management," *Business History Review* 39 (Spring 1965): 37.

16. Peter Mathias, *The First Industrial Nation: an Economic History of Britain, 1750–1914* (New York: Charles Scribner's Sons, 1969), pp. 275–78, 280.

17. Shepherd B. Clough, *France: a History of a National Economy, 1789–1939* (New York: Charles Scribner's Sons, 1939), p. 146.

18. Cochran, *Railroad Leaders*, p. 97.

19. Alfred D. Chandler, Jr., *Henry Varnum Poor: Business Editor, Analyst and Reformer* (Cambridge: Harvard University Press, 1956), p. 22.

20. Irene D. Neu, *Erastus Corning: Merchant and Financier, 1794–1862* (Ithaca: Cornell University Press, 1960), p. 62.

21. Chandler, "The Railroads," p. 37.

22. Chandler, *Poor*, p. 155.

23. Ibid.

24. Ibid.

25. Ibid.

26. Ibid.

27. Ibid.

28. Leland H. Jenks, "Early History of Railway Organization," *Business History Review* 35 (Summer 1961): 155; and Cochran, *Railroad Leaders*, pp. 82–84, 303–4, 326.

29. Quoted from *American Railroad Journal* 30 (July 1858): 108.

30. Jenks, "Early History," p. 158.

31. Jacob M. Price, *France and the Chesapeake: A History of the French Tobacco Monopoly, 1674–1791, and of its Relationship to the British and American Tobacco Trades*, 2 vols. (Ann Arbor: University of Michigan Press, 1973).

32. Cochran, *Railroad Leaders*, pp. 435–36.

33. For an example, see Jurgen Kocka, "The Family and Bureaucracy in German Industrial Management, 1850–1914: Siemens in Comparative Perspective," *Business History Review* 45 (Summer 1971): 143 ff.

34. Ralph W. and Muriel E. Hidy, *Pioneering in Big Business, 1882–1911: History of the Standard Oil Company* (New Jersey) (New York: Harper, 1955); 1: 25.

35. Ibid., pp. 35–65, 322–34.

36. Cochran, *Railroad Leaders,* p. 85.

37. Joseph A. Litterer, "Systematic Management: the Search for Order and Integration," *Business History Review* 35 (Winter 1961): 467.

5: *Adaptive Americans*

1. Nathan Rosenberg, "Technological Change in the Machine Tool Industry 1840–1910," *Journal of Economic History* 23 (Dec. 1963): 431 ff.

2. Merle E. Curti and associates, *The Making of an American Community* (Stanford: Stanford University Press, 1959), p. 147.

3. J. H. Clapham, *The Economic Development of France and Germany 1815–1914* (Cambridge, England: Cambridge University Press, 1951), pp. 310–12.

4. See William Z. Ripley, *Railroad Rates and Regulation* (New York: Longmans, Green & Co., 1915).

5. Thomas C. Cochran, *Railroad Leaders, 1845–1890: The Business Mind in Action* (Cambridge: Harvard University Press, 1953), pp. 170–71.

6. Clapham, *Economic Development,* pp. 375–98.

7. Alfred D. Chandler, "The Railroads: Pioneers in Modern Corporate Management," *Business History Review* 39 (Spring 1965): 16 ff.

8. Elisha P. Douglass, *The Coming of Age of American Business: Three Centuries of Enterprise, 1600–1900* (Chapel Hill: University of North Carolina Press, 1971), pp. 491–92.

9. Daniel J. Boorstin, *The Americans: The Democratic Experience* (New York: Random House, 1973), pp. 398–99.

10. Ibid., pp. 200–205.

11. Sir S. Martin Peto, *Resources and Prospects of America* (New York: Arno Press, 1973), p. 270.

12. See Roy F. Foulke, *Sinews of American Commerce* (New York: Dun & Bradstreet, 1941).

13. James H. Madison, "The Evolution of Commercial Credit Reporting Agencies in the Nineteenth Century," *Business History Review* 48 (Summer 1974), pp. 164–86.

14. James Willard Hurst, *The Growth of American Law: The Law Makers* (Boston: Little, Brown, 1950).

15. See Ralph M. Hower, *The History of an Advertising Agency: N. W. Ayers & Son at Work, 1869–1939* (Cambridge: Harvard University Press, 1939).

16. See A. C. Littleton, *Accounting Theory* (New York: American Institute of Public Accountants, 1933).

17. Thomas C. Cochran, *The Pabst Brewing Company: The History of an American Business* (New York: New York University Press, 1948), pp. 94–101, 183–88. It is interesting that in Boris Emmett and John E. Jeuck, *Catalogues and Counters: A History of Sears, Roebuck & Company* (Chicago: University of Chicago Press, 1950), an excellent mercantile company history, the index has no headings for accounting, auditing, bookkeeping, costs, depreciation or finance.

18. Littleton, *Accounting*, p. 194.

19. See Michael Chatfield, *A History of Accounting Thought* (Hinsdale, Ill.: Dryden Press, 1974).

20. Roy J. Simpson, "American Accounting Education, Textbooks and Public Practice Prior to 1900," *Business History Review* 34 (Winter 1960): 465 ff.

21. Jurgen Kocka, paper on German business in press for Second International Business History Conference, Tokyo, 1974, mss. p. 22.

22. Victor S. Clark relied on it heavily in Volume II of his *History of Manufacture in the United States*, 3 vols. (published for the Carnegie Institute of Washington by the McGraw-Hill Book Co., Inc., 1929).

23. Louis Galambos, *Competition and Cooperation: the Emergence of a National Trade Association* (Baltimore: Johns Hopkins University Press, 1966), p. 49.

24. Theodore N. Beckman and Nathaniel N. Engle, *Wholesaling: Principles and Practice* (New York: Ronald Press, 2d ed. 1949), p. 75.

25. Glenn Porter and Harold C. Livesay, *Merchants and Manufacturers: Studies in the Structure of Nineteenth Century Marketing* (Baltimore: Johns Hopkins University Press, 1971), p. 115.

26. See Lewis Atherton, *Pioneer Merchant in Mid-America* (Columbia: University of Missouri Press, 1954).

27. Cochran, *Pabst*, pp. 160–79.

6: Real Estate and Finance

1. See Robert P. Swierenga, *Pioneers and Profits: Land Speculation on the Iowa Frontier* (Ames: University of Iowa Press, 1968).

2. Ibid., p. 95.

3. Thomas C. Cochran, *Railroad Leaders, 1845–1890: The Business Mind in Action* (Cambridge: Harvard University Press, 1953), p. 96.

4. Lance E. Davis, "The Investment Market, 1870–1914," *Journal of Economic History* 25 (Sept. 1965): 385–86.

5. William G. Kerr, "Foreign Investments in the United States," in *The Dictionary of American History* (New York: Charles Scribner's Sons, 1976); and *Scottish Capital on the American Frontier* (Austin: Texas State Historical Association, 1976), p. 168.

6. Fritz Redlich, *The Molding of American Banking: Men and Ideas*, 2 vols. (New York: Hafner, 1951), 2: 76.

7. Walter Bagehot, *Lombard Street: A Description of the Money Market* (London, 1873; rev. ed. 1904), p. 20.

8. Paul R. Trescott, *Financing American Enterprise: The Story of Commercial Banking* (New York: Harper & Row, 1963), p. 23.

9. Benjamin J. Klebaner, *Commercial Banking in the United States: A History* (Hinsdale, Ill.: Dryden Press, 1974), pp. 18–21.

10. Redlich, *American Banking* 2: 69 ff.

11. Trescott, *Financing American Enterprise*, p. 32.

12. Davis, "Investment Market," p. 363.

13. Klebaner, *Commercial Banking*, p. 6.

14. Redlich, *American Banking* 2: 156.

15. Ibid., p. 316 ff.

16. Cochran, *Railroad Leaders*, pp. 51, 362.

17. David S. Landes, *Bankers and Pashas: International Finance and Economic Imperialism in Egypt* (Cambridge: Harvard University Press, 1958), chap. I passim.

18. Ibid., p. 59 ff.

19. Margaret G. Myers, *The New York Money Market:* Vol. I, *Origins and Development* (New York: Columbia University Press, 1931), pp. 292–93.

20. Shepherd B. Clough, *France: A History of a National Economy, 1789–1939* (New York: Charles Scribner's Sons, 1939), p. 254.

7: *Marketing and Manufacturing*

1. "Trends in the Structure of American Economics," in Robert W. Fogel and Stanley L. Engerman, eds., *The Interpretation of American Economic History* (New York: Harper & Row, 1971), p. 33.

2. Clive Day, *A History of Commerce* (New York: Longmans, Green, 1907), p. 404.

3. Melvin Thomas Copeland, *Principles of Merchandising* (Chicago: A. W. Shaw, 1924), pp. 45–47.

4. Boris Emmet and John E. Jeuck, *Catalogues and Counters: A History of Sears, Roebuck and Company* (Chicago: University of Chicago Press, 1950), p. 266.

5. Copeland, *Merchandising*, p. 52.

6. Alfred D. Chandler, Jr., ed., *Giant Enterprise: Ford, General Motors, and the Automobile Industry* (New York: Harcourt, Brace & World, 1964), p. 161 ff; and "How to Sell Automobiles," *Fortune* (Feb. 1939): 71–78, 105–9.

7. Edward A. Duddy and David A. Revzan, *Marketing: An Institutional Approach* (New York: McGraw-Hill, 1947), pp. 156, 199.

8. Theodore N. Beckman and Nathaniel N. Engle, *Wholesaling: Principles and Practice*, 2d ed. (New York: Ronald Press, 1949), p. 230.

9. Copeland, *Merchandising*, pp. 4–8.

10. Ibid., pp. 330–60.

11. Ralph M. Hower, *The History of an Advertising Agency: N. W. Ayer & Son at Work, 1869–1939* (Cambridge: Harvard University Press, 1939), p. 93.

12. Ibid., p. 98.

13. Frank S. Presbrey, *The History and Development of Advertising* (Garden City, N.Y.: Doubleday, Doran, 1929), p. 432.

14. Otis Pease, *The Responsibilities of American Advertising* (New Haven: Yale University Press, 1958), p. 13.

15. Presbrey, *Advertising*, p. 550.

16. Thomas C. Cochran, *Railroad Leaders, 1845–1890: The Business Mind in Action* (Cambridge: Harvard University Press, 1953), pp. 185–89.

17. Alan R. Raucher, *Public Relations and Business, 1900–1929* (Baltimore: Johns Hopkins University Press, 1966).

18. Ralph L. Nelson, *Merger Movements in American Industry, 1895–1956* (Princeton: National Bureau of Economic Research, 1959), Appendix C.

19. For Germany, see Hermann Levy, *Industrial Germany: A Study of its Monopoly Organizations and their Control by the State* (Cambridge, England: Cambridge University Press, 1935); for Japan, see M. Y. Yoshimo, *Japan's Managerial System: Tradition and Innovation* (Cambridge: M.I.T. Press, 1968).

20. David S. Landes, *The Unbound Prometheus: Technological Change and Development in Western Europe from 1759 to the Present* (Cambridge, England: Cambridge University Press, 1969), p. 336.

21. See U.S., Congress, Senate, Temporary National Economic Committee, *Investigation of Concentration of Economic Power: Monograph 17, Problems of Small Business*, 76th Cong., 3d sess., Senate Committee Print (Washington, D.C.: Government Printing Office, 1941).

22. Copeland, *Merchandising*, pp. 72–74.

23. James H. Soltow, "Origins of Small Business Metal Fabricators and Machinery Makers in New England, 1890–1957," American Philosophical Society, *Transactions* (Philadelphia: American Philosophical Society, 1965): 10.

8: *The Growing Importance of Business Services*

1. Warren C. Scoville, *Revolution in Glassmaking: Entrepreneur-ship and Technical Change in the American Industry, 1880–1920* (Cambridge: Harvard University Press, 1948), p. 218.

2. Professor Doris King is about to publish a history of hotel management, and I am indebted to her for her help.

3. Kenneth Sturges, *American Chambers of Commerce* (New York: Moffat Bard & Co., 1915), p. 140.

4. See Business Training Corporation, *Accounting* (New York: Business Training Corporation, 1911), pp. 164–70.

5. Thomas C. Cochran, *The Pabst Brewing Company: The History of An American Business* (New York: New York University Press, 1948), p. 185.

6. James D. Edwards, "Accounting in the United States from 1913 to 1926," *Business History Review* 32 (Spring 1958): 74–101.

7. Henry C. Bentley, *Bibliography of Works on Accounting*, 2 vols. (Boston: H. C. Bentley, 1934–35).

8. Edwards, "Accounting," p. 83.

9. See Owen J. Stalson, *Marketing Life Insurance: Its History in America* (Cambridge: Harvard University Press, 1942), and Shepard B. Clough, *A Century of American Life Insurance: A History of the Mutual Life Insurance Company of New York* (New York: Cambridge University Press, 1946).

10. Benjamin J. Klebaner, *Commercial Banking in the United States: A History* (Hinsdale, Ill.: Dryden Press, 1974), p. 58.

11. Hugh Neuberger and Houston H. Stokes, "German Banks and German

Growth, 1883–1913: An Empirical View," *Journal of Economic History* 34 (Sept. 1974): 712–14.

12. J. H. Clapham, *Economic Development of France and Germany, 1815–1914* (Cambridge, England: Cambridge University Press, 1936), pp. 391–95.

13. Kano Yamamura, "Japan," in Rondo Cameron, *Banking and Economic Development* (New York: Oxford University Press, 1972), pp. 184–85.

14. See Vincent Carosso, *Investment Banking in the United States: A History* (Cambridge: Harvard University Press, 1970).

15. Neuberger and Stokes, "German Banks," p. 729.

16. R. S. Sayers, *Lloyds Bank in the History of English Banking* (Oxford, England: Clarendon Press, 1957), p. 163.

17. Lance E. Davis, "The Investment Market, 1870–1914: The Evolution of a National Market," *Journal of Economic History* 25 (Sept. 1965): 369–72.

18. Margaret G. Myers, *A Financial History of the United States* (New York: Columbia University Press, 1970), pp. 250–51.

19. Ibid., p. 246.

20. F. Cyril James, *The Growth of Chicago Banks*, 2 vols. (New York: Harper, 1938), 2: 953.

21. Carosso, *Investment Banking*, p. 267.

22. See Milton Friedman and Anna Jacobson Schwartz, *The Great Contraction, 1929–1933* (Princeton: Princeton University Press, for the National Bureau of Economic Research, 1963).

9: *Rationalizing the Big Firm*

1. See Henry R. Seager and Charles A. Gulick, *Trust and Corporation Problems* (New York: Harper & Row, 1929, Arno Press, 1973).

2. Ralph L. Nelson, *Merger Movements in American Industry, 1895–1956* (Princeton: Princeton University Press, 1959; published for the National Bureau of Economic Research), p. 6.

3. Hermann Levy, *Industrial Germany: A Study of its Monopoly Organizations and their Control by the State* (Cambridge, England: Cambridge University Press, 1935), pp. 2–3.

4. Ibid.

5. David S. Landes, "Japan and Europe: Contrasts in Industrialization," in William W. Lockwood, ed., *The State and Economic Enterprise in Japan* (Princeton: Princeton University Press, 1965), p. 175. See also Hugh Neuberger and Houston H. Stokes, "German Banks and Growth, 1883–1913; An Empirical View," *Journal of Economic History* 34 (Sept. 1974): 729.

6. Peter Mathias, *The First Industrial Nation: An Economic History of Britain, 1750–1914* (Charles Scribner's Sons, 1969), pp. 390–93.

7. David Granick, *The European Executive* (Garden City, N.Y.: Doubleday, 1962), p. 16.

8. Each scholar since John Moody's *The Truth About the Trusts* (New York: Moody, 1904), has compiled slightly different data for illustration, but they all emphasize the unequaled size of this turn-of-the-century merger movement.

9. Alfred D. Chandler, Jr., "The Structure of American Industry in the Twentieth Century: A Historical Overview," *Business History Review* 43 (Autumn 1969): 256–57.

10. Joseph A. Litterer, "Systematic Management: The Source for Order and Integration," *Business History Review* 26 (Winter 1961): 463.

11. Daniel A. Wren, *The Evolution of Management Thought* (New York: Ronald Press), p. 180.

12. Wren, *Management Thought*, pp. 289–97.

13. See M. Y. Yoshino, *Japan's Managerial System: Tradition and Innovation* (Cambridge: M.I.T. Press, 1968).

14. A. Dunsire, *Administration: The Word and the Science* (New York: John Wiley & Sons, 1973), p. 196.

15. Antony Jay, *Corporation Man* (New York: Pocket Books, 1973), chapter 3.

16. Jürgen Kocka, "Family and Bureaucracy in Germany Industrial Management 1850–1914: Siemens in Comparative Perspective," *Business History Review* 45 (Spring 1971): 145–47.

17. Alfred D. Chandler, Jr., and Stephen Salsbury, *Pierre S. du Pont and the Making of the Modern Corporation* (New York: Harper & Row, 1970), p. 73 ff.

18. Ibid., pp. 428–29.

19. General Motors Corporation Organizational Study, Defendant's Trial Ex. No. GM 1, Defendant's Exhibit No. 300 (Mss., Eleutherian Mills-Hagley Library, Greenville, Delaware).

20. Ibid., p. 7.

21. Alfred D. Chandler, Jr., *Strategy and Structure: Chapters in the History of American Industrial Enterprise* (Garden City, N.Y.: Doubleday, Anchor Books, 1966), p. 185.

22. Ibid., p. 197.

23. Ibid., pp. 398–99.

24. Ibid., p. 396, and passim.

25. Michel Crozier, "The French Business System of Organization," in Stanley M. Davis, ed., *Comparative Management: Organizational and Cultural Perspectives* (Englewood Cliffs, N.J.: Prentice-Hall, 1971), pp. 414–19.

26. Edith Penrose, *The Theory of the Growth of the Firm* (New York: John Wiley & Sons, 1959), p. 34.

10: *New Relations Between Business and Government*

1. See Raymond Goldsmith, *A Study of Saving*, 2 vols. (New York: National Bureau of Economic Research, 1954), 1: 48–59.

2. Joseph S. Davis, *The World Between the Wars, 1919–1939: An Economist's View* (Baltimore: Johns Hopkins University Press, 1975), p. 365.

3. Margaret G. Myers, *The New York Money Market: Origins and Development*, 2 vols. (New York: Columbia University Press, 1931), 1: 310.

4. Davis, *World Between Wars*, p. 397.

5. Vincent Carosso, "Washington and Wall Street: The New Deal and

Investment Bankers, 1933–1940," *Business History Review* 44 (Winter 1970): 426.

6. See Thomas C. Cochran, *The Great Depression and World War II 1929–1945* (Glenview, Ill.: Scott, Foresman, and Co., 1968), pp. 52–53.

7. See Michael E. Parish, *Securities Regulation and the New Deal* (New Haven: Yale University Press, 1970), p. 40.

8. Henry R. Seager and Charles A. Gulick, *Trust and Corporation Problems* (New York: Harper, 1929; Arno Press, 1973), p. 576 ff and 598 ff.

9. Carosso, "Washington and Wall Street," pp. 434–35.

10. Herman E. Krooss, *Executive Opinion: What Business Leaders Said and Thought, 1920–1960* (Garden City, N.Y.: Doubleday, 1970), p. 208.

11. For more see Thomas C. Cochran, *Business in American Life: A History* (New York: McGraw-Hill, 1972), chapter 17.

12. Wallace B. Donham, *Business Adrift* (New York: McGraw-Hill, 1931), p. 34.

13. Cochran, *The Great Depression*, p. 81.

14. Norman Beasley, *Knudsen* (New York: McGraw-Hill, 1947), p. 270.

15. See Thomas C. Cochran, *American Business in the Twentieth Century* (Cambridge: Harvard University Press, 1972).

16. See Albro Martin, *Enterprise Denied: Origins of the Decline of American Railroads, 1897–1917* (New York: Columbia University Press, 1971).

17. David S. Landes, "Japan and Europe: Contrasts in Industrialization," in William E. Lockwood, ed., *The State and Economic Enterprise in Japan* (Princeton: Princeton University Press, 1965), and M. Y. Yoshimo, *Japan's Managerial System* (Cambridge: M.I.T. Press, 1968).

18. See Oliver E. Williamson, *Corporation Control and Business Behavior* (Englewood Cliffs, N.J.: Prentice-Hall, 1970).

11: *Marketing Shapes Management*

1. See James J. Flink, *The Car Culture* (Cambridge: M.I.T. Press, 1975), and John B. Rae, *The American Automobile: A Brief History* (Chicago: University of Chicago Press, 1965).

2. Alfred D. Chandler, Jr., "Structure of American Industry in the 20th Century," *Business History Review* 43 (Autumn 1969): 255–99.

3. Thomas Berg, *Mismarketing: Case Histories of Marketing Misfires* (Garden City, N.Y.: Doubleday, Anchor Books, 1971), p. 88.

4. J. Woodward, "Management and Technology," in Tom Burns, ed., *Industrial Man: Selected Readings* (Baltimore: Penguin Books, 1969), p. 196.

5. James Soltow, "Origins of Small Business Metal Fabricators and Machinery Makers in New England, 1890–1957," American Philosophical Society, *Transactions* (Philadelphia: American Philosophical Society, 1965), pp. 10–11.

6. Renato Tagiuri, et al., *Behavioral Science Concepts in Case Analysis: The Relationship of Ideas to Management Action* (Boston: Graduate School of Business Administration, Harvard University, 1968), p. 67.

7. See Edward A. Duddy, John E. Jeuck, and David A. Revzan, *Marketing: An Institutional Approach* (New York: McGraw-Hill, 1947).

8. Mabel Newcomer, "The Little Businessman: A Study of Business Proprietors in Poughkeepsie, New York," *Business History Review* 35 (Winter 1961): 509–11.

9. U.S., Congress, Senate, Temporary National Economic Committee, *Investigation of Concentration of Economic Power: Monograph 17, Problems of Small Business* 76th Cong., 3d sess., Senate Committee Print (Washington, D.C.: Government Printing Office, 1941), p. 81.

10. Newcomer, "Little Businessman," p. 512.

11. Philip Shabecoff, "S. B. A. Under Fire," *New York Times* (May 12, 1971), sec. 3, p. 3.

12. *Statistical Abstract of the United States, 1973*, p. 471.

13. David S. Landes, *The Unbound Prometheus: Technological Change and Development in Western Europe from 1750 to the Present* (Cambridge, England: Cambridge University Press, 1969), p. 336.

14. *Time* (July 28, 1975): 54.

15. Oliver E. Williamson, *Corporate Control and Business Behavior* (Englewood Cliffs, N.J.: Prentice-Hall, 1970), p. 138.

16. In addition to Alfred D. Chandler, Jr., *Strategy and Structure: Chapters in the History of American Industrial Enterprise* (Garden City, N.Y.: Doubleday, Anchor Books, 1966), see his *Great Enterprise: Ford, General Motors and the Automobile Industry* (New York: Harcourt, Brace, World, 1964), and Peter F. Drucker, *Concept of the Corporation* (New York: John Day, 1946).

17. Herbert Simon, "Designing Organizations for an Information Rich World" in Martin Greenberger, ed., *Computers, Communication and the Public Interest* (Baltimore: Johns Hopkins University Press, 1973), p. 41.

18. Chandler, *Strategy and Structure*, p. 414.

19. Daniel A. Wren, *The Evolution of Management Thought* (New York: Ronald Press, 1972), p. 358.

20. Peter F. Drucker, *The Practice of Management* (New York: Macmillan Co., 1954), p. 196.

21. Edward C. Bursk and John F. Chapman, eds., *New Decision-Making Tools for Managers: Mathematical Programming as an Aid in the Solving of Business Problems* (Cambridge: Harvard University Press, 1963), p. 1.

22. *Fortune* (Oct. 1953): 151, 260.

23. Henrietta M. Larson, Evelyn H. Knowlton, and Charles S. Popple, *New Horizons, 1927–1950: A History of the Standard Oil Company* (New Jersey) (Harper & Row, 1971), p. 617.

24. See Michael Chatfield, *A History of Accounting Thought* (Hinsdale, Ill., Dryden Press, 1974). For foreign requirements see American Institute of Certified Public Accountants, *Professional Accounting in 30 Countries* (n.p., 1975).

25. *International Encyclopedia of the Social Sciences*, s. v. "Accounting."

26. *Fortune* (Oct. 1969): 3.

27. Simon, "Designing Organizations for an Information Rich World," Greenberger, ed., *Computers*, p. 46.

28. William Barrett, *Time of Need* (New York: Harper & Row, Torchbooks, 1973), p. 5.

29. *Time* (Feb. 24, 1975): 26.

30. See *New York Times* (June 15, 1975), Business and Finance sec., p. 1.

12: *Finance Expands Its Markets*

1. For details of these intricate operations see Henry E. Hoagland and Leo D. Stone, *Real Estate Finance*, 5th ed. (Homewood, Ill.: R. D. Irwin, 1973), or other recent textbooks.

2. Ibid., p. 460.

3. Ira V. Cobleigh, *All About Investing in Real Estate Securities* (New York: Weybright and Talley, 1971), pp. 38–48.

4. *Finance* (April 1974): 43–45.

5. Hoagland and Stone, *Real Estate Finance*, p. 263.

6. Roy F. Foulke, *Sinews of American Commerce* (New York: Dun & Bradstreet, 1941), pp. 215–17.

7. See J. Owen Stalson, *Marketing Life Insurance: Its History in America* (Cambridge: Harvard University Press, 1942).

8. William A. Carr, *Perils Named and Unnamed* (New York: McGraw-Hill, 1967), p. 294 ff.

9. Shepard B. Clough, *A Century of American Life Insurance: A History of Mutual Life Insurance Company of New York, 1843–1943* (New York: Columbia University Press, 1946), pp. 303–30.

10. Such statistics are in large part available in the *Statistical Abstract of the United States,* but Benjamin J. Klebaner's *Commercial Banking in the United States: A History* (Hinsdale, Ill.: Dryden, 1974) is more statistically useful for historical comparisons.

11. Paul R. Trescott, *Financing American Enterprise: The Story of Commercial Banking* (New York: Harper & Row, 1963), p. 238.

12. W. H. Steiner and Eli Shapiro, *Money and Banking: An Introduction to the Financial System,* 4th ed. (New York: Henry Holt & Co., 1958), p. 98.

13. Klebaner, *Commercial Banking,* p. 185.

14. Steiner and Shapiro, *Money and Banking,* p. 86.

15. Klebaner, *Commercial Banking,* p. 180.

16. See Charles Popple, *Development of Two Bank Groups in the Central Northwest: A Study in Bank Policy and Organization* (Cambridge: Harvard University Press, 1944).

17. Klebaner, *Commercial Banking,* p. 184.

18. Steiner and Shapiro, *Money and Banking,* pp. 137–46.

19. See Peter F. Drucker, "American Business's New Owners," *Wall Street Journal,* May 27, 1976.

13: *The Changing Environment*

1. See W. Paul Strassmann, *Risk and Technological Innovation: American Manufacturing Methods during the Nineteenth Century* (Ithaca: Cornell University Press, 1959).

2. See Charles P. Kindelberger, "Origins of United States Direct Investment in France," *Business History Review* 48 (Autumn 1974): 382–413.

3. Ibid., pp. 398–99.

4. Ibid., pp. 389, 393.

5. Myra Wilkins, *The Maturing of Multinational Enterprise: American Business Abroad* (Cambridge: Harvard University Press, 1974), p. 56.

6. Ibid., p. 170 ff.

7. Ibid., p. 300.

8. See Thomas Berg, *Mismarketing: Case Histories of Marketing Misfires* (Garden City, N.Y.: Doubleday, Anchor Books, 1971).

9. David Granick, *The European Executive* (Garden City, N.Y.: Doubleday, 1962), pp. 242–58.

10. Ibid., pp. 171–73.

11. See Rosemary Stewart, *The Reality of Organizations: A Guide for Managers and Students* (Garden City, N.Y.: Doubleday, 1972), and Roy Lewis and Rosemary Stewart, *The Managers: A New Examination of the English, German, and American Executive* (New York: Mentor, 1961).

12. *Fortune* (Sept. 1974): 116 ff.

13. Michel Crozier, "The French Business System of Organization," in Stanley M. Davis, ed., *Comparative Management: Organizational and Cultural Perspectives* (Englewood Cliffs, N.J.: Prentice-Hall, 1971), pp. 412–16.

14. M. Y. Yoshino, *Japan's Managerial System: Tradition and Innovation* (Cambridge: M.I.T. Press, 1968).

15. *Fortune* (Aug. 1973): 60.

16. Morrell Heald, *The Responsibilities of Business: Company and Community* (Cleveland: Press of Western Reserve University, 1970), p. 107.

17. Ibid., p. 261.

18. Jules Cohn, *The Conscience of the Corporations: Business and Urban Affairs, 1967–1970* (Baltimore: Johns Hopkins University Press, 1971), pp. 24–28.

19. Charles B. McCoy, Address before the Governor's Conference on Business and Industry, Wilmington, Delaware, April 4, 1968.

20. *Time* (July 28, 1975): 55.

21. Mason Haire, Edwin E. Ghiselli, and Lyman Porter, *Managerial Thinking: An International Study* (New York: John Wiley & Sons, 1966), p. 171.

22. *New York Times* (June 30, 1974), sec. 4, p. 4.

SOURCES AND
SUGGESTIONS FOR
FURTHER READING

There is no comprehensive history of modern business in either the United States or any of the other leading industrial nations. Specialized writing in English is naturally most voluminous on America and Britain, in that order, and probably more so on Japan than on either France or Germany as separate nations. In fact, business as distinct from economic history has not become a separate discipline on the Continent. A good deal of information useful for business history, however, may be gained in all nations from economic history texts such as *The Economic History of the United States* (New York: Rinehart) in nine volumes or the six-volume *Cambridge Economic History of Modern Europe* (Cambridge, England: Cambridge University Press), but the entrepreneurial aspects of subjects such as marketing, real estate, or finance are likely to be omitted or slighted.

Some General Works

In *The Coming of Age of American Business* (Chapel Hill: University of North Carolina Press, 1971), Elisha P. Douglass has written a detailed and readable narrative that ends in 1900. Jonathan Hughes has assembled a number of biographies of American businessmen in *The Vital Few: American Economic Progress and Its Protagonists* (Boston: Houghton-Mifflin, 1965). There is also a brief textbook by Herman E. Krooss and Charles Gilbert, *American Business History* (Englewood Cliffs, N.J.: Prentice-Hall, 1972), that does not attempt comprehensive coverage of business activities in the recent periods, and displays the usual bias of economic histories toward emphasis on big manufacturing companies. Nevertheless it was a valuable first step in the synthesis of American business history and still represents the only scholarly book covering the whole period from Jamestown to 1970.

Specialized Scholarly Writing

There are a number of good monographs dealing with special phases of business history but leaving many subjects untouched. The following are some of the best studies. Robert G. Albion, *The Rise of New York Port* (New York: Charles Scribner's Sons, 1939), is basic to an understanding of the specialization of mercantile enterprise. Lewis E. Atherton's *The Pioneer Merchant in Mid-America* (Columbia: University of Missouri Press, 1939), and *The Southern Country Store, 1800– 1860* (Baton Rouge: Louisiana State University Press, 1949), give understanding treatment to backcountry retailing. Alfred D. Chandler, Jr., in *Strategy and Structure* (Cambridge: Harvard University Press, 1962), has written an important interpretation of the forces shaping modern management. Richard P. Rumelt, *Strategy, Structure, and Economic Performance* (Boston: Harvard Business School, 1974) is a quantitative study inspired by Chandler. Michael Chatfield's *A History of Accounting Thought* (Hinsdale, Ill.: Dryden Press, 1974), covers both England and America from the late seventeenth century on. In *Business in Its Social Setting* (Cambridge: Harvard University Press, 1959), Arthur H. Cole emphasizes the wide range of factors bearing on business. Louis Galambos, in *Competition and Cooperation* (Baltimore: Johns Hopkins University Press, 1966), deals with a trade association's efforts to organize its industry; in *The Public Image of Big Business in America, 1880–1914* (Baltimore: Johns Hopkins University Press, 1975) he attempts to weigh public reaction toward corporate power. Bray Hammond, in *Banks and Politics in America,* and *Sovereignty and an Empty Purse* (Princeton: Princeton University Press, 1957, 1970, respectively), traces the interaction of banking regulations and politics from 1800 to 1865. Morrell Heald's *The Social Responsibilities of Business, 1900–1960* (Cleveland: Case Western Reserve University Press, 1970) is penetrating and judicious. Arthur M. Johnson and Barry E. Supple, *Boston Capitalists and Western Railroads* (Cambridge: Harvard University Press, 1967), is a valuable study in need of replication for New York and Philadelphia. On an aspect of later foreign investment see William G. Kerr, *Scottish Capital on the American Frontier* (Austin: Texas State Historical Commission, 1976). The business aspects of early Massachusetts textile mills are discussed in Hannah Josephson's *The Golden Threads* (New York: Duel, Sloan and Pierce, 1940). Morton Keller, *The Life Insurance Enterprise, 1885–1910,* is an interpretive study of business and politics. Edward C. Kirkland, in *Thought and Dream in the Business Community, 1860–1900* (Ithaca: Cornell University Press, 1956) discusses business attitudes. Benjamin J. Klebaner's *Commercial Banking in the United States* (Hinsdale, Ill.: Dryden Press, 1974) is a useful condensation. In *Executive Opinion* (Garden City: Doubleday, 1970), Herman E. Krooss wittily comments on the period from 1920 to 1960. A. C. Littleton's *Accounting Evolution to 1900* (New York: American Institute, 1933) is not exciting, just indispensable. Gerald D. Nash, *United States Oil Policy, 1890–1964* (Pittsburgh: University of Pittsburgh Press, 1960) is obviously of current importance. Vishnu N. Oak's *The Negro's Adventure in General Business* (Yellow Springs: Antioch, 1949) is a first step in this subject. In *Merchants and Manufacturers* (Baltimore: Johns Hopkins

University Press, 1971), Glenn Porter and Harold C. Livesay interpret heavy industry marketing in the nineteenth century. Marketing in the mid-twentieth century is well covered in Reavis Cox, C. S. Goodman, and T. C. Fichlander, *Distribution in a High Level Economy* (Englewood Cliffs: Prentice-Hall, 1965). Alan R. Raucher's *Public Relations and Business, 1900–1929* (Baltimore: Johns Hopkins University Press, 1968) provides the facts of a generally mis-interpreted history. The two-volume work *The Molding of American Banking*, (New York: Hafner Press, 1947), by Fritz Redlich, is a major study that un-fortunately ends in 1910. In *The Age of Giant Corporations* (Westport: Green-wood Press, 1972), Robert Sobel writes on the sectors of business dominated by big companies from 1914 to 1970. James H. Soltow's *Origins of Small Business Metal Fabricators and Machinery Makers in New England, 1890–1957* (Philadelphia: American Philosophical Society, 1965) is one of the few qualitative studies of small- to medium-sized manufacturing. Francis X. Sutton and associates, *The American Business Creed* (Cambridge: Harvard University Press, 1958) is on the twentieth century but suggestive for the thought of earlier periods. Robert T. Swierenga's *Pioneers and Profits* (Ames: Iowa State University Press, 1968) is one of a very few studies in the history of real estate operations. In *The Urban Frontier* (Cambridge: Harvard University Press, 1959), Richard C. Wade explores early municipal business influence. Two volumes by Mira Wilkins, *The Emergence of Multinational Enterprise*, and *The Maturing of Multinational Enterprise* (Cambridge: Harvard University Press, 1970, 1974, respectively), contain by far the most thorough history of this subject. Daniel A. Wren's *The Evolution of Management Thought* (New York: Ronald Press, 1972) is the most historically oriented recent text. In *Business in American Life* (New York: McGraw-Hill, 1972) I have tried to assess the effects of business on other social institutions. Harold F. William-son's *Winchester, the Gun That Won the West* (Washington, D.C.: Combat Forces Press, 1952), several other of his company histories, and studies of the petroleum industry (with Arnold Daum) and of the carpet industry (with Arthur H. Cole) are important and substantial contributions to business history.

The Harvard Studies in Business History, growing well beyond a score of volumes, is chiefly a collection of excellent company biographies, but also includes some more general monographs. Other universities and some com-panies have sponsored scholarly business histories, most notably Standard Oil (New Jersey), in four volumes written and published through the Business History Foundation. There are also a number of books bearing upon business history by freelance writers and journalists, among which the best known are the *Robber Barons* (New York: Harcourt Brace, 1934) and other works by Matthew Josephson.

Many interesting articles have appeared only in collections too numerous to list in any detail. Hugh G. J. Aitken, ed., *Explorations in Enterprise* (Cam-bridge: Harvard University Press, 1965), and William Miller, ed., *Men in Business* (Cambridge: Harvard University Press, 1952) may serve as examples.

In spite of what may seem to be a great deal of writing, major areas of business history have to be studied largely from contemporary surveys at various periods or unsystematic references in studies of economic history. Any bibliography of such books, however, would be impossibly long and need much explanation of the usefulness of each volume. The reader wanting to make a start on any particular topic should first consult the appropriate footnotes in the preceding chapters of this book.

On Four Foreign Nations

Even if all the literature in foreign languages were available to the reader, the history of business would be inadequately told. As in the case of the United States, however, it is impossible here to more than give samples of the major studies in English. Articles in the periodicals listed in the next section also give much new information on foreign business. Many observations in the text of this work have come from personal interviews and research in foreign nations over the last quarter century, rather than from printed sources. I have also found that businessmen operating outside their own country often have an excellent perspective on practices "back home."

The following books with their notes and bibliographies may open the way to understanding business development in Britain, France, Germany, and Japan. An excellent beginning is John A. Armstrong, *The European Administrative Elite* (Princeton: Princeton University Press, 1973), in which he discusses this group in relation to active participation in national economic growth. Walter Bagehot's *Lombard Street* (London: rev. ed. 1873, 1904) is not only an overview of world banking in relation to London, but a famous book of the 1870s. In *Essays in French Economic History* (New York: Oxford University Press, 1972), Rondo Cameron has collected a large number of useful essays by leading scholars. His *France in the Economic Development of Europe* (Princeton: Princeton University Press, 1961) is also useful. J. H. Clapham's *The Economic Development of France and Germany* (Cambridge, England: Cambridge University Press, 1951) is still important for the period 1815 to 1914. Shepard B. Clough, *France: The History of National Economics* (New York: Charles Scribner's Sons, 1939) is not much concerned with business practices, but useful as a general guide. Phyllis Deane's *The First Industrial Revolution* (Cambridge, England: Cambridge University Press, 1965) has become a standard account. David Granick, in *The European Executive* (Garden City, N.Y.: Doubleday, 1962), gives the results of a large number of interviews. F. H. Harbison and C. A. Myers, in *Management in the Industrial World* (New York: McGraw-Hill, 1959), have brief discussions of management in each of the major nations. A very good comparative study giving considerable weight to business practices is Charles P. Kindelberger's *Economic Growth in France and Britain, 1851–1950* (Cambridge: Harvard University Press, 1964). David Landes, in *The Unbound Prometheus* (Cambridge, England: Cambridge University Press, 1969), has written the best general economic history of Europe since 1750. Solomon B. Levine's *Industrial Relations in Post War Japan* (Urbana: University of Illinois Press, 1958) discusses the peculiarities of employee relations. *Industrial Germany*, by Herman Levy (Cambridge, England: Cambridge University Press, 1935), is primarily a study of cartels and syndicates. André Liesse's *The Evolution of Credit and Banks in France* (Washington D.C.: Government Printing Office, 1909) is a useful study prepared for the U.S. National Monetary Commission. While only historical to the extent of its time of preparation, *The Managers* (New York: Mentor, 1958), by Roy Lewis and Rosemary Stewart, is devoted to penetrating comparisons of English, German, and American executives. The essays collected by William Lockwood in *The State and Economic Growth in Japan* (Princeton: Princeton University Press, 1965) include some excellent comparisons with business in other nations. *The First Industrial Nation*, by Peter Mathias (New York: Charles Scribner's Sons, 1969), is the economic history of England from 1750 to 1914 that supplied the theoretical background for the concept of the Business Revolution. In *Japanese Economic Growth* (Stanford: Stanford University Press, 1973), Kazushi Ohkawa and Henry Rosovsky give basic environmental factors necessary for an understanding of business and growth. Guy Palmade's *French Capitalism in the Nineteenth Century*, trans. (New York: Barnes & Noble, 1972) is rather brief and uninterpretive but useful for material usually omitted from economic history. In *The Genesis of Modern Management* (Cambridge: Harvard University Press, 1965), Sidney Pollard gives useful early comparison with the United States and other nations. *Lloyds Bank in the History of English Banking* (Oxford: Clarendon, 1957), by R. S. Sayers, amply fulfills the promise of its title, and with special reference to business practices. *English Accounting* (London: Gee, 1954), by Nicholas A. Stacey, places the specialized history in a social and economic context. Gustav Stolper's *German Economy, 1870–1940* (New York: Reynal & Hitchcock, 1940) is unsatisfactory from the standpoint of business history but adds usefully to the small literature in English. A Dutch executive, H. Van Der Haas, in *The Enterprise in Transition: an Analysis of European and American Practice* (New York: Tavistock, 1967), writes with a long and discriminating historical view. In *English Theories of Central Banking Control, 1819–1858* (Cambridge: Harvard University Press, 1939), Elmer Wood surveys early European ideas regarding central banks. The most useful, although somewhat controversial, study of recent Japanese business practice is M. Y. Yoshino's *Japanese Managerial System* (Cambridge: M.I.T. Press, 1968).

As in the United States there are some good histories of particular companies, chiefly British ones, such as Charles Wilson's *The History of Unilever*, 2 vols. (London: Cassell, 1954). There are a great number of memorial histories of family firms, and some scholarly studies in German, but only a few that would merit translation.

This brief sketch of foreign accounts in English has omitted some substantial and useful studies. Selection has inevitably been influenced by the holdings of the Eleutherian Mills Historical Library, where as Senior Resident Scholar, I did the final reading for the present book. Although surprisingly strong in books in English, the library quite properly has not regarded comprehensive coverage of foreign business literature as within its chosen field of American economic history.

Periodicals and Bibliographies

The Business History Review, published in its present form quarterly at Harvard since 1954, when it succeeded the shorter Bulletin of the Business History Society, is the best general source of information. Starting as a mimeographed or offset quarterly in 1949 and continuing in more conventional format after 1960, Explorations in Entrepreneurial History is also of major importance. Most issues of the Journal of Economic History, published since 1941, include some direct or indirect references to American business. Among foreign journals with articles in English are: The Economic History Review (Great Britain), the Journal of European Economic History (Italy), and the Japan Business History Review. In accordance with the English language bias of this list, other publications such as the Annales in France and Tradition in Germany are not included. No less valuable than articles in the historical quarterlies are those in contemporary periodicals that go back to Hunt's Merchants Magazine, The Bankers' Magazine, and De Bow's Review in the 1840s, and the Commercial and Financial Chronicle from the late 1860s on. Currently there are Forbes, Business Week, Fortune, the Harvard Business Review, and the quarterlies of a number of other business schools.

There is a large biographical literature on business leaders which, along with other materials, was first assembled by Henrietta M. Larson in A Guide to Business History (Cambridge: Harvard University Press, 1948), and continued by Lorna Daniells in Studies in Enterprise (Cambridge: Harvard University Press, 1957). From 1959 to 1964, the latter bibliography was kept up to date in summer or autumn issues of the Business History Review. Since then the field has been resurveyed by Robert W. Lovett in American Business and Economic History Information Sources (Detroit: Gale Research, 1971), and by Ralph W. Hidy in the Winter 1970 issue of The Business History Review.

Useful Miscellaneous Data

In addition to special academic writing there is a great deal to be learned, chiefly of a statistical nature, from the books and pamphlets of the National Bureau of Economic Research (New York City), from Historical Statistics of the United States, the annual Statistical Abstract, and from innumerable other government published reports and hearings before commissions and committees of Congress. This latter type of literature is so large and hard to locate that it is best to consult the special guides to government documents. There is also a vast and generally unindexed amount of information in the books and periodicals of trade, professional, and management associations, of which an example is Professional Accounting in 30 Countries, by the American Institute of Certified Public Accountants (New York: 1964, 1975).

The truly great possibilities for new knowledge and understanding hidden in the published but unexplored literature bearing on business history should be a stimulating challenge to present and future generations of scholars.

INDEX